Mixed Martial Arts'
Most Wanted™

Related Potomac Titles

Boxing's Most Wanted™: The Top 10 Book of Champs,
Chumps, and Punch-Drunk Palookas
—*David L. Hudson Jr. and Mike Fitzgerald Jr.*

Wrestling's Most Wanted™: The Top 10 Book of
Pro Wrestling's Outrageous Performers,
Punishing Pile Drivers, and Other Oddities
—*Floyd Conner*

Mixed Martial Arts' Most Wanted™

The Top 10 Book of Crazy Combat, Great Grappling, and Sick Submissions

Adam T. Heath and David L. Hudson Jr.

Potomac Books
WASHINGTON, D.C.

Library of Congress Cataloging-in-Publication Data

Heath, Adam T.
Mixed martial arts' most wanted : the top 10 book of crazy
combat, great grappling, and sick submissions / Adam T. Heath
and David L. Hudson Jr.
p. cm.—(Most wanted)
Includes bibliographical references and index.
ISBN 978-1-59797-549-0 (paperback: alk. paper)
ISBN 978-1-61234-041-8 (electronic edition)
1. Mixed martial arts. I. Hudson, David L., 1969–II. Title.
GV1102.7.M59H43 2012
796.815—dc23
2011024862

Printed in the United States of America on acid-free paper that meets the
American National Standards Institute Z39-48 Standard.

Potomac Books
22841 Quicksilver Drive
Dulles, Virginia 20166

First Edition

10 9 8 7 6 5 4 3 2 1

I dedicate this book to my parents, Tom and Sharon Heath;
my sister, Amy Heath; and
my partner in crime, Christina Messino.
—Adam

To Thomas Wayne Watson: rest in peace, my friend!
—David

Contents

List of Photographs   xi
Acknowledgments   xiii

Where It All Comes From
1. MMA Originals: The First Mixed Martial Art Styles   3
2. Why They Call It MMA: The Most Common Martial
   Arts in MMA   10
3. MMA Coaches: The Brains behind the Brawn   16

Fighting on the Rebound
4. I Hate You: Grudge Matches   23
5. Tough Trilogies: They Fought Three Great
   Fights against Each Other   29

Not Everything Goes According to Plan
6. Downright Dirty: Fighters Who Cheat   39
7. Low Blows: The Most Telling Foul Shots in the Sport   45
8. Ouch: The Worst Injuries in MMA   51

The Best There Are
9. Tough Women: The Best Female Fighters   61
10. Regal Reigns: Champions Who Ruled Their Class   67

11. Fedor's Finest: The Greatest Victories of the
    Last Emperor   72
12. Fighting Families: The Best Bloodlines in MMA   78
13. Great Unknowns: The Best Fighters Who
    Never Stepped into the Cage   84

Countries That Love to Brawl

14. Brazilian Battlers: The Greatest Fighters from Brazil 93
15. Dominating Dutchmen: The Best from the
    Netherlands   99
16. Japanese Juggernauts: The Best Fighters
    from Japan   103

Fighting Occupations

17. Fighting Fires: They Put Out Fires outside the Cage   111
18. Law Dawgs: They Serve the People   115
19. GI Fighters: Soldiers in the Octagon   119

Not Your Average Fighter

20. Age Is Nothing but a Number: Defying Father Time   129
21. Fighting Phenoms: Bursting on the Scene at
    a Young Age   134
22. Extra Large: Human Anomalies   138

It's All Showbiz

23. Best Nicknames: Most Interesting Appellations   147
24. Wannabes: Celebrities Who Cross Train   151
25. Fake Wrestlers Fighting for Real: Professional
    Wrestlers in MMA   157
26. MMA on the Big Screen: The Best and
    Worst MMA Movies   163
27. MMA Actors: Fighters Who Have Made the
    Great Leap   169
28. MMA Goes Global: MMA Promotions and Bodies
    throughout the World   174

29. Not Quite Boxing: Biggest MMA Paychecks   180

Competitive Cousins: Boxing and MMA
30. Boxers' Biggest Failures in MMA: Should Have
    Stayed in the Sweet Science   189
31. Mixed Martial Artists Who Boxed Professionally:
    Trying the Sweet Science   194
32. Same Nickname Game—Mixed Martial Artists and
    Boxers: Sharing Nicknames with Famous Boxers   198

Somebody Usually Wins
33. Stunning Surprises: The Greatest Upsets in
    MMA History   205
34. Winning on Points: They Get Decisions   211
35. Captivating Comebacks: They Pulled It Out
    from Behind   215
36. Quickest Knockouts: These Fights Ended Early   221
37. Controversial Decisions: The Wrong Fighter Won   228
38. Biggest Losers: Fighters on a Perpetual
    Losing Streak   233
39. Debut Disappointments: They Lost Their First Fight 238

Fighters Have to Start Somewhere
40. It Takes More than a Singlet: Collegiate Wrestlers 245
41. Gridiron Grapplers: They Loved the Football Field   250
42. Kickboxers in MMA: Heavyweight Kickers
    Turned to MMA   256
43. Olympic Glory before MMA: They Won Gold
    Medals in the Olympics   261

MMA Standouts
44. Greatest Grapplers in MMA: Submission Specialists
    Who Dominate on the Ground   269
45. Brains and Brawn: Highly Educated Mixed
    Martial Artists   275

46. Combat Craziness: Crazy Moments in MMA History   279
47. Crazy Kickers: Hardest Kickers of the MMA   286

Selected Bibliography   293
Index   297
About the Authors   305

Photographs

A military MMA competition   13

Two women grounding and pounding   63

Paul Vunak and Adam Heath   86

A Japanese production, New Year's 2007   106

John "the Saint" Renken   121

Dan Severn on the mat   130

A *Total Combat* match   177

Brian Stann in action   223

Rodney Wallace on the football field   252

David Martinez countering an armbar   273

Acknowledgments

I would like to thank head instructor Eric Wnek of Elite Jeet Kune Do and my training partners Mike Racine, Albert Heinrich, Nathan Marinone, Chris Ipacs, and James Robinson for their time and dedication. I would also like to thank Aryana Hendrawan, Liz Norris, and Elizabeth Demers of Potomac Books for all of their help.

—Adam

I would like to thank my coauthor, Adam Heath, the people at Potomac who made the book possible, Scott "Flattop" Pope of Fightnews.com, and Jim Casey of *FIGHT!* magazine. Thank you all for either helping with the book or giving me other MMA writing opportunities.

—David

Where It All Comes From

1

MMA Originals

The First Mixed Martial Art Styles

The media and sports fans tend to believe that the sport of mixed martial arts (MMA) is a new development. Nothing could be further from the truth. It's likely older than any other competitive sport. There can be little doubt that our ancestors were actively beating each other senseless long before they had even invented the wheel. Not only did the ancient Greeks practice MMA more than two thousand years ago, but records also indicate that the Chinese were doing it even three thousand years before that. In all likelihood every ancient culture had versions of mixed martial arts that have been lost to the ages. Calling MMA a modern sport is nothing more than a marketing ploy that does an injustice to the great warriors who have come and gone.

1. KATO PANKRATION

If there was one thing the ancient Greeks were good at, it was kicking each other's asses. With only two rules—no eye gouging and no biting—*kato pankration* symbolized the Greek tradition of going to extremes and was as close to life-and-death combat as could be justified outside of warfare. Nobody knows exactly when the various forms of pankration came into existence, but by 648 BCE they had found their

3

way into the Olympic Games. However, the noble Greeks had added an additional, important rule: It was illegal for competitors to kill their opponents "voluntarily."

Of course, it wouldn't be a Greek sport if there weren't a few deaths now and again. Perhaps the most famous death in the history of kato pankration was that of Arrichion of Phigalia. While being choked Arrichion managed to apply a toe lock to his opponent, causing the man to raise a hand in submission. Unfortunately for Arrichion the submission came too late, as his opponent continued to choke him until the referee stopped the bout, by which time Arrichion had already taken his last breath. Arrichion was posthumously appointed the victor, and his legend has survived nearly three millennia.

2. GLADIATORIAL COMPETITIONS

Not only were Roman gladiators skilled in hand-to-hand combat, they were also accomplished with a wide variety of weapons and regularly used them to good effect. Although Hollywood portrays gladiator games as events held in public venues, the vast majority of such competitions were held in private between representatives of rival ludi (gladiatorial schools). Public gladiatorial games only became common in the late republic, as societal instability drove leaders to seek cost-effective ways to curry favor from cohorts and plebeians.

The majority of gladiators were slaves and criminals who had been sentenced to the arena, but as the games became more commonplace and the rewards grew, paid volunteers began to fill the ranks. Despite being the denizen of rogues and unsavory characters, well-known figures occasionally entered the games, often for no other reason than to spite their more moderate colleagues. Although Spartacus is the most revered gladiator, a number of emperors also entered the coliseum, including Commodus, who regularly appeared in character as Hercules and is credited with no fewer than a thousand appearances (albeit often on a pedestal from which he lanced creatures and men).

3. CLASSIC PUGILISM

The word pugilism may be synonymous with boxing in the modern lexicon, but the pugilism of old was a far cry from what we now see in the squared circle. The Greeks and Romans had their own version of the sport, where fighters wore various forms of knuckle dusters and often beat each other until they were dead. Banned sometime around AD 400, pugilism continued in a number of forms throughout Europe and the rest of the world.

It wasn't until the eighteenth century that we again have substantial written evidence of commonplace pugilism, as attempts were made to apply various rules to what was, in essence, free-for-all combat. In early classical matches combatants regularly grappled, tripped, and threw each other. They also pulled hair, gouged eyes, and used all manner of dirty techniques as long as they helped ensure victory. Beginning with Broughton's Rules of 1743, sportsmen made numerous attempts to limit the savagery of pugilism. These attempts culminated with the late-nineteenth-century Queensberry Rules, which are the basis for modern boxing regulations.

4. BARTITSU

A largely unknown and secretive fighting method from the late nineteenth century, Bartitsu was more of a learning style than it was a specific art form. Formulated by the Englishman Edward William Barton-Wright, who had spent a number of years in Japan, Bartitsu was primarily composed of Asian martial arts but advanced the idea of training in fighting disciplines regardless of their origin. Unlike many combat sports and traditional fighting methods of the day, Bartitsu also promoted the idea of weapons training.

Far from being just another dojo, the Bartitsu Club openly promoted competition between diverse martial arts and recommended that members maintain a strict regime of physical fitness. Unfortunately for the world of MMA, the Bartitsu Club was short lived, first opening its doors in 1898 and closing them permanently in 1902. If Sir Arthur Conan Doyle had not made Sherlock Holmes a Bartitsu practitioner in his books, the fighting style would have passed into obscurity long ago.

5. KAMPFRINGEN

Exactly who founded this system has been lost to the fog of history, but we do know that *Kampfringen*, combining elements of wrestling with striking along with the use of various weapons, was heavily practiced during the Middle Ages and the Renaissance. What little we know about this discipline has been passed down to us through a few illustrated manuscripts. Some of the imagery suggests a high degree of grappling sophistication that rivals anything seen in the Asian martial arts of the period. Kampfringen was obviously intended for warfare and commonly employed during judicial combat and duels. Many of the original techniques resemble a combination of Western clinch fighting and judo, with ground fighting deemphasized as it was considered too dangerous when weapons were involved.

6. VAJRAMUSHTI

Created in India more than two thousand years ago, Vajramushti is easily one of the oldest martial arts on record. While little can be substantiated about the initial formulation of Vajramushti, it is widely accepted that the art is a combination of other Indian martial arts that cover the gamut of fighting ranges. In traditional Vajramushti, the combatant wears a knuckle duster on one hand and uses many grappling techniques specifically designed to nullify his opponent's wielding of this deadly weapon. Experts disagree as to how Vajramushti impacted the development of other Asian martial arts, with the Chinese side arguing that the Indian martial arts that spawned Vajramushti were themselves the product of Chinese influence. The Indian side, of course, rebuts this point by showing early manuscripts that suggest Vajramushti may in actuality be the great-granddaddy of all Chinese martial arts. Either way, the art is verifiably ancient and certainly deserves great respect for its completeness and ferocity.

7. SHUAI JIAO

This Chinese martial art is a hybrid that combines both striking and wrestling, with the wrestling component being descended from the Mongolian steppes nearly five thousand years ago. With numerous variations of the style in existence, it is now difficult to differentiate between ancient and modern versions, but the majority of them incorporate the grappling techniques that can be found in tai chi chuan. Because *Shuai Jiao* is a combative system first and competitive style second, most competitions focus on throwing and off-balancing opponents while maintaining a lock so that a weapon may be brought to bear.

Deemed to be the practical form of tai chi chuan, the most combative version of Shuai Jiao was handed down to the emperor's guards and is still taught to Chinese police and military personnel. Unlike many modern grappling arts, where clothing is used to facilitate throws and improve one's position, Shuai Jiao focuses on grabbing muscle and bone in order to execute techniques properly. Competitions are regularly held throughout China, but the most brutal and truest events are primarily found on the plains of Mongolia.

8. BANDO (BURMESE BOXING)

Bando first came to the attention of Westerners at the end of World War II when a tame version of the system was brought to the United States. The modern, sportive version of Bando is often compared to the striking art of *Muay Thai*, but traditional Bando is a complete self-defense system, with native competition allowing high-velocity throws, grappling, and headbutts.

Normally regarded as a dirty sister art to Muay Thai, Bando is in fact much older. Unfortunately, while Bando has persevered for more than two thousand years, the original system is becoming increasingly obscure as the more common sporting version rapidly surpasses it in popularity. Never gaining much traction outside Myanmar, traditional Bando is quickly disappearing as the more skilled fighters make the move to the highly lucrative sporting version and Muay Thai.

9. SILAT

Often referred to as a single system, *silat* is actually a term that encompasses all of the related arts from the Malay Archipelago. Versions of silat focus on every range and aspect of fighting, from the use of sticks and knives to grappling and even biting. Because so many systems fall under the silat name, it is difficult to characterize them all. However, almost all variations encompass grappling, striking, and weapons, often with great emphasis on trips and throws.

As with many martial arts intended specifically for self-defense, silat tends to place great emphasis on using weapons. As various forms of silat evolved to meet the needs of specific practitioners, it was discovered that modern silat was becoming too focused on specific ranges. Practitioners have now begun mixing forms in order to reestablish the authenticity and original intention of the art.

10. **KALI (ESCRIMA/ARNIS)**

A comprehensive term that refers to all native Filipino martial arts, *Kali* differs from Western martial arts in that it teaches the use of weapons first and empty hand techniques last, with the goal of smoothly transitioning from one type of fighting to another. Many Western martial arts schools have adopted the weapon-based aspects of the Filipino martial arts for their self-defense value, but few practice the empty hand techniques.

Within Kali there are three basic types of unarmed fighting: *panantukan* (boxing), *pananjakman* (kicking), and *dumog* (wrestling). Although these components can be taught separately, they are most often taught as part of an integrated system. Differing from most Western fighting methods, Kali focuses not only on strikes to the opponent's head, body, and legs but also to the nerve centers on the limbs in order to destroy mobility and create openings for compound attacks.

2

Why They Call It MMA

The Most Common Martial Arts in MMA

When the sport of mixed martial arts first became fa-mous in the United States, people viewed it as a venue where different styles of martial arts could come together and compete to discover which system was the best. While Royce Gracie's jiu-jitsu was shown to be the dominant style in the early Ultimate Fighting Championship (UFC) tourna-ments, it didn't take long before competent fighters became familiar enough with the jiu-jitsu bag of tricks to eventually put the hurt on him. By the fifth UFC tournament (UFC 5), the Gracie phenomenon had effectively come to an end, and with it the modern version of mixed martial arts, where fighters adopt techniques and training methodologies from a myriad of systems, began to form. That being said, fighters still have their strengths, weaknesses, and preferred styles. Following is a list of the most commonly found martial arts in MMA, many of which have proven quite valuable.

1. WESTERN BOXING

When it comes to throwing a good punch, no fighting style can quite compare with the "sweet science." Long disre-garded as a sport by martial artists, boxing has proven its worth in the cage by leaving black belts and fighters of all styles lying battered and bleeding on the canvas. Despite the moderate success of journeyman boxers in the MMA, there have been no prime, top-level fighters who have been willing to venture into the cage. Poor pay is often cited as the primary reason, and though an aging James "Lights Out" Toney decided to pick up the gauntlet only to be put away by former UFC champ Randy Couture, few insiders consider him to be a top fighter and no decent pugilists have been willing to follow in his footsteps.

2. MUAY THAI KICKBOXING
Considered to be the hardest (and most painful) of the striking arts, Muay Thai fighters are legendary for their low kicks and ability to withstand punishment. Thailand is the native home to the sport and boasts the best Muay Thai fighters in the world. Unfortunately for MMA fans, hardly any Muay Thai champions from Thailand have ventured into the cage. However, a number of Western Muay Thai champions have competed, and almost every MMA fighter uses at least some Muay Thai techniques. Anderson Silva, perhaps the best-known striker in MMA, uses a hybrid version of Muay Thai consistently to outstrike his opponents and take grapplers out of their game plans.

3. BRAZILIAN JIU-JITSU
The impact of Brazilian jiu-jitsu (BJJ) and specifically Gracie jiu-jitsu on the sport of MMA cannot be overstated. Like boxing and Muay Thai, an MMA fighter of any value has spent countless hours on the mat either learning to implement or defend against this versatile art. Before the first UFC matches took place, few North Americans had any idea what submission grappling was all about, and Brazilian jiu-jitsu adherents capitalized on this deficit to win early tournaments. As time

went on and the cloak of secrecy surrounding Brazilian jiu-jitsu began to lift, however, the art lost much of its mystique. That being said, more professional MMA fighters still cite BJJ as their primary fighting style than any other martial art.

4. JUDO

The grandfather of Brazilian jiu-jitsu and Russian sambo, judo has a long history that can be traced back to Japan, where it was officially created in 1882. Primarily focused on throwing opponents but supplemented with a heavy dose of ground fighting, judo was one of the earliest martial arts to gain great popularity and by the mid-twentieth century had spread around the globe. Known as the "gentle way," judo allows combatants to practice full-speed techniques without substantial danger of crippling or maiming their opponents. This methodology gives judo a degree of realism that other arts lacked, and many other martial arts have since adopted a similar training philosophy.

5. JEET KUNE DO

Considered to be the direct forefather of mixed martial arts, Jeet Kune Do was developed by Bruce Lee as a practical form of street fighting that emphasized the ability to fight and flow through all ranges of combat. Adopting the best training methods of professional athletes and combining them with the most effective fighting techniques available, Jeet Kune Do is regularly described as a hybrid style that emphasizes speed, pressure, and aggressiveness over strength and power. Known as much for its strategy and philosophy as it is for its practical application, the basic tenets of Jeet Kune Do are often cited as important influences in the way MMA has developed, particularly because many of today's top coaches have at one time or another trained in Jeet Kune Do.

In recent years the U.S. Army added many MMA techniques to its hand-to-hand curriculum. Here, two soldiers compete in a military MMA competition. *United States Army*

6. SHOOT WRESTLING

One of the first fighting systems to give Brazilian jiu-jitsu practitioners significant problems, shoot wrestling combines techniques taken from various martial arts with a primary focus on grappling. A modification of the age-old "catch wrestling" that was popular at carnivals in the United States, modern shoot wrestling was developed after longtime catch wrestler Karl Gotch taught his techniques to a number of professional Japanese fighters. Shoot Fighting is technically an adaptation of shoot wrestling where additional emphasis is placed on striking. To date the most famous shoot fighter in history is Ken Shamrock, who was the first man to fight Royce Gracie to a draw. Gracie needed to be carried from the ring after their match, and with his beaten form went the myth of Brazilian jiu-jitsu's invincibility.

7. COMBAT SUBMISSION WRESTLING

Developed by MMA legend Erik Paulson, combat submission wrestling (CSW) draws on Paulson's diverse knowledge of both stand-up and ground fighting that he acquired while fighting all over the globe. Unlike most other MMA coaches, Paulson is a former champion and holds instructor-level credentials in numerous martial arts. A permanent student of Dan Inosanto's, Paulson's CSW takes Bruce Lee's philosophies into the ground fighting realm by effectively bridging the gap between stand-up and grappling, a talent that has made him one of the most popular coaches in professional mixed martial arts.

8. COMBAT SAMBO

The preferred fighting method of Fedor Emelianenko, combat sambo is one of the few systems that was meant to be a mixed martial art from its conception. Developed as a hand-to-hand combat system for the Soviet military, combat sambo was heavily influenced by judo and karate but also contains a healthy dose of traditional wrestling techniques taken from regional fighting styles in the Soviet satellite states. Intended to be a combination of the world's most effective fighting methods, combat sambo is primarily known for sophisticated leg locks but is slowly gaining notoriety for the unique looping strikes thrown by many of its practitioners.

9. GRECO-ROMAN WRESTLING

Historically, wrestling of all varieties has played a prominent role in the development of mixed martial arts. Greco-Roman wrestling has been particularly influential as many UFC champions have spent years studying the style. Differing from freestyle wrestling in that it doesn't allow fighters to trip each other or use their legs, Greco-Roman instead empha-sizes throws, arm drags, and headlocks to dominate and pin opponents. This emphasis on limited technique means that practitioners are more likely to master specific maneuvers. MMA stalwarts such as Randy Couture and Dan Henderson have made a science of using Greco-Roman wrestling to dominate larger and stronger opponents in the cage.

10. **KARATE**

There are dozens of variations of karate, and uneducated MMA fighters and fans repeatedly denigrate many of them. In reality, many of today's top MMA stars, including Georges St-Pierre, Chuck Liddell, and Lyoto Machida, have substantial karate backgrounds. Traditional karate training tends to be more structured and less flexible than the other arts that have seen success in no-holds-barred (NHB) competition, but the simple truth is that good fighters can make any system work, and the sheer number of people who have participated in karate means that we will continue to see it in the cage for many years to come.

3

MMA Coaches

The Brains behind the Brawn

Behind every good fighter is an even better coach. Sports teams generally have a variety of coaches and trainers to develop different athletic attributes, including muscular development, cardiovascular fitness, and endurance. The sport of mixed martial arts is a little bit different because professional fighters need development not only in traditional athletic areas but also in a variety of fighting disciplines. MMA coaches generally specialize in one area of fighting and bring in experts to instruct in others. However, several unique coaches can be considered experts in all areas of fighting and have gone on to become recognized as the most influential instructors in the fight game.

1. ERIK PAULSON

Erik Paulson was an MMA champion long before the sport gained popularity in the United States. A longtime disciple of Guro Dan Inosanto, Paulson became enamored with grappling in the late 1980s and was the first Westerner to win a *Shooto* title in Japan. Credited by his many opponents with being an absolute "wizard" on the ground, Paulson went on to develop his own grappling system and now teaches it to a number of professional MMA fighters. Soft-spoken and fairly refined by MMA standards, Paulson has instructed some of the best combatants in history, including Brock Lesnar, Sean Sherk, and Josh Barnett. In 2007 Paulson came out of retirement for one last match, defeating Muay Thai kickboxer Jeff Ford via armbar in the first round.

2. GREG JACKSON

Few coaches can boast the stable of fighters that Greg Jackson manages. A lifelong martial artist who was born into a family of wrestlers, Jackson was heavily influenced by the success of grappling in the early UFC events. With ten world champions fighting out of his gym, Jackson has one of the most decorated and highly publicized clubs in the world. Living and working in Albuquerque, New Mexico, Jackson is known for taking already great fighters and making them better. His best-known fighter at the time of this writing is Georges St-Pierre, who, although hailing from Canada, spends an inordinate amount of time in New Mexico to train with his illustrious coach.

3. GREG NELSON

Owner of the Academy in Minnesota, Greg Nelson is another student of Dan Inosanto and makes a living by training exceptional fighters. A former gymnast and college wrestler, Nelson is also a former competitive Muay Thai fighter and gold medalist in Brazilian jiu-jitsu. Nelson has a diverse martial arts background that allows him to focus on his student's weaknesses and turn them into strengths. He is also a cancer survivor, an experience that gives him a sense of compassion that many MMA coaches are lacking. Nelson has trained a number of exceptional fighters, including former Bodog Fight champion Nick Thompson and Muay Thai champion Nat McIntyre.

4. PAT MILETICH

Claiming to have trained more world champion fighters than any other coach in the world, Miletich is a former UFC champion who also coached two International Fight League (IFL) teams. With a fighting background that goes back to the mid-1990s, Miletich has been one of the most important names in mixed martial arts for more than a decade. He also sports one of the most impressive winning streaks in recent history, having fifteen wins before finally succumbing to Matt Hume in Extreme Fighting 4. Holding one black belt in Shuri-ryu karate and another in Brazilian jiu-jitsu, Miletich is known for being a tough, no-nonsense coach. With a fighting roster that features a who's who list of MMA stars, some of the more notable figures from the Miletich camp are Tim Sylvia, Mark Coleman, Matt Hughes, and Jens Pulver.

5. JOHN HACKLEMAN

As one of the few men to ever be inducted into the Kajukenbo Hall of Fame, Hackleman began his martial arts studies in Hawaii and later joined the U.S. Army Boxing Team. After leaving the service he was picked up by Don King and had seventeen wins and three losses on the professional circuit. Now known as the owner of the Pit gym in Arroyo Grande, California, Hackleman is a highly respected MMA coach who makes no bones about his love of brawling. Creator of Hawaiian Kempo, Hackleman is an easy conversationalist with an exceptionally well-rounded martial arts pedigree. His most accomplished student is former UFC lightweight champion Chuck Liddell, who sports the school's logo, a hooded skull, as a tattoo on his left arm.

6. RUDY VALENTINO

One of the lesser-known but still influential coaches in MMA, Rudy Valentino is another Hawaiian fighter with a background in Kajukenbo and a master instructor in Muay Thai under Dana Goodson. More important than his credentials, however, is his status as B. J. Penn's primary coach. More than anyone else, Valentino is responsible for helping his Hawaiian colleague obtain three world championships. Besides coaching Penn, Valentino has also appeared as a coach on *The Ultimate Fighter.* Valentino grabbed attention when he accused Georges St-Pierre's team of greasing its fighter, an accusation that was widely heard but the Nevada State Athletic Commission did not heed.

7. **RICARDO LIBORIO**
As co-owner of the American Top Team, Ricardo Liborio has had a significant impact on the direction of mixed martial arts in the United States. Liborio, who specializes in instructing grapplers, is in the NAGA Grappling Hall of Fame and was made head coach of the U.S. Grappling World Team in 2009. Highly respected as a competitor in his own right, Liborio has won numerous grappling competitions and is one of only a handful of black belts under Carlson Gracie. Liborio's American Top Team is one of the largest MMA teams in the world and has developed some of the sport's best fighters, including Mike Brown, Thiago Silva, Ben Saunders, Kevin "Kimbo Slice" Ferguson, and Eric "Butterbean" Esch.

8. **MATT HUME**
Matt Hume's name is practically a household word among MMA fans who have been following the sport since its beginning in the United States. Although Hume's professional career was fairly short, he did fight a number of exceptional fighters, including Erik Paulson, Pat Miletich, and Ken Shamrock, at a time when their names reflected the top tier of the sport. Retired from professional fighting since 2002,

Hume has turned his attention to training some of MMA's top athletes, such as the legends Rich Franklin, Bob Sapp, and Chris Leben.

9. MARC LAIMON

Marc Laimon is one of the younger coaches on this list, but his reputation as an excellent grappling coach far exceeds his physical age. Even though Laimon can lay claim to half a dozen significant grappling titles, the one win that put him in the spotlight was his defeat of Ryron Gracie. Soon after the match he was selected to appear on *The Ultimate Fighter* and gained further recognition after a particularly bitter dispute with competitor Matt Serra. Some of Laimon's more outstanding students include Jake Rosholt, Shane Roller, Ulysses Gomez, and Jason Carpenter.

10. FREDDIE ROACH

MMA coaches come in two varieties—specialists and non-specialists. Many of the better-known MMA coaches cut their teeth during years of grappling training, which puts them strictly in the specialist category. Freddie Roach is a little different in that he is a former professional boxer who came close to winning world titles on two different occasions. He has trained many of the best professional boxers in history, including Manny Pacquiao and Oscar De La Hoya. Roach came to the forefront of MMA training when the world witnessed Andrei Arlovski's overnight transformation into a highly technical striker, a miracle that quickly made him a much more dangerous opponent and put Roach on the MMA map. With more than twenty-five world champions under his tutelage, Roach is currently the striking coach for three of MMA's best fighters: Georges St-Pierre, Anderson Silva, and B. J. Penn.

Fighting on the Rebound

4

I Hate You

Grudge Matches

The sport of mixed martial arts seems to have many athletes who don't like each other. Before the sport really took off in America, much of this animosity seemed to be real and founded on genuine dislike. As the years have passed and the sport has become more profitable, many MMA fighters have assumed personalities similar to those of professional wrestlers, and the feuds have stemmed more from showmanship than actual hate. That being said, MMA has certainly seen any number of real grudges, some of which made for some damn good fights.

1. KEN SHAMROCK VS. ROYCE GRACIE

This is the original MMA grudge match, with accusations and hatred flying back and forth from the fighters' first encounter. Before these two men were legends, they were both simply fighters who were intent on cementing their legacies in the United States. Gracie won their first encounter by submission, but the fight was later clouded by controversy as Shamrock accused Gracie of using the sleeve of his *gi*, which would be considered a weapon, to work the choke. Their second match was a draw, but Shamrock had beaten Gracie so badly that he had to be carried from the ring. Since then the two have

23

thrown verbal jabs at each other on various occasions but have never fought a rematch.

2. MATT HUGHES VS. MATT "THE TERROR" SERRA

These two guys have reputations as being a bit unfriendly, and each has characterized the other as the ultimate jerk. Their feud stems from various incidents on *The Ultimate Fighter* television show, where Hughes was a coach and Serra a contestant. The bitterness only gained momentum until they met in the cage. The result was a hard-fought contest that saw both men give their all, but Hughes emerged victorious. The two embraced at the end of the fight, and the feud was over.

3. RASHAD "SUGAR" EVANS VS. QUINTON "RAMPAGE" JACKSON

The Ultimate Fighter seems to produce a great deal of bad blood. Anyone who studiously watched the program could hardly miss the brewing anger between Evans and Jackson that was supposed to culminate in a match between the two at the end of the season. Unlike MMA grudge matches that are invented to boost ratings, the feud between these two seemed real enough, and fans were greatly disappointed when Jackson announced his retirement before the fight took place. In all likelihood this "retirement" was just a stunt so he could act in the film remake of *The A-Team*, and the two eventually fought at UFC 114. Both fighters fought hard, but Evans was awarded the victory. The fight ended with the usual hugs and backslaps that signify the end to a feud.

4. JENS "LITTLE EVIL" PULVER VS. B. J. "THE PRODIGY" PENN

The rivalry between Penn and Pulver began in UFC 35 when Penn looked all but unstoppable as he fought his way through the UFC lightweight ranks. In what will go down as one of the greatest matches in MMA history, Pulver and Penn battled it out on the ground and on their feet with Pulver surprising everyone not only by stifling Penn's every attack but also by beating the formerly unstoppable fighter in every range. Pulver stuffed Penn's ground attacks in such a dominant manner that Penn decided to keep the last round standing, and in the process Pulver rocked him with a number of tremendous blows. Midway through the round, Penn connected with what appeared to be an intentional kick to Pulver's groin, and the fight was restarted after a minute's delay. Pulver came back with more punches to win the round and the fight. Five years later they met again as coaches on the set of *The Ultimate Fighter*, and this time Penn emerged victorious from their final bout, defeating Pulver by a rear naked choke.

5. ANDREI "THE PIT BULL" ARLOVSKI VS. TIM "THE MAINE-IAC" SYLVIA

Exactly why Arlovski and Sylvia dislike each other is a matter of conjecture. Whatever the case may be, we do know for sure that the men fought three times and that the first fight went to Arlovski by way of submission from an ankle lock, crowning him the interim UFC heavyweight champion. When organizers realized that Frank Mir, the reigning but injured heavyweight champion, would not be able to compete, they awarded the official crown to Arlovski. Around six months later Arlovski fought Sylvia again, this time losing by way of a technical knockout (TKO). By Sylvia's request the two fought again, and this time the fight went the distance. Once more Sylvia defeated Arlovski, who seriously injured his leg during the match. Some suspect that had he been able to throw effective kicks, the outcome of the fight may have been different.

6. BROCK LESNAR VS. FRANK MIR

This hate-filled feud might have gone differently if it hadn't been for a referee. When the duo first met in the ring, there was no love lost between the two, and the fight began with fireworks and ended up on the ground. As Lesnar obtained the dominant position, the referee stepped in and stood them up, even docking Lesnar a point for illegal punches. Shortly afterward Mir got Lesnar in a kneebar, ending the fight. After that there was no end to the insults hurled from both parties, and when they finally met in the ring again, Lesnar was visibly agitated. Unfortunately for his opponent, Lesnar's lack of composure did not slow his assault, and Mir lost the bout from referee stoppage in the second round.

7. BAS "EL GUAPO" RUTTEN VS. JASON DeLUCIA

To say that this rivalry is strange is an understatement, mainly because it isn't quite clear whether Rutten felt there was a rivalry at all. DeLucia certainly did, and he made it known throughout the media and, eventually, cyberspace. At one point DeLucia even sent Rutten a strange, mystical painting that supposedly required a drop of blood to make it "operate properly." This painting, of course, was a bit of voodoo, or black magic, and was intended to cost Rutten his fight against Frank Shamrock. Maybe it even worked, because Rutten did end up losing the fight. But that painting didn't do DeLucia any good, because Rutten beat him on three separate occasions and even ruptured DeLucia's liver with a series of his infamous liver shots.

8. FRANK "THE LEGEND" SHAMROCK VS. PHIL BARONI

When professional MMA starts to resemble the World Wrestling Entertainment (WWE) brand, you know that something's up. In this case MMA competitors turned to new media in order to take shots at each other, with Frank Shamrock releasing several online videos lampooning his opponent. Baroni fired back with some choice words of his own. The whole feud was obviously staged to gain publicity for the promotion, but both men trained hard for the fight and each entered the first round sporting fairly serious injuries (sustained in training). The match started hard with Shamrock knocking Baroni to the ground repeatedly in the first round. It ended in the second when Shamrock rendered Baroni unconscious with a rear naked choke.

9. GEORGES "RUSH" ST-PIERRE VS. B. J. "THE PRODIGY" PENN

When it comes to MMA there are no greater stars than St-Pierre and Penn. Not only are these two superior grapplers, their personalities have earned them legions of devoted fans. It should come as no surprise, then, that these two outspoken athletes developed something of a feud, especially when they're fighting for the same crown. The two fought twice over a period of three years, with Penn getting the worst of it both times. During the first fight Penn lost a close split decision. The second fight, which was for the UFC welterweight title, showed an initially confident Penn lose steam in the second round. By the fourth round Penn was in trouble, and his corner threw in the towel. The controversy began as Penn later claimed that St-Pierre's corner man had intentionally greased St-Pierre between rounds during the fight. Penn filed a complaint with the Nevada State Athletic Association, but it took no action. The UFC, meanwhile, instituted new rules governing the use of petroleum jelly in the ring. Penn has since unofficially accepted a rematch with St-Pierre, but he has also called for the suspension of his opponent's fighting license.

10. KEN SHAMROCK VS. TITO "THE HUNTINGTON BEACH BAD BOY" ORTIZ

Ken Shamrock seems to dislike many people, and for a number of years Tito Ortiz was high up on his list. It all began when Ortiz started knocking off the top fighters from Shamrock's club, the Lion's Den, one at a time. The feud grew to full swing after a controversial fight between Guy Mezger and Ortiz, where it appeared to most spectators that Mezger had tapped after taking a series of knees to the head. The referee saw it differently and restarted the fight standing, which allowed Mezger to secure a guillotine that forced Ortiz to tap. They met again at UFC 19, and this time Ortiz dominated Mezger, forcing a stoppage. Ortiz then went back to his corner, donned an offensive T-shirt, and flipped off the opposing team.

Ken Shamrock took the insult personally, and despite a torn anterior cruciate ligament (ACL) injury, he fought Ortiz three years later at UFC 40, losing when his corner threw in the towel. Naturally, then UFC president Dana White saw fit to make the enemies competing coaches on *The Ultimate Fighter*, which made things worse. The two met again in UFC 61 only to have the referee, who determined Shamrock wasn't defending himself after a series of elbows, stop the bout in the first round. Nobody agreed with this decision, and Dana White immediately set up a rematch. The third fight, which was broadcast on Spike TV, saw Shamrock lose the fight in the first round. Naturally Ortiz put on another offensive T-shirt and began talking smack, but after a brief discussion with Shamrock, the two declared that it was all "just business" and said amiable things about each other.

5

Tough Trilogies

They Fought Three Great Fights against Each Other

Some epic trilogies have elevated sports to mythic proportions. In boxing the classic series between Muhammad Ali and Joe Frazier is the stuff of legends, culminating in the unforgettable "Thrilla in Manila." Mixed martial arts also has had its share of famous trilogies. Some have been terrific, such as the pitched battles between Chuck "the Iceman" Liddell and Randy "the Natural" Couture. Others have been decidedly one sided, as in Tito Ortiz's dismantling of the older Ken Shamrock.

1. CHUCK "THE ICEMAN" LIDDELL VS. RANDY "CAPTAIN AMERICA" COUTURE

These two Ultimate Fighting Championship Hall of Famers waged perhaps the most famous rivalry in UFC—and perhaps MMA—history for light heavyweight supremacy. In June 2003, Liddell entered the octagon on a four-year winning streak. He was expected to dismantle an aging Couture on his way to a title shot against then-champion Tito Ortiz. Couture shocked the sporting world by standing, trading, and outstriking the vaunted Iceman. Couture captured a knockout win in the third round. Nearly two years later, Liddell wreaked revenge, crushing Couture with his devastating right hand. That defeat set the stage for the rubber match, the most highly anticipated match in UFC history, in February 2006. Liddell again avoided the clinch and managed to take Couture out with his punches in the second round. While the Iceman vaulted to the mythical pound-for-pound supremacy, Couture announced his retirement—though he did return and later won the UFC heavyweight title.

2. SHINYA "TOBIKAN JUDAN" AOKI VS. JOACHIM "HELLBOY" HANSEN

One of the most competitive and thrilling trilogies in mixed martial arts history featured two lightweights—Shinya Aoki from Japan and Joachim Hansen from Norway. The two first met in a Pride bout in 2006. Aoki managed to pull off a *gogoplata* (a type of chokehold) submission, one of the few times such a move has been successfully accomplished in a professional MMA bout. Hansen lived up to his nickname in their July 2008 rematch in the finals of a Dream tournament. He used his superior punching power to stop Aoki in the second round and won the lightweight championship. Then came the rubber match, which also took place under the Dream promotional banner, in October 2009. After a competitive first round, Aoki managed to sink in an armbar and submitted Hansen in the second round.

3. WANDERLEI "THE AXE MURDERER" SILVA VS. QUINTON "RAMPAGE" JACKSON

Two of the most explosive fighters of all time, Wanderlei Silva and Quinton Jackson, staged an epic rivalry first in Pride and then in the UFC with their three thrilling battles. Their feud started in Pride, where Silva was firmly ensconced as the middleweight champion and Jackson wanted his shot. The two first met in the finals of the Pride 2003 Middleweight Grand Prix. Jackson aggressively attacked for much of the fight, but Silva stopped him with a series of devastating knee strikes more than six minutes into the first round. Nearly a year later, Jackson got his rematch in October 2004, but unfortunately he suffered a much worse fate. Silva unloaded an even deadlier batch of knee strikes that knocked Rampage senseless. Those defeats left an indelible impression on Jackson, who vowed he would avenge them. He finally got his chance after both fighters were in the UFC. In December 2008, Jackson knocked out Silva with one devastating left hook and stopped his rival.

4. GEORGES "RUSH" ST-PIERRE VS. MATT HUGHES

For the past decade the two greatest 170-pounders in the world have been Matt Hughes and his successor, the ridiculously athletic Georges St-Pierre. The two first collided in October 2004 for the UFC welterweight championship. St-Pierre showed his striking advantage in the first round, but Hughes managed a couple of takedowns. He also showed the value of experience, as he managed to secure an armbar and submit the challenger. St-Pierre had to wait a little more than two years for the rematch in November 2006 at UFC 65. This time St-Pierre stopped Hughes in the second round with a series of strikes. Finally, the two squared off at UFC 79 in December 2007. In this bout the difference in the men's athleticism was glaring. St-Pierre took Hughes down and dominated him, eventually submitting him near the end of the second round with an armbar. It truly was the passing of the torch from one champion to another.

5. WANDERLEI "THE AXE MURDERER" SILVA VS. KAZUSHI "GRACIE HUNTER" SAKURABA

Two of the most talented and entertaining mixed martial artists in the history of Pride squared off three times at Pride 13,

Pride 17, and the opening round of the Pride 2003 Middle-weight Grand Prix tournament. The combatants were the Brazilian striker Wanderlei Silva and the Japanese wrestler Kazushi Sakuraba. The style matchup simply didn't favor Sakuraba, who faced a stronger and more powerful striker. At Pride 13 in March 2001, Silva introduced the Japanese legend to his kicks and delivered a soccer kick knockout less than two minutes into the fight. At Pride 17 in November 2001, Sakuraba fought better and showed great courage in surviving the first round. However, he took a brutal beating, and the doctor stopped the contest at the end of the ten-minute round. Then, in August 2003, the two squared off for the third time. Once again, Silva dispatched Sakuraba in the first round, this time with a knockout punch.

6. RANDY COUTURE VS. VITOR "THE PHENOM" BELFORT

Many MMA fans forget that Randy Couture and Vitor Belfort fought three times in their careers. At UFC 15 in 1997, the two squared off as undefeated prospects. Belfort entered the octagon at 4-0 and Couture at 3-0. Couture surprised many by stopping the faster Belfort with strikes in the first round. The two would not meet again for nearly seven years, when in February 2004 at UFC 46, Couture defended his UFC light heavyweight title against the Phenom. This time Belfort's speed was phenomenal, and forty-nine seconds into the bout he opened up a serious gash on Couture's left eyelid. Attending physician Dr. Margaret Goodman stopped the fight. Later that year in August, Couture exacted his revenge and regained his title by stopping Belfort in the third round.

7. TIM "THE MAINE-IAC" SYLVIA VS. ANDREI "THE PIT BULL" ARLOVSKI

Frank Mir had been the UFC heavyweight champion, dominating the division with his superior submission skills. Sadly, he suffered a near-fatal motorcycle accident that derailed his MMA career and left a void in the UFC's heavyweight division. Two fighters stepped in to fill that void—six-foot-nine Tim Sylvia and an exciting striker from Russia named Andrei Arlovski. The two first met in February 2005 at UFC 51. Arlovski landed a devastating right hand that dropped the big man. Arlovski, a sambo expert, then quickly secured an Achilles lock, and Sylvia tapped. Sylvia won the rematch at UFC 59 in April 2006, surviving another early Arlovski assault and then using his underrated boxing skills to stop his opponent. It led to the rubber match on July 2006 at UFC 61, which turned into a bit of a snoozer. Neither fighter did significant damage, though Sylvia worked enough to earn a five-round unanimous decision victory and keep the heavyweight crown.

8. TITO "THE HUNTINGTON BEACH BAD BOY" ORTIZ VS. KEN SHAMROCK

An entertaining though one-sided trilogy took place between the brash, trash-talking Tito Ortiz and one of the sport's pioneers who was nearly as brash, battler Ken Shamrock. The two first met in November 2002 at UFC 40, with Ortiz defending his light heavyweight title for the fifth time. Ortiz, a South Park fan, drew roars for wearing a shirt up to the cage that read, "I Killed Kenny. You Bastard!" He dominated the fight over his older opponent. A game Shamrock took as much punishment as he could, but he did not answer for the fourth round.

The rivalry between the two increased after they served as opposing coaches on season 3 of the popular show *The Ultimate Fighter.* They eventually fought a second match in July 2006 at UFC 61. Ortiz took Shamrock down and pounded him with elbow strikes, stopping him in the first round. Shamrock apparently protested loudly enough that it was a premature stoppage to merit a third fight. In October 2006 Ortiz closed the show with another impressive striking display. He once again stopped Shamrock in the first round to end this one-sided trilogy.

9. MIRKO "CRO COP" FILIPOVIĆ VS. JOSH "THE WARMASTER" BARNETT

Two of the best heavyweights in Pride and MMA history during the mid-2000s were former kickboxing sensation Mirko "Cro Cop" Filipović and wrestling standout Josh Barnett. Though both fell under the inescapable shadow of the dominant Fedor Emelianenko, these two waged battle three times. They first met in October 2004 at Pride 28 with a bad result. Early into the fight Barnett suffered a shoulder injury and had to submit. Nearly a year later at Pride 30 in October 2005, Barnett was able to fight the full three-round distance but dropped a unanimous decision to the flashier striker, Cro Cop.

In 2006, the two squared off again in the finals of the 2006 Pride Grand Prix Open Weight Tournament. Anticipation abounded as the two combatants had looked quite good in reaching the finals. Cro Cop had knocked out the dangerous Wanderlei Silva with a kick to the head, while Barnett had outpointed the great Antônio Rodrigo Nogueira via split decision in his semifinal match. The finals once again proved a bit anticlimactic, as Barnett suffered an eye injury during the first round and the fight was stopped.

10. MASAKATSU FUNAKI VS. VERNON "THE TIGER" WHITE

Masakatsu Funaki was a cofounder of Pancrase hybrid wrestling in 1993 and a skilled submission fighter who was simply ahead of the competition by a mile. He showed that over the course of his career in Pancrase by defeating the likes of Frank Shamrock and Bas Rutten. He dominated another fighter, the up-and-coming Vernon White. A skilled striker with good kicks, White simply didn't have the experience to deal with Funaki's submission skills. The two fighters fought three times in Pancrase matches—March 1994, December 1994, and June 1996—but in all three, White failed to reach the end of the first round. Funaki knocked him out in the first fight and won submissions in the next two.

Not Everything Goes According to Plan

6

Downright Dirty

Fighters Who Cheat

Early mixed martial arts fights had few, if any rules. During those matches it was essentially up to the opponents to reach gentlemen's agreements before and during the bouts, agreements that often were forgotten as soon as the fight started. Since then numerous rules have been instituted to protect fighters and to make for more entertaining matches. As the old saying goes, though, rules are meant to be broken. When the blood starts pouring and adrenaline kicks in, some fighters give in to their natural instincts and turn legitimate MMA matches into no-holds-barred street fights.

1. KEITH "THE GIANT KILLER" HACKNEY

Hair pulling, groin shots, and headbutts were what the early Ultimate Fighting Championship was all about, and it was a far different event than what we see today. Yet, as noted, the UFC had gentleman's agreements and most, if not all, fighters shied away from using the aforementioned tactics, but on occasion, when faced with defeat or even a grueling match, some fighters would resort to anything to win. To say that Keith Hackney relied on such techniques is inaccurate. He resorted to those techniques when others wouldn't. They also served him well. Whether he was trying to kick Emmanuel

Yarborough in the groin or repeatedly punching Joe Son in his, Keith Hackney secured a place in history as a man who would do anything to win.

2. GILBERT "THE HURRICANE" YVEL

Fight fans around the world know Gilbert Yvel not only for his fighting prowess but also for his recourse to foul tactics in desperate matches. With a hangdog face and permanent scowl, Yvel even looks mean. He has been disqualified twice for biting opponents and once for blatantly eye gouging Don Frye. Through the years Yvel has been accused of all sorts of other unfair tactics, but his most notorious gambit took place in a 2004 match against Atte Backman. The two fighters were in a clinch, with Yvel on the ropes and getting the worse of it. To keep the fighters from going into the crowd, the referee separated them and tried to restart them in the center of the ring. Yvel refused to remain in the disadvantaged position for the restart. After the referee tried for what seemed like the tenth time, Yvel finally had had enough and flung the referee across the ring. As if he hadn't gone too far already, Yvel gave the referee a kick for good measure in what is easily one of the lowest points in MMA history.

3. BRANKO "THE CROATION TIGER" CIKATIĆ

The majority of dirty fighters tend to stick to the basics, such as hitting below the belt and poking people in the eyes, but not Branko Cikatić. Before every fight he seems to take a look at the rules and make note of the more mundane ones that he wants to break. Making elbow strikes to the top of the head, kicking on the ground, and grabbing the ropes—all are staples of Cikatić's normal game plan. His most publicized dirty shots occurred when fighting Mark Kerr, as Cikatić constantly elbowed him in the back of the neck during their match. His most effective foul shot, however, was when he shin kicked a fallen Ralph White in the head during a K-1 bout. When White stood up, he was sporting a goose egg that grew by the second until it was the size of a softball, causing the match to be immediately stopped.

4. GERARD GORDEAU

Gordeau has been the subject of much controversy throughout his long career. During the first Ultimate Fighting Championship the Aryan-looking Gordeau made the strange mistake of giving the American crowd a series of what appeared to be Nazi salutes, something he stopped doing in later matches. During the same tournament he bit Royce Gracie's ear. Gracie responded by throwing him a few side headbutts. Gordeau's most sensational tactic was used against Japanese fighter Yuki Nakai. Despite outweighing the Japanese fighter by nearly fifty pounds, Gordeau decided to eye gouge the smaller man, a move that resulted in Nakai losing his vision in one eye.

5. BOB "DIRTY BOB" SCHRIJBER

Bob Schrijber has all sorts of unflattering nicknames, but the most revealing is Dirty Bob. Hardly known to American audiences, Schrijber's fighting career spans nearly fifteen years and has taken him all over the world. A man who considers the rules in MMA bouts too restrictive, Schrijber is as notorious for his behavior outside the ring as he is for his behavior inside it. An admitted partier who spent his youth carousing and brawling, Schrijber and his fighting wife, Irma, have reputations for being two of the biggest hard asses in MMA. Looking more like a pit bull than a human, Schrijber thinks nothing of resorting to dirty tactics in the ring, be it holding ropes, headbutting, or kicking a man while he's down. Although Schrijber has held a number of championships, his best fight occurred on a smaller ticket against Gilbert Yvel. During the bout, both fighters ignored any sort of defensive strategy and just pounded away at each other, making for an exciting–and very bloody–match. Yvel won after the doctor stopped the fight because Schrijber could no longer see. The fight is still regarded as one of the most violent in MMA history.

6. MIKE KYLE

The sport of mixed martial arts has been substantially cleaned up since it first debuted in the United States. The idea of no-holds-barred rules greatly boosted its initial following, but as the sport grew in popularity, the "bad boy" image of MMA had to change for the sport to reach a broader audience. In recent memory not many fighters have made a point of breaking the rules, but Mike Kyle is a leading exception. Supporters claim that he gets caught up in the heat of battle, while others say he strategically uses dirty tactics to defeat superior opponents. Regardless of whether it is by intent or accident, Kyle seems to use an unusually high number of illegal techniques. Kyle has poked a number of adversaries in the eyes and once upped the ante by biting Wes Sims. In another match he soccer kicked opponent Brian Olsen in the face when Olsen was down and continued the attack even after the referee stepped in. This infraction resulted in an eighteen-month suspension and in many fans' eyes forever colored Kyle as a dirty and dishonorable opponent.

7. WES "THE PROJECT" SIMS

Wes Sims stands six foot ten, which currently makes him one of the tallest fighters ever to compete in the UFC. That height gives him a major advantage over many of his opponents and even allowed him to put a serious body triangle on Mike Kyle during their match, to which Kyle responded by biting his chest. Since then Sims has had more than two dozen fights and appeared on the show *The Ultimate Fighter*. With such a pedigree you would think that he would be remembered for some of his best battles, but that's not the case. When Sims is no longer a contender, he likely still will be remembered for his performance against Frank Mir in UFC 43, where he held onto the cage and attempted to stomp Mir's head into jelly. This move cost him the fight and has gone down as one of MMA's most fiendish moments.

8. CHEICK "THE FRENCH SENSATION" KONGO

As someone who claims *not* to be a dirty fighter, Kongo certainly has a long history of landing illegal blows. Whether it was kneeing a downed opponent or hitting Mirko "Cro Cop" Filipović repeatedly in the groin, Kongo's actions seem to be the subject of continual controversy. His fight against Cro Cop was such that it has colored his entire career, and every time he steps into the ring, announcers and fans alike can't help but comment on the probability that Kongo will offer a repeat performance. And it isn't just the low blows against the erstwhile Croatian that fans think about, either. Kongo has "accidentally" kneed a number of opponents, including Mustapha Al-Turk, when it was specifically against the rules.

9. ALEX "EL TORO" ANDRADE

In a sport where otherwise civilized people try their damnedest to smash other people's heads in, a few foul blows can be expected. Most of these foul shots occur in the form of knees to the groin during a clinch, and if a few accidentally slip through during a fight, nobody pays much attention. But when Andrade fought Krzysztof Soszynski, Andrade made at least half a dozen such groin shots that *connected* before prompting a disqualification. Andrade is no newcomer to illegal blows. In UFC 26 Andrade, while wearing grappling shoes, fought Amaury Bitetti. When Bitetti went to the ground, Andrade immediately kicked him in the head, connecting with the shoe. Andrade kicked his opponent two more times, but on the last one the referee stepped in and disqualified him.

10. **REПATO "BABALU" SOBRAL**

Not known for his social skills, for all intents and purposes Sobral seems to be one of the most disliked fighters in mixed martial arts. His poor reputation began with his fight against Brad Kohler in 2000, and while Kohler was out on the ground, Sobral decided to soccer kick him in the head, winning the fight. It wasn't until his match with David Heath, however, that Sobral really earned the crowd's fury. During the fight, Sobral dominated his opponent through ground and pound and transitioned to an anaconda choke. After a few seconds Heath tapped out, but Sobral refused to release the hold even though the referee was trying to pry his hands apart. Sobral held the choke until Heath passed out. The fight cost him his UFC contract and a fine from the Nevada State Athletic Commission.

7

Low Blows

The Most Telling Foul Shots in the Sport

One of the big differences between a professional fight and a street fight is that professional fights have rules. Depending on the fight's location, the rules can change, but in general there are always blows and tactics that are considered illegal and dishonorable. While rules are meant to broken—indeed, every rule in mixed martial arts competition has been broken dozens, if not hundreds, of times—most of these infractions go unnoticed. Some breaches, however, stand out as being so egregious that fans and promoters both cringed—the fan because of the perceived pain and the promoters because of the bad publicity that such foul tactics bring to their sport, which is still banned in several states.

1. CHEICK "THE FRENCH SENSATION" KONGO VS. MIRKO "CRO COP" FILIPOVIĆ

In a sport where most low blows are accidental and the offender often shows remorse or at least apologizes, a few fighters still claim innocence but have a history of throwing the foulest blows at the most optimal times. Cheick Kongo is one of those fighters, and his infamy grew when he battled Mirko Filipović in Ultimate Fighting Championship 75. The fight began with Kongo stalking his opponent around the ring, using his reach advantage to keep the smaller fighter at a distance. As the long-range sparring continued into later rounds, Kongo pinned his opponent against the cage and landed a series of devastating knees to the groin that went uncorrected by the referee, "Big" John McCarthy. As the fight moved into round 3 and it became clear that it would go to the judges, Kongo once again pinned Cro Cop against the cage and landed another low blow. This time McCarthy stepped in, but instead of deducting points, he simply warned Kongo and the fight continued. The decision eventually went to Kongo, but had the official deducted the appropriate points for Kongo's low blows, Cro Cop would have emerged victorious.

2. ALISTAIR "DEMOLITION MAN" OVEREEM VS. MIRKO "CRO COP" FILIPOVIĆ

If there's one thing that Cro Cop should get used to at this point in his career, it is getting kneed in the groin. The fight began with Overeem as the aggressor, keeping the former champion off balance and taking him to the ground twice. After the second restart for inaction, a flurry of strikes followed, and Cro Cop was pushed against the ropes, where Overeem landed multiple groin strikes. Cro Cop became incapacitated when Overeem threw him to the ground, and the referee quickly stopped the match. The doctor stepped in and wouldn't allow Cro Cop to continue. The match was declared no contest. In later interviews Cro Cop admitted that his testicle had been driven up into his body and that the injury was still causing him distress.

3. RON FAIRCLOTH VS. ALESSIO "LEGIONARIUS" SAKARA

Known for his amateur boxing record and ability to throw down with some of the best pugilists in MMA, Sakara took on veteran MMA fighter Ron Faircloth in UFC 55. The fight was pretty much a one-way contest, with Sakara giving Faircloth a boxing tutorial from the beginning of the first round and Faircloth doing everything he could just to make it into the second. At the start of the new round, Faircloth stepped forward and landed a mighty kick directly against Sakara's groin. Sakara went down and couldn't continue. The fight was a ruled a "no contest," but the sensational kick made Faircloth an overnight Internet sensation.

4. ANTHONY "RUMBLE" JOHNSON VS. KEVIN "THE FIRE" BURNS

Although most of us think that the world of mixed martial arts produces the toughest fighters on the planet (and rightfully so), sometimes we forget just how fragile the human body really is. One fight that stands out for its display of poor sportsmanship and bad luck occurred in 2008, when Anthony Johnson took on Kevin Burns. Both opponents were tough and in prime condition, with the fight seesawing back and forth for three rounds. As the fight progressed Burns kept getting warned about eye poking, but the warnings went unheeded. Then, twenty-eight seconds into the third round, Burns landed one of the best eye jabs in UFC history when he threw an open hand at Johnson's face. Recoiling in pain and shock, Johnson fell to the floor, and the referee ended the fight. To everyone's surprise, despite receiving repeated warnings, Burns was awarded the victory. In the post-fight interview, Burns claimed that he couldn't make a fist with his left hand because of repeated breakages so there was no way he could avoid jabbing with his fingers.

5. FRANK "TWINKLE TOES" TRIGG VS. MATT HUGHES

As a match that would go down in history, Hughes versus Trigg was one of the highlights of UFC 52. It can only be expected that two world-class wrestlers who don't like each other will put on a great show, but the intensity and anger that both fighters displayed in this match was unusual. The fight began with both men throwing a few shots, followed by a fast clinch. Everything was going as planned until Trigg punched Hughes cleanly in the groin, sending the former champion scrambling backward in anticipation of a warning. Instead, the referee did nothing. Trigg took advantage of the inaction to shoot in, taking Hughes to the mat and gaining his back. Hughes fought his way out, went for a ground and pound, and then turned the tables against Trigg by implementing a rear naked choke of his own.

6. KEITH "THE GIANT KILLER" HACKNEY VS. JOE SON

Younger no-holds-barred aficionados probably forget that the early UFC had few hard-and-fast rules. What it did have was an unwritten code of contact whereby contestants abstained from using certain questionable techniques. Those agreements, however, mean very little when someone is trying to choke you unconscious or tear your head off. In this particular match, Hackney was on the receiving end of both moves at the same time and didn't like it. His answer was to punch Joe Son repeatedly in the groin, and Son retaliated—by doing absolutely nothing. If anything can be said about this match, it is that no technique, however painful, will work each and every time against all opponents.

7. WANDERLEI "THE AXE MURDERER" SILVA VS. GILBERT "THE HURRICANE" YVEL

Few kicks in MMA history rang with such authority as the one Wanderlei Silva perpetuated against Gilbert Yvel. In a fight that lasted only twenty-one seconds, Silva managed to land a perfectly timed cut kick to Yvel's groin, resulting in an audible crack that reverberated through the arena. Yvel spent the next three minutes writhing in pain on the canvas, after which the fight was ruled a no contest. Even though Silva had thrown an admittedly foul blow, most MMA fans were inwardly pleased by his actions. Yvel is widely considered to be one of the dirtiest fighters in MMA, and fans viewed the kick as a little bit of payback for his less-than-honorable actions.

8. JOACHIM "HELLBOY" HANSEN VS. TATSUYA "CRUSHER" KAWAJIRI

Sporting the prerequisite sleeve tattoo and matching bad attitude, Joachim Hansen is a seasoned grappler who wears his cauliflower ears with pride. Fighting out of Norway, Hansen's most noteworthy opponent to date is Eddie Alvarez, who defeated him via unanimous decision back in 2008. What really put Joachim on the map, however, was his championship Shooto bout against Tatsuya Kawajiri. The match took place in Japan and lasted a staggering eight seconds, ending when Hansen delivered a powerful rear leg kick to Kawajiri's groin. When Kawajiri couldn't continue, the match was called off, and Hansen was disqualified.

9. JOSH BARNETT VS. SIALA-MOU "MIGHTY MO" SILIGA

A heavyweight kickboxer turned MMA fighter, "Mighty Mo" Siliga isn't exactly a household name. Josh Barnett, meanwhile, is known to NHB enthusiasts worldwide and has fought many top-flight competitors. Unfortunately, at this point in his career, Barnett is probably just as well known for his dismissal from the UFC. In one of his more entertaining matches, Barnett, who was wearing shoes, managed to tag Siliga in the groin with a savate toe kick. Siliga instantly dropped to the mat. He was able to recover but lost shortly afterward via submission. When the match concluded, Barnett went over to apologize to Siliga, who promptly kneed him in the groin in retaliation.

10. DARIUS SKLIAUDYS VS. NAOYUKI KOTANI

Legal or not, every type of strike and submission has found its way, at one time or another, into MMA competition. At least that's what many people had thought until they witnessed the shocking Skliaudys vs. Kotani fight in 2005. The fight was fast and competitive from the beginning, with neither fighter able to gain a significant advantage over the other. Then, in the third round, Kotani was taken to the ground and landed with his head against the ropes. Skliaudys went for the mount, but Kotani fought him off with a barrage of upkicks. Frustrated in his attempt, Skliaudys stepped in with a plunging hammerfist that smashed Kotani's groin in a very disturbing manner. Despite the freak shot, the fight continued and was judged a draw.

8

Ouch

The Worst Injuries in MMA

People are prone to getting hurt, and every serious contact sport has its fair share of injuries. Mixed martial arts differs from other competitive activities in that the whole point of the competition is for one fighter to literally beat his or her opponent into unconsciousness or submission. Certainly other sports promote full contact and, in some, pummeling one's opponent senseless is vital to success. That being said, no other sport gives participants such a wide variety of tools for harming each other. Following is a list of some of the most graphic, if not worst, injuries ever to occur in the cage.

1. CAL WORSHAM VS. ZANE "NASTY" FRAZIER

The Internet has been an unbelievably successful tool for dispersing images of carnage and violence around the globe, and the sport of MMA has certainly seen its share of both. The battle between Worsham and Frazier wasn't a particularly gory one, but the internal damage done to one of the opponents stands as the worst injury ever to occur in the cage. It all began when Worsham charged Frazier and took a tremendously powerful knee that crushed his chest, damaged his heart, and reportedly collapsed a lung. Despite the horrific injury—and thanks to Frazier being knocked off balance—Worsham went on to win the fight by taking Frazier to the ground and beating him into submission. Worsham later collapsed backstage and was rushed to the hospital. He eventually made a full recovery and returned to the ring.

2. TIM "THE MAINE-IAC" SYLVIA VS. FRANK MIR

The sport of MMA has been around long enough that most fans have grown fairly nonchalant about seeing breaks and dislocations. Every once in a while, however, cringe-inducing injuries still occur, and Ultimate Fighting Championship 48 had one that was worthy of retelling. The evening's main event featured Frank Mir and Tim Sylvia competing for the vacant heavyweight title slot, and Sylvia almost immediately made the cardinal mistake of going to the ground with Mir, who just as quickly pulled him into an armbar. As Sylvia tried to fight his way out of it, Mir pulled the big man's forearm against the inside of his thigh, and everyone in the audience saw the bones give way. Although Sylvia claimed that he could continue, the referee stopped the bout and awarded Mir the win. Sylvia eventually had a titanium plate implanted in his arm and was back in action six months later.

3. SHINYA "TOBIKAN JUDAN" AOKI VS. KEITH "THE POLISH CONNECTION" WISNIEWSKI

Japanese fighters are known for their intense grappling skills, and Shinya Aoki is one of the best. In the Shooto 2005 tournament, he fought Keith Wisniewski in a match that rapidly became a clinch contest. Midway through the first round, Aoki had Wisniewski against the ropes but was suffering a barrage of knees for the effort. To avoid retaliatory knee strikes, Wisniewski reached down to put his arm underneath Aoki's underhook. In a display of classical jiu-jitsu that is rarely seen in competition, Aoki stepped back and wrenched Wisniewski's arm against his midsection, breaking the American's elbow. Wincing in pain and sporting a useless arm, Wisniewski was taken to the ground, where the referee stopped the match.

4. KARO "THE HEAT" PARISYAN VS. DIEGO "THE NIGHTMARE" SANCHEZ

A feared grappler, competent striker, and worshipper of the personal empowerment coach Tony Robbins, Diego Sanchez is known for fast-paced contests where he and his adversaries spend a great deal of time getting thrown on their heads. Although he lost a match to the legendary B. J. Penn, Sanchez is perhaps best known for his win against troubled fighter Karo Parisyan. In a match that showcased an abnormally high number of successful judo throws between bursts of effective striking, Sanchez pinned his opponent against the cage and delivered a beautifully executed knee that struck Parisyan right in the mouth. Although it wasn't a fight-ending blow, Parisyan did end up spitting out a tooth that the fight cameras captured for posterity in high-definition clarity. Since that day, slow-motion images of Parisyan spitting out a bloody tooth have gone on to become the screen saver of choice for fight fans across America.

5. GABRIEL "NAPAO" GONZAGA VS. MIRKO "CRO COP" FILIPOVIĆ

When Cro Cop battled it out with Gonzaga at UFC 70, everyone expected the fight to end with a kick to the head, but nobody expected Cro Cop to be on the receiving end of it. A skilled grappler and former member of the Chute Boxe Academy, Gonzaga came out surprisingly strong and managed to keep his opponent off balance. To everyone's surprise, Gonzaga threw a well-timed kick to Cro Cop's head, knocking him out. Unbeknownst to the referee or even Gonzaga, when the unconscious former Pride champion fell, he went straight down and to the side while one of his feet was still planted firmly beneath him. As Cro Cop landed on the floor, his knee remained vertical but the foot on the same leg turned all the way to the *rear*. Despite the gruesome spectacle, Cro Cop claimed that the injury was minor, and he was back fighting again four months later.

6. MARK "THE HAMMER" COLEMAN VS. MAURICIO "SHOGUN" RUA

Anyone who follows MMA knows that Mark Coleman is a fantastic wrestler who combines the strength of a gorilla with the attitude of an angry old man. Likewise, Mauricio Rua is known for being an amazing Brazilian jiu-jitsu practitioner who has no problem trying unorthodox techniques in the ring, including flying stomps on downed opponents. When the two fighters finally met in the ring, everyone expected fireworks, and the first minute of the fight showcased Coleman's wrestling skills and power against Rua's superior ground work. Midway through the first round, Rua was working for a leg lock when Coleman managed to escape and stand. As Rua followed him to his feet, Coleman shot for a single leg, slamming Rua to the mat, where he landed awkwardly, dislocating his elbow. Coleman proceeded to pound on his injured opponent, and when the referee intervened, Coleman flung him away. Supporters of both sides entered the ring, and a thirty-second brawl erupted, ending only when Coleman took to the ropes and began shouting at the crowd. Coleman made no friends that night, and Rua took his revenge in UFC 93, defeating Coleman via technical knockout.

7. ROSI SEXTON VS. TOMOMI "WINDY" SUNABA

Showcasing two accomplished athletes who possess amazing striking and grappling skills, the Sexton-Sunaba fight would have gone down in the record books as one of the most memorable fights in women's MMA history even without the freak injury. Although they acknowledge their lust for blood, MMA fans tend to agree that this battle was so good that they would rather have had the fight continue than have it stopped because of an injury, and such a position is rare among a group of people who thrive on the unique and painful. Unfortunately for the fans and the two fighters alike, the contest ended when a game but frustrated Sexton chased Sunaba around the ring, looking for a takedown to avoid Sunaba's more accurate punches. A worn-down Sunaba allowed Sexton to get behind her and was taken to the ground. During the fall Sunaba dislocated her ankle, resulting in her foot facing in the wrong direction. Fans and fighters alike were horrified by the injury, and naturally it became one of the most popular female MMA video clips in history.

8. VITOR "THE PHENOM" BELFORT VS. MARVIN "THE BEASTMAN" EASTMAN

MMA fans have become virtually immune to seeing all manner of minor injuries. From the early UFC when broken noses and missing teeth were the norm to modern-day competitions where dislocations and breaks are much more common, undoubtedly the longtime MMA aficionado has seen only slightly less carnage than an emergency room doctor has. As MMA fighters develop more sophisticated defensive skills, they are less successful at landing clean blows and cause fewer large, bloody cuts. Every once in a while, though, we are all reminded of just how damaging a good knee or elbow strike can be, and Vitor Belfort presented us with a perfect example of why these joints, when used as weapons, are to be genuinely feared. In a fight that lasted less than three minutes, Belfort hit Marvin Eastman with a knee and followed with a series of punches that opened up a three-inch-long gash across Eastman's forehead, causing a referee stoppage. What makes the wound so unique is that it was also roughly an inch wide and devoid of blood, meaning that as Eastman walked around after the fight, spectators got a good look at Eastman's flesh and skull.

9. JOSÉ "PELÉ" LANDI-JONS VS. BRIAN "MANDINGO" GASSAWAY

While some will always argue over what counts as disturbing or disgusting when it comes to professional sports injuries, most insiders agree that the fight between Pelé and Gassaway fits perfectly into these categories. Both fighters were seasoned veterans although Pelé had a bit more experience with world-class competition, having defeated Pat Miletich and Matt Hughes while losing to Carlos Newton. The fight went back and forth before going into the second round, when Pelé threw a low Thai kick that impacted Gassaway's knee. An audible pop could be heard in the audience, but Pelé was unaware that anything was wrong. While his foot dangled toward the ground at a ninety-degree angle, Pelé retracted his leg and tried to step backward, collapsing to the mat. The referee stopped the match before any more damage could be done.

10. COREY "THE REAL DEAL" HILL VS. DALE "THE DEMON" HARTT

From the beginning there seemed to be something unnatural about this fight. Corey Hill, standing six foot four, came into the ring weighing 155 pounds. His opponent, Dale Hartt, was a full eight inches shorter but the same weight. Despite his massive reach advantage, Hill fought the shorter man's fight, taking Hartt to the ground repeatedly throughout the match. Failing to use long-range kicks and punches, Hill threw a single, low Thai kick early in the second round. The kick impacted with Hill's knee, resulting in a catastrophic and gruesome injury that left Hill's foot dangling loosely in the air. Capitalizing on his opponent's sudden weakness, Hartt took the side mount and proceeded to go to work on Hill's face. He was stopped by the referee, who seemed to be oblivious to Joe Rogan's high-pitched screams of disgust from the commentator's booth.

The Best There Are

q

Tough Women

The Best Female Fighters

Everyone has heard about the famous Amazon warriors of lore, and most of us can even recall at least one or two famous female warriors who inspired fear in the men they faced on the battlefield. Barred from combat positions in modern times, women have been denied proper venues to display their martial prowess for decades. Some societies have been more accepting of women warriors, and the Japanese have supported female mixed martial arts competitions since the 1990s. Following are some of the fiercest female MMA competitors to ever step into the cage, many of whom can even pose significant challenges to their accomplished male counterparts.

1. MEGUMI "MEGA MEGU" FUJII

Also known as the "Queen of Sambo," Fujii is one of the most highly accomplished female grapplers in history. Holding black belts in judo and Brazilian jiu-jitsu, Fujii is a five-time world sambo champion runner-up and is the 2006 BJJ Pan-Am champion. While many consider her to be the best pound-for-pound female fighter in the world, Fujii is just as respected for her coaching skills as she is for her killer technique. Primarily a submission fighter, Fujii even has a toehold named after her that she has used to defeat a number of opponents. Often likened to a female version of Fedor Emelianenko, Fujii has a 24-1 record and has defeated two of the most highly touted female fighters in the world—Lisa Ellis-Ward and Tomomi "Windy" Sunaba.

2. YUKA "VALE TUDO QUEEN" TSUJI

One of the more storied female fighters to come out of Japan, Tsuji has twenty-four fights to her record and only two losses. An accomplished grappler, Tsuji is known for her ballistic takedowns and ability to intercept her opponent's submission attempts long before they can be applied. Looking frail and slight in comparison to her more robust adversaries, Tsuji has the uncanny ability to constantly take her opponent's backs and has consistently embarrassed some of the sport's top grapplers by riding them for entire rounds. Her best-known match to date was a shocking rematch loss to underdog Mei Yamaguchi when Tsuji practically fell into a rear naked choke during the first round.

3. TARA LaROSA

An accomplished and highly respected MMA fighter, Tara LaRosa has been fighting since 2002 and has had more than twenty professional bouts. Long considered to be the best 125 pounder in the world, LaRosa is one of the few female fighters who actually enjoys going blow for blow with her adversaries. This gameness and ability to absorb punishment put her in the top tier of entertaining fighters. A physically strong specimen who can often dominate other fighters through brute strength, LaRosa finally came face to face with her kryptonite after a fifteen-fight winning streak when she encountered Roxanne Modafferi. The duo fought three long, hard rounds, where both contestants were exhausted and

Women's MMA has grown rapidly in popularity. In this photo, a female fighter exhibits a perfect display of classic ground and pound. *Courtesy of Matthew Walsh*

battered, but in the end Modafferi was awarded the decision. The fight was close enough that it could have gone either way, with fans on both sides pushing for a rematch to end the debate once and for all.

4. MIKU "SUPERNOVA" MATSUMOTO

Currently retired, Matsumoto started off as a music student and ended up as one of the top Japanese MMA champions, scoring the DEEP Women's Lightweight Championship in 2007. Like most Japanese fighters, Matsumoto is more comfortable on the ground than on her feet, using her superior

positioning skills and dexterity to defeat more technical opponents. Considered by some to be unbeatable, Matsumoto
retired in her prime at the end of a twelve-fight winning
streak. Along the way she defeated rivals Lisa Ellis-Ward and
Tomomi Sunaba. Matsumoto chose to end her fighting career
out of boredom rather than a lack of talent.

5. CRISTIANE "CYBORG" SANTOS

A Brazilian jiu-jitsu purple belt and member of the famed
Chute Boxe Academy, Santos rocketed to fame when she
overpowered MMA superstar Gina Carano via technical
knockout for the Strikeforce featherweight title. Looking
more like a machine than a human, Santos adopted the
name Cyborg and has lived up to the moniker. Santos is
unique in women's MMA because she combines outstanding strength with tremendous punching power. In fact, she's
one of the few female fighters who has more wins by strikes
than she does by submissions. This power makes her a con-
founding opponent for even the toughest MMA competitors
because their training partners can rarely deliver the same
kind of pressure that Santos does.

6. GINA "CONVICTION" CARANO

Credited with bringing life to the women's division of MMA,
Carano is an accomplished Muay Thai fighter and is known
for her excellent footwork and exceptional good looks. A
more technical stand-up fighter than most MMA competitors, Carano effectively combines striking speed and power
to keep away from better grapplers. Tremendously strong
and persistent for her weight class, Carano was nonetheless
defeated by an overly aggressive Cristiane Santos in 2009.
Unlike many of Santos's opponents, however, Carano appeared to be as physically powerful, if not quite as ballistic,

as her opponent was. A cerebral fighter who analyzes all of her opponents, it is expected that the next time Carano enters the cage she will be a much stronger and hardened fighter.

7. SATOKO "PRINCESS" SHINASHI

One of the more interesting characters in Japanese MMA, Satoko Shinashi tips the scale at a pint-sized 100 pounds but packs a tremendous amount of muscle on her diminutive frame. A sambo world champion and Japanese BJJ gold medalist, Shinashi is a submission machine with few equals. Differing from other fighters who rely either on ground skills or striking abilities, Shinashi takes a judo-sambo approach by focusing on high-amplitude throws while still maintaining enough cohesion for a submission.

8. ROSI "THE SURGEON" SEXTON

One of the more learned fighters to be found in MMA, Sexton not only holds black belts in Tae Kwon Do and Brazilian jiu-jitsu but also a PhD in theoretical computer science. Although Sexton isn't averse to throwing punches during her matches, she lacks the power to dominate her opponents standing up. She is, however, an accomplished ground fighter who has a firm understanding of her strengths and weaknesses. To date she's only lost two fights, and the first was to Gina Carano, who managed to avoid the majority of Sexton's takedown attempts while cutting away her base with thigh kicks. Carano persistently peppered Sexton with right hands and eventually laid Sexton out at the end of the second round with an overhand right.

9. ROXANNE MODAFFERI

A jack of all trades, Modafferi has studied Tae Kwon Do, Kempo karate, judo, Brazilian jiu-jitsu, and Muay Thai. This mix of arts gives Modafferi an eclectic fighting style that has allowed her to capitalize on the preconceived notions of more conventional opponents. With a thin frame that hides surprising punching power, Modafferi uses her speed and ability to transition quickly between ranges and keep her adversaries guessing. A disproportionate number of her wins have come by decision, many of which she accomplished through her accurate striking and her slippery defense, which keeps blows from landing even when she's in a disadvantageous position.

10. ERIN "STEEL" TOUGHILL

A top-ranked male boxer might have no desire to enter the cage, but elite female pugilists have no such qualms. A competitor known for her imposing physique, Toughill is a savage fighter who relies on her long arms and punching power to stay out of harm's way. Even with her imposing size and strength, Toughill is considered one of the most technically proficient strikers in MMA and backs up her boxing ability with a serious ground game. Although she temporarily retired from fighting in 2007 and joined the *American Gladiators* television team, Toughill returned to MMA the following year and won her next three fights only to lose to Ashley Sanchez in 2011. With a size and punching-power advantage that could very well be the antidote to Cristiane Santos's aggression, rumors abound of a matchup between the two in what could be female MMA's first super fight.

10

Regal Reigns

Champions Who Ruled Their Class

Every fighter would love to be a world champion. It is the ultimate accomplishment in the life of a professional athlete. A special few competitors not only win a world title, but they also maintain a viselike grip on their prized possession. The following ten competitors enjoyed lengthy and regal reigns as world champions in mixed martial arts.

1. ROYCE GRACIE
Royce Gracie was the undisputed king of mixed martial arts in the early to mid-1990s. The early Ultimate Fighting Championship events were tournaments where fighters would have to win three or four fights in a single night to be crowned the champion. Royce Gracie successfully represented his family's name and Brazilian jiu-jitsu in those early tournaments, winning eleven times at the first four UFC events. He won three bouts to win UFC 1, four bouts to win UFC 2, and three bouts to win UFC 4. During his reign, he often submitted much larger men, such as his classic submission win over Dan Severn to capture the title at UFC 4. He withdrew from UFC 3 in the second round after a particularly grueling, punishing victory over the powerful Kimo Leopoldo. That withdrawal aside, in 1993 and 1994, Royce Gracie was the virtual and real king of mixed martial arts.

2. ANDERSON "THE SPIDER" SILVA

Anderson Silva, at the time of this writing, still maintains a tight choke hold over the UFC's 185-pound middleweight championship. In October 2006, he overwhelmed Rich Franklin to capture the belt. He has never let it go, defending his title seven times (eight if you count his win over Travis Lutter, who did not make weight). In that span, Silva has even moved up to the 205-poundlight heavyweight division and taken out James Irvin and former light heavyweight champion Forrest Griffin in easy first-round knockouts. In August 2010, Silva narrowly lost his title, as Chael Sonnen used his superior wrestling to win four of the first five rounds of the title bout. However, the champion showed exceptional heart in surviving and then managed to score a come-from-behind submission victory in the fifth and final round to retain his title. In August 2011, Silva made his ninth successful defense of his title with a second-round stoppage of Yushin Okami.

3. FEDOR "THE LAST EMPEROR" EMELIANENKO

Fedor Emelianenko won the Pride heavyweight championship by upsetting the Brazilian great Antônio Rodrigo Nogueira at Pride 25 in August 2003. He never lost his Pride championship, and when the organization folded in 2007, Emelianenko was still the titleholder. In fact, Emelianenko never lost a fight in Pride from his debut win over Semmy Schilt in June 2002 to his last bout in Pride in December 2006.

4. MATT HUGHES

Matt Hughes is an active Hall of Fame fighter with two reigns as the UFC 170-pound welterweight champion. He won the title in November 2001 with a memorable slam knockout of Carlos Newton. He successfully defended his title five times with wins over such great fighters as Hayato Sakurai, Sean

Sherk, and rival Frank Trigg. B. J. "the Prodigy" Penn upset Hughes to end his first reign. But Hughes went back to
work, regaining the title with a win over the athletic Georges
St-Pierre at UFC 50 in October 2004. During his second
reign as welterweight kingpin, he defeated Trigg again and
exacted revenge against Penn before falling in a rematch
with St-Pierre. Whether he ever captures another UFC world
title, Hughes will always be considered as one of the sport's
all-time greats.

5. ALEXANDRE FRANCA NOGUEIRA
Brazil's Alexandre Franca Nogueira held the Shooto lightweight championship for more than six and a half years,
from September 1999 to May 2006. It is believed to be the
longest title reign of any major mixed martial arts organization. Nogueira won the title in 1999 with a victory over
Noboru Asahi and successfully defended his title against the
likes of Hiroyuki Abe, Stephen Palling, and Katsuya Toida.
He never lost his Shooto championship in the ring. A knee
injury forced the organization to strip him of his title in May
2006 because he could not make another title defense in the
requisite time period.

6. WANDERLEI "THE AXE MURDERER" SILVA
Wanderlei Silva is one of the world's most exciting mixed
martial artists in the history of the sport. At his peak, he
dominated the Pride Fighting Championships' middleweight
division, terrorizing opponents with an all-out blitzkrieg of
strikes. His knee strikes against Quinton "Rampage" Jackson
resulted in some of the most visceral and brutal knockouts in
the sport's history. At Pride 17 in November 2001, Silva won
the title with one of his three career victories over Japan's
Kazushi Sakuraba. He successfully defended his title against

the likes of Rampage Jackson and Ricardo Arona. For much of his reign, he took bigger challenges literally, as he stepped up to face much larger opponents, such as Mirko "Cro Cop" Filipović, Mark Hunt, and Kazuyuki Fujita. He finally lost his middleweight title to "Dangerous" Dan Henderson in February 2007 at Pride 33.

7. CHUCK "THE ICEMAN" LIDDELL

Chuck Liddell was one of the most feared strikers in the history of the sport. At his peak, the Iceman knocked out opponents with his devastating right-hand bomb. His great stand-up defense and ability to sprawl usually prevented superior wrestlers from taking him to the ground. If they did, he got back up quickly and looked to pound them. He won the UFC light heavyweight title in April 2005 with a knockout win over Randy "the Natural" Couture, a win made all the sweeter because Couture had upset him in the June 2003 match for the interim UFC title. Liddell successfully defended his title against Jeremy Horn, Couture (in their third bout), Renato Sobral, and former champion Tito Ortiz. He lost his title in May 2007 to Quinton "Rampage" Jackson.

8. GEORGES "RUSH" ST-PIERRE

Georges St-Pierre—better known by his initials GSP—is arguably the most complete mixed martial artist in the world. Ridiculously athletic, GSP often breaks fighters down by outperforming them at their own particular brand of fighting discipline. In November 2006, he defeated longtime division kingpin Matt Hughes in a rematch to win the UFC welterweight championship for the first time. He lost in a shocking upset to Matt Serra in his first title defense. GSP rededicated himself and trained even harder to regain his title. In December 2007, he dominated Hughes again to win the interim title and then battered Serra in their rematch to take the world title in April 2008. He remains the champion as of this writing with successful defenses against Jon Fitch, B. J. Penn, Thiago Alves, Dan Hardy, Josh Koscheck, and Jake Shields.

9. URIJAH "THE CALIFORNIA KID" FABER

Urijah Faber is one of the most successful and popular fighters in the lower weight divisions in modern MMA history. He captured the World Extreme Cagefighting (WEC) featherweight championship in March 2006 with a victory over Cole Escovedo and held the title for more than two years. Faber was an active champion, successfully defending his belt against Joe Pearson, Dominick Cruz, Chance Farrar, Jeff Curran, and Jens Pulver. He lost his title in November 2008 to Mike Brown and the rematch in 2009. Faber remains active, hoping to add a UFC title to his resume.

10. TITO "THE HUNTINGTON BEACH BAD BOY" ORTIZ

People may forget that Tito Ortiz was one of the longest reigning UFC champions in history. Instead, he is better known for wearing provocative T-shirts to mock opponents, for his relationship with former porn superstar Jenna Jameson, and for his on-again, off-again feud with Dana White. Tito Ortiz, however, once held a stranglehold over the UFC light heavyweight division. He captured the title in April 2000 with a win over Wanderlei Silva. He successfully defended his title five times, going up against Yuki Kondo, Evan Tanner, Elvis Sinosic, Vladimir Matyushenko, and Ken Shamrock. He finally lost his title to Randy Couture in June 2003.

11

Fedor's Finest

The Greatest Victories of the Last Emperor

Many experts believe that the greatest mixed martial artist to walk the planet is Fedor "the Last Emperor" Emelianenko. He built his legend by dominating the heavyweight division in Pride for several years. He defeated Antônio Rodrigo Nogueira twice and otherwise cleaned out the Pride heavyweight division. The Russian sambo expert is well versed in all aspects of the fighting game. He also possesses an iron chin and an unflappable spirit, which enable him to fight through adversity with seeming ease. For nearly a decade, he was considered virtually unbeaten until a shocking submission loss to Fabricio Werdum in 2010. Here are ten of Fedor's greatest victories in his professional MMA career.

1. FEDOR VS. ANTÔNIO RODRIGO NOGUEIRA I

In March 2003 Fedor challenged Brazilian submission master Antônio Rodrigo Nogueira for the Pride heavyweight championship. At the time, Nogueira was considered an unstoppable force. He had won thirteen consecutive bouts, including five wins in 2002 alone. Meanwhile, Fedor had won only two bouts under the Pride banner at the time, defeating two fighters Nogueira had also defeated—Semmy Schilt and Heath Herring. Fedor proved too powerful for Nogueira, blasting his way through the Brazilian's vaunted guard with never-before-seen power strikes. Only Nogueira's legendary ability to absorb punishment kept him from losing via knockout. Fedor dominated the twenty-minute bout and earned a unanimous decision. Fedor never lost his Pride championship, holding it until the organization folded.

2. FEDOR VS. MIRKO "CRO COP" FILIPOVIĆ

Fedor reigned as the Pride heavyweight champion since dethroning the great Brazilian Nogueira; however, a significant challenger loomed on the horizon in the form of a Croatian striker named Mirko "Cro Cop" Filipović, who was mowing down opponents with his devastating strikes. Cro Cop had won seven straight bouts before entering the showdown with Fedor, including wins over Josh Barnett, Mark Coleman, Kevin Randleman, and Fedor's brother Aleksander. The two finally met in August 2005, at Pride: Final Conflict 2005 for Fedor's belt. Cro Cop inflicted some damage in the first round, including breaking Fedor's nose, but Fedor managed to take Cro Cop down and administered enough blows to wear him out. As the fight progressed, Fedor began to win even the stand-up exchanges. At the end of the three rounds, Fedor clearly proved his dominance with a convincing unanimous decision victory.

3. FEDOR VS. TIM SYLVIA

In July 2008, Fedor traveled to fight in the United States for only the second time in his storied career. Affliction brought the two top heavyweights together for this much-anticipated matchup. His opponent was former two-time Ultimate Fighting Championship heavyweight champion Tim Sylvia, a fighter and tough competitor with a long reach and excellent striking skills. A confident Sylvia entered the match believing that Fedor was overrated and had not fought the best competition. The two met in the center of the ring, and it was immediately apparent that Fedor's quickness would be the difference. He landed a couple of right-hand bombs that dropped the champion. Fedor then rapidly moved around the larger man and set in a rear naked choke. Sylvia tapped, ending the contest after only thirty-six seconds. After the bout, Sylvia had a much different impression of Fedor, calling him a stud and questioning whether he was even human.

4. FEDOR VS. ANDREI "THE PIT BULL" ARLOVSKI

After dismantling Tim Sylvia, Fedor's next bout under the Affliction banner was with another former UFC champion, Andrei Arlovski. Once again, doubters wondered whether Fedor could handle the fellow sambo expert, a man who was much quicker than Fedor was. Arlvoski trained under the tutelage of famed boxing trainer Freddie Roach, who maintained that Arlovski could exploit Fedor's lack of good boxing technique. For the first round, Roach seemed prescient, as Arlovski landed more blows and appeared to frustrate Fedor. The pattern continued for about a minute into the second round. Arlovski then backed Fedor up against the ropes and apparently thought he had hurt him. Arlovski attempted a flying knee strike, which Fedor answered with a right-hand bomb that landed flush. Arlovski was out cold. Once again, the Last Emperor reigned supreme.

5. FEDOR VS. KEVIN "THE MONSTER" RANDLEMAN

In June 2004, Fedor squared off against Kevin Randleman in a Pride 2004 Grand Prix quarterfinal match. Randleman, a former college wrestling standout, was one of the most athletic individuals ever to compete in mixed martial arts. He had won the UFC heavyweight championship in 1999 with a win over Pete Williams, but he never fulfilled his potential for some reason. He came into the Grand Prix matchup, though, fired up against Fedor. He used his quickness to slide in and power slam Fedor to the ground in the first thirty seconds. Fedor attempted to escape and managed to stand up with his back to Randleman. The Monster put his hands around the Russian's waist, lifted him up, and performed a scary-looking German suplex slam on the Russian. Randleman actually slammed Fedor on his head. Amazingly, Fedor recovered, managed to move to a side mount position on Randleman, and began raining blows to the Monster's head. When Randleman raised his hand to ward off the blows, Fedor promptly took Randleman's arm and submitted him via an armbar.

6. FEDOR VS. GARY "BIG DADDY" GOODRIDGE

In August 2003, Fedor returned to Japan to face the dangerous Gary Goodridge. Fedor wasted no time, landing a few winging hooks. He then unloaded consecutive left hook body shots, and Big Daddy looked weary. Fedor then landed a left knee to Goodridge's midsection and took him down. Fedor escaped Goodridge's guard and unleashed his trademark ground and pound. The referee mercifully called a halt to the fight a little longer than a minute into the fight.

7. FEDOR VS. MARK COLEMAN I

Fedor defeated Mark Coleman twice in his career. Their first fight took place in April 2004 during the first round of the Pride Grand Prix tournament. Coleman had the advantage early, using his amazing wrestling abilities to take Fedor to the ground. He attempted to implement a rear naked choke hold on the Russian but couldn't sink it in far enough. Fedor spun around and managed to land a few blows on Coleman.

The persistent Coleman took Fedor down to the canvas, where Fedor showed he can fight effectively off his back. Fedor then surprised Coleman by pulling guard and submitted him with an armbar.

8. FEDOR VS. SEMMY SCHILT

In June 2002, Fedor had one of the most significant fights in his career, his debut in the Pride Fighting Championships at Pride 21 against dangerous striker Semmy Schilt. Fedor had not yet fought on the biggest stages of mixed martial arts, while Schilt entered the ring with a 3-0 record in Pride and with previous UFC experience. Additionally, at nearly seven feet tall, Schilt presented a tall order—literally and figuratively. Although Schilt was one of the greatest kickboxers of all time, Fedor proved his greatness by continually taking Schilt down to the canvas and controlling him. He also showed resilience, as early in the fight, Schilt nailed Fedor with a knee strike as the Russian went for the takedown. The fight showed that Fedor was a force to be reckoned with in mixed martial arts.

9. FEDOR VS. NAOYA OGAWA

People forget that when Fedor faced Japan's Naoya Ogawa in August 2004 in the semifinals of the Pride 2004 Grand Prix heavyweight tournament, Ogawa was undefeated. Indeed, Ogawa, the silver medalist in judo at the 1992 Barcelona Olympic Games, entered the matchup with a perfect 7-0 record. No fighter had been able to go the distance with the talented Japanese judoka. Already he had defeated Gary Goodridge, Stefan Leko, and Matt Ghafarri. Fedor was a different story. Ogawa refused to shake Fedor's hand as the referee gave prefight instructions. Whatever the reason for the insolence, it had no impact on the fight. Fedor quickly launched a flurry of hooks, some of which landed. He softened Ogawa up on the ground and then eventually transitioned to a successful armbar submission less than a minute into the fight.

10. FEDOR VS. HIROYA TAKADA

Fedor's third professional MMA fight showcased the devastating power of his left hook. In September 2000, he faced Japanese fighter Hiroya Takada. The two fighters circled each other for a few seconds. Fedor then threw a right hand followed by two left hooks, and the fight stopped. It had lasted only twelve seconds. Takada simply couldn't take the power of the Last Emperor.

12

Fighting Families

The Best Bloodlines in MMA

Mixed martial arts is a most demanding sport. It takes dedication and discipline to master so many different styles of fighting. It also requires the support of family and friends. Some families not only offer their support but also the camaraderie from brothers, fathers, or uncles who have also been involved in the sport. The following ten families have made an impact in professional mixed martial arts.

1. GRACIE

The first fighting family of mixed martial arts is without a doubt the Gracie family. The masters of the art of Brazilian jiu-jitsu, the family boasts an unrivaled legacy of achievement in mixed martial arts. Legend has it that Gastão Gracie befriended Japanese fighting expert Mitsuyo Maeda, who offered to teach his knowledge of fighting to Gastão's son Carlos. Carlos in turn taught the art to his youngest brother, Helio.

While Carlos's son Carlson Gracie became a great teacher of the sport, several sons of Helio's—Rickson, Relson, Royler, Rorion, and Royce Gracie—carried the sport to the next level and are household names in the MMA community. A BJJ instructor, Rorion cofounded the Ultimate Fighting Championship organization. Rickson is considered one of the greatest MMA fighters in the world and reportedly has never lost an official bout. Royce, however, has the greatest name recognition of any Gracie because he competed in and won three of the four initial UFC tournaments.

2. SHAMROCK

Bob Shamrock ran a facility in Susanville, California, for troubled kids. Among the hundreds of kids he helped, two became not only his adopted sons but also two of the most famous fighters in the sport. In tribute to Bob, Ken took the name Shamrock. Also known as the World's Most Dangerous Man, Ken became one of the top fighters in MMA in the early 1990s. He won early UFC events and is one of the few fighters inducted into the UFC Hall of Fame.

Bob's other adopted son, twelve-year-old Frank Juarez, also changed his last name and later became known to the world as Frank Shamrock. In the eyes of many experts, Frank was the most complete mixed martial artist of his day. He became the first UFC middleweight champion in history.

The Shamrock family continues to compete in mixed martial arts as three of Ken's sons train and fight. Sean Shamrock made his professional MMA debut at a King of the Cage event in August 2010. He actually filled in for his older brother Ryan, who had also made a successful debut in MMA in August 2007. Younger brother Connor also expects to fight in a professional MMA event soon.

3. NOGUEIRA

Arguably the greatest fighting tandem of brothers in mixed martial arts history belongs to the Brazilian twins Antônio Rodrigo Nogueira and Antônio Rogerio Nogueira. Antônio Rodrigo, known as Minotauro, is the more famous of the twins, primarily from his reign as the first heavyweight champion in Pride. He has shown a legendary ability to absorb punishment and then come back with a trademark submission victory, as he did against Tim Sylvia, Mirko "Cro Cop" Filipović, and the giant Bob Sapp.

Antônio Rogerio also has reached the pinnacle of MMA in Pride and hopes to become a champion in the UFC as well. He is not only an excellent submission specialist but also an accomplished boxer. He owns victories over Alistair Overeem (twice), Dan Henderson, and Guy Mezger in his distinguished career.

The Nogueiras have passed on their skill set to some of their pupils, including the vaunted Anderson "the Spider" Silva and Junior dos Santos.

4. COUTURE

Randy "the Natural" Couture may be the most popular mixed martial artist in the history of the sport. The former UFC light heavyweight and heavyweight champion still excels in the sport in his late forties. A former Olympic alternate, Couture inspires many with his work ethic, discipline, and courage in the octagon.

His third wife (he filed for divorce in early 2010), Kim, also has fought professionally in mixed martial arts. She made her professional MMA debut in June 2008. Although she lost the match, she showed great courage in battling to the end with a broken jaw that she suffered in the first round.

Ryan Couture, Randy's son from his first marriage, fought his first amateur MMA bout in 2008. In August 2010, he made his professional debut in a Strikeforce event, winning in the first round.

5. EMELIANENKO

In many people's eyes, the greatest mixed martial artist in

the history of the sport is Fedor "the Last Emperor" Eme-lianenko. A specialist in sambo, Emelianenko held the Pride heavyweight championship for many years and has defeated five former UFC heavyweight champions. But he is not the only member of this fighting family.

One of his two younger brothers, Aleksander, also com-petes in mixed martial arts. Aleksander's only losses in his professional career have been to Josh Barnett, Mirko "Cro Cop" Filipović, Fabricio Werdum, and Peter Graham. He also tried his hands at professional boxing in 2009.

The youngest of the three Emelianenko brothers is Ivan. He is expected to make his professional MMA debut in the near future.

6. RUA

Mauricio and Murilo Rua have two of the more entertaining nicknames in mixed martial arts—Shogun and Ninja, respec-tively. They also possess entertaining fighting styles. The former UFC light heavyweight champion after knocking out fellow Brazilian Lyoto Machida, Mauricio lost the title to Jon Jones in March 2011. Before the UFC, Shogun dominated the ranks in Pride, defeating Quinton "Rampage" Jackson, Antônio Rogerio Nogueira, Kevin Randleman, Ricardo Arona, and Alistair Overeem.

Older brother Murilo also fought in Pride for several years. where he tangled with the likes of Dan Henderson, Mario Sperry, Arona, Randleman, and Paulo Filho. After los-ing to Tom Watson for the BAMMA middleweight champion, Murilo indicated he would retire from the sport.

7. DIAZ

Brothers Nick and Nate Diaz are Cesar Gracie–trained Brazilian jiu-jitsu black and brown belts, respectively, who compete on the highest stages of mixed martial arts. Older brother Nick is the current Strikeforce welterweight champion but has also competed in the UFC, Pride, and Dream in his career. He is known for his excellent all-around skills and his combative nature and personality. Nick plans to vacate his Strikeforce welterweight title and challenge UFC welterweight champion Georges St-Pierre in October 2011.

Younger brother Nate won season 5 of *The Ultimate Fighter* and currently competes in the UFC.

8. MILLER

Dan and Jim Miller are fighters in the UFC middleweight and lightweight divisions. They both excel at wrestling and jiu-jitsu learned under the tutelage of Jamie Cruz, who awarded both brothers black belts. They did not begin training in mixed martial arts until 2005, but both had wrestled in high school in their hometown of Sparta, New Jersey. The brothers made their professional MMA debuts on the same fight card in Atlantic City, New Jersey, in November 2005. They both signed with the UFC in July 2008. Both brothers remain on the active roster of the UFC.

9. LAUZON

Joe and Dan Lauzon are brothers who both fight professionally in MMA in the lightweight division. Joe, the older brother by three years, made his professional debut in September 2006 with an unexpected knockout of former UFC champion Jens Pulver. It earned Joe Knockout of the Night honors. He still competes in the UFC.

Younger brother Dan made his professional debut in April 2006. In October of that year, he became the youngest fighter ever to fight in the octagon when he lost to Spencer Fisher. He left the UFC and returned in 2010; however, the premier promotional company dropped him after two straight losses. He still competes professionally.

10. HUGHES

There is a good chance that anyone even vaguely familiar with mixed martial arts has heard of Matt Hughes, a former UFC welterweight champion and UFC Hall of Famer. He has won forty-five fights in his distinguished professional career and owns victories over B. J. Penn, Georges St-Pierre, Renzo Gracie, and Royce Gracie. What some may not know is that Matt has a twin brother, Mark, who also fought professionally in MMA. Mark won his only fight in the UFC at UFC 28: High Stakes with a decision win over Alex Stiebling. He last fought professionally in 2003.

13

Great Unknowns

The Best Fighters Who Never Stepped into the Cage

Professional fighters around the world will regularly admit that there are plenty of top-level competitors who never fight for money. Some of these folks might be too old or injured, others have more money than they know what to do with, and still others may not be able to maintain professional licenses. Whatever the case may be, every professional MMA fighter generally has at least one highly respected trainer or training partner who never ventured into the professional realm and has no inclination to do so. The following individuals have greatly impacted modern mixed martial arts without ever having stepped into the professional ring themselves.

1. JIM ARVANITIS

As with many fighters on this list, Jim Arvanitis was too old for competition when the Ultimate Fighting Championship first debuted in America. He is considered to be a highly skilled mixed martial artist and is also esteemed as the father of modern pankration. With a background in boxing, judo, and savate, in the 1970s Arvanitis sought to revitalize one of the earliest forms of MMA and did so by promoting the lost art's Greek origins. Recognized for his crazy Greek afro and his strange attempts to gain a following by promoting his feats of strength, Arvanitis is nonetheless an important innovator and is currently working to see pankration readopted as an Olympic sport.

2. PAUL VUNAK

A disciple of Dan Inosanto and an adherent to the fighting method and philosophies of Bruce Lee, Paul Vunak has been instrumental in popularizing sportive techniques and practical self-defense among mainstream martial artists. Beginning his martial arts career in the early 1970s, Vunak was an early adopter of cross training and holds instructor-level credentials in a variety of disciplines. He is credited with being one of the early supporters of Gracie jiu-jitsu in the United States and has added substantial elements of the art to his common curriculum. Unlike the Gracies, he has steered away from competition and focused his studies entirely on self-defense and combat applications.

With his scarred visage reflecting a chaotic lifestyle that was dedicated to real-world violence, Paul Vunak is widely held as one of the most respected street fighters of all time. Such was his real-world fighting prowess that in the late 1980s the U.S. Navy SEALs paid him an unannounced visit and requested that he perform as their chief hand-to-hand combat instructor. Eventually they awarded him a multiyear contract.

3. MARC "CRAFTY DOG" DENNY

A strong proponent of the Filipino martial arts and a longtime student of Dan Inosanto, Marc Denny began his martial arts training during his final year of law school and never looked back. Older than most students when he began his martial arts career, Denny made up for lost time by working twice as hard and eventually sought the tutelage of numerous ac-

Former Navy Seal H2H combat instructor Paul Vunak (left) and Jeet Kune Do instructor Adam Heath (right). *Courtesy of Adam Heath*

complished instructors, including Paul Vunak, Edgar Sulite, and the Machado brothers.

Unlike most martial artists of his time, Denny was primarily focused on the use of weapons—particularly sticks—as a method fighting. To that end he and several students began full-contact stick fighting, eventually forming an organization known as the Dog Brothers. The Dog Brothers promote realistic combat among like-minded individuals through the use of every medium but with an emphasis placed on blunt weapons. They, along with Denny, gained notoriety when the early UFC turned down their request to introduce stick fighting to the UFC as being "ahead of its time."

4. DAN INOSANTO
Considered by many to be the most learned martial artist ever, Dan Inosanto's reputation blossomed with the death of his instructor, Bruce Lee. Known for his dedication to preserving the Filipino martial arts and other fighting systems that are on the verge of extinction, Inosanto has achieved instructor rankings in more than a dozen martial arts, includ-

ing achieving the rank of black belt in Machado jiu-jitsu while in his seventies. A natural athlete and a former U.S. Army paratrooper, Inosanto has maintained his outstanding physical attributes throughout his entire life and has continued to teach a full schedule of diverse martial arts classes.

5. NEIL MELANSON

To say that Neil Melanson is respected within the grappling community is an understatement. At six foot four and more than two hundred pounds, he combines the power of a top heavyweight with the agility of a lightweight and the ground game of a Gracie. A U.S. Navy veteran and former air marshal who lost some of his vision due to illness, Melanson is considered one of the friendliest and most skilled grappling instructors in the United States. Incredibly strong and entirely dedicated to his profession, Melanson currently holds the coveted job of head jiu-jitsu coach at Xtreme Couture.

6. IMRICH "IMI" SDE-OR

An old man long before most of today's mixed martial artists were even born, Imi deserves recognition, not just because he was an early proponent of combining martial arts styles, but because he did so in order to kick Nazi ass. A champion boxer, wrestler, and gymnast, Imi used his skills to fight anti-Semitic gangs that were terrorizing Jewish neighborhoods in Slovakia in the 1930s. As one of the last Jews to escape from Central Europe to Palestine, Imi went on to become the chief instructor of physical training for the Israel Defense Force and founded Krav Maga (literally, close combat). While it may be strange to see a man who was born in 1910 on this list, Imi and his legacy have been extremely important to the development and acceptance of diverse fighting methodologies throughout the world.

7. EDDIE "THE TWISTER" BRAVO

Known for his laid-back personality and affinity for marijuana, Eddie Bravo has done a tremendous amount to enhance the sport of Brazilian jiu-jitsu within the United States. Bravo first came to the attention of the grappling world when, as a brown belt, he defeated Royler Gracie in 2003 at the Abu Dhabi Submission Wrestling championships. Bravo's unique take on Brazilian jiu-jitsu soon became the subject of intense interest among competitive fighters, and many flocked to his school. Not a competitive fighter himself, Bravo is nonetheless considered an unequalled submission artist who poses a danger to even the highest-level grapplers.

8. ADRIANO EMPERADO

Another ancient fellow who was fighting before Bruce Lee was even a sparkle in his mother's eye, Emperado trained in a wide range of fighting disciplines that spanned all ranges of hand-to-hand combat. Born in a poor section of Honolulu, Emperado lived in a world of violence and was fighting for his life almost on a daily basis. Roving from one side of town to the other in search of competent instructors, he soon became known as a tough fighter and at the age of twenty-four, along with four other black belts, created a fighting style called Kajukenbo. Known for his brutal training methods and intense workouts, Emperado stressed reality and combined his knowledge of martial arts with his experiences as a police officer in order to provide his students with a fundamental education in street depravity. As one of the earliest proponents of combining grappling with striking, Emperado was a consistent supporter of innovation. He even went so far as to allow multiple disciplines within his own system to meet the needs of a wider variety of students.

9. LEO GIRON

A Filipino American who served in the U.S. Army during World War II, Giron is one of the most remarkable martial artists in recent times. Indoctrinated in the Filipino warrior culture and weapons arts when he was a child, Leo put his fighting skills to good use while combating the Japanese in the jungles of his homeland. Taking part in a war where rifles, grenades, and aerial bombardment were the norm, the close quarters of the Philippine jungle limited the effectiveness of these weapons and brought combat down to its most primitive level. Using edged weapons, clubs, and fists, Leo fought and killed a number of skilled Japanese warriors in hand-to-hand combat. In California after the war, he became one of the world's foremost instructors in the realities of life-and-death fighting.

10. SCOTT SONNON

A respected MMA coach with an impressive amateur record, Sonnon is best known for being one of the first Americans to study sambo in Russia. Furthermore, he went on to become an acclaimed master of the system and has been instrumental in disseminating the art throughout the world. Sonnon has had a major impact on the sport of mixed martial arts and has introduced a number of experienced fighters to the intricacies of Russia's most famous fighting system. Sonnon has gone on to enhance his fighting expertise by investigating numerous other fighting systems, including Chinese Sanshou kickboxing.

Countries That Love to Brawl

14

Brazilian Battlers

The Greatest Fighters from Brazil

Mixed martial arts events were being held in Brazil long before the sport ever came to the United States. The Brazilians may not have invented MMA competition, but at a time when most countries were seeking more civilized sports, the Brazilians were busy bringing no-holds-barred fighting to a new level of sophistication. Without our South American cousins and the legendary Gracie family, the sport of mixed martial arts likely would not exist in the United States today. Following are some of the most noteworthy fighters ever to come out of Brazil.

1. ROYCE GRACIE

Few names are as revered in the MMA community as Royce Gracie's is. Without a doubt it was Royce who put Brazilian jiu-jitsu on the international map and brought the grappling arts to the forefront of mixed martial arts competition. Instrumental in the early development of the Ultimate Fighting Championship, Royce was chosen by his older brother Rickson to represent the Gracie family in the original tournament. He defeated all comers, including the accomplished savate champion Gerard Gordeau. Despite Royce's initial success,

Ken Shamrock fought him to a draw only a year and a half later, ending the Gracies' MMA dominance. Royce returned to the octagon one last time in 2006 only to be soundly beaten by Matt Hughes.

2. MAURICIO "SHOGUN" RUA

Like most Brazilian no-holds-barred fighters, Mauricio Rua is a skilled grappler who began competing in Brazilian jiu-jitsu at a young age. Unlike many of his compatriots, however, Rua is also a skilled striker who prefers to fight on his feet. Rua has had a number of famous bouts, including a fight against Mark Coleman where Rua slipped, fell on his arm, and caused one of the most cringe-inducing breakages in MMA history. Formerly the reigning UFC light heavyweight champion, Rua had captured the title after soundly defeating Lyoto Machida in a much-anticipated rematch, only to lose the title to Jon Jones in March 2011.

3. PAULO "ELY" FILHO

Few fighters are as well built for grappling as Paulo Filho is. With a squat body and tremendous power, Filho combines outstanding submission skills with the strength and speed of a world-class wrestler. A Carlson Gracie black belt who is also an accomplished judo practitioner, Filho won a number of hard-fought BJJ competitions before entering mixed martial arts. First earning his MMA stripes fighting on Japanese cards, Filho went on to become the World Extreme Cage-fighting middleweight champion in 2007. He has since had almost a dozen fights including a loss to the Chael Sonnen, the man he originally beat in order to win the WEC belt. Plagued by substance abuse problems and reliability issues, Filho continues to fight for lesser-known promotions.

4. LYOTO "THE DRAGON" MACHIDA

There can be little doubt that Lyoto Machida has been one of the most influential fighters of the last ten years. A firm proponent of traditional martial arts such as karate, Machida has taken what many consider to be a rigid fighting system and given it new life. With his wide stance and broken rhythm, Machida confounds opponents with his quick, linear retreats and bulletproof defense. Moving faster backward than most fighters can move forward, Machida relies heavily on his powerful lead punch to off balance opponents and interrupt their attacks. Machida lost his light heavyweight title to Mauricio Rua, but there can be little doubt that Machida's unique, cerebral fighting style will continue to confound opponents for years to come.

5. RICARDO "THE BRAZILIAN TIGER" ARONA

A powerhouse wrestler with awesome submission skills, Arona is also known as being exceptionally strong and explosive. Throughout his career Arona has consistently fought the top fighters in Pride, many of whom went on to become champions in their own right. Even though he has fought and defeated many accomplished MMA stars during his career, Arona's most interesting fight occurred early in 2000 when he lost a unanimous decision to a young Fedor Emelianenko. The fight began the same way as it ended, with Arona as the aggressor, shooting in on Emelianenko and gaining the dominant position. Emelianenko stymied all of Arona's submissions efforts, and by the end of the match a visibly tired Arona lost the ability to control Emelianenko while on the ground. The decision went to Emelianenko, but many believe that Arona should have won the fight.

6. ANTÔNIO "MINOTAURO" RODRIGO NOGUEIRA

Hardly any MMA fighters alive can boast having faced the level of competition that Nogueira has fought against during his eleven years in mixed martial arts. A championship grappler before he took up professional fighting, Nogueira began beating the odds early in life after literally being crushed by a truck when he was a child. He defied the doctors' prognoses by not only walking again but also by becoming a superb athlete to boot. A well-rounded fighter who has seen success on his feet as well as on the ground, Nogueira is the only fighter ever to hold championships simultaneously in both Pride and the UFC.

7. THALES LEITES

Even in the storied Brazilian jiu-jitsu community, among those grapplers who stand out is Thales Leites. A technical fighter who goes about his submission game in a protracted and systematic manner, Leites has often been accused of being a slow, unentertaining fighter. This lack of action isn't entirely his fault. Opponents are loath to engage him because of his expertise on the ground. To date Leites has fought a number of bouts throughout North and South America, and his most noteworthy opponent, Anderson Silva, won the split decision for the UFC middleweight championship in 2005. Since then Leites has only fought in the UFC once more, losing a questionable decision to Alessio Sakara during a fight that fans derided as slow and uneventful. Even though his fights tend to be less flashy than those of some of his stable mates, Leites is still considered one of the best BJJ artists in his weight class and a dangerous opponent.

8. FABRICIO "VAI CAVALO" WERDUM

With black belts in Brazilian jiu-jitsu and judo, Werdum is a respected ground tactician with exemplary stand-up abilities. His few early fights were for little-known promotions in Europe and South America before he moved on to Pride. In recent years Werdum's career has been hit or miss, with wins against Gabriel Gonzaga and Aleksander Emelianenko but losses against Junior dos Santos and Andrei Arlovski. Nonetheless, since 2009 Werdum has gained a reputation as a fearsome fighter who excels at clinch work. This distinction was further reinforced after his shocking upset victory in June 2010 over Fedor Emelianenko, whom many people considered unbeatable. Whether this astounding success was a fluke remains to be seen, but one thing is certain: Fabricio Werdum has ensured his place in the record books and done so in grand style. Werdum lost to Alistair Overeem in June 2011, arguably showing too much deference to Alistair's stand-up fighting prowess.

9. CRISTIANE "CYBORG" SANTOS

As one of the top female fighters in the world, Cristiane Santos needs no introduction. Regarded as the strongest fighter in her weight class, Santos beats most of her competition through sheer punching power and aggression. Though many of her opponents maintain professional boxing and kickboxing records, few have encountered the type of systematic pressure that Santos brings into the ring. Commentators often question her grappling ability, but none can dispute the fact that Santos has a rare combination of attributes that tends to confound more skilled opponents. She prominently displayed this ability when she took on Gina Carano for the Strikeforce featherweight championship. During the fight Santos came out swinging, using a series of rushing combinations to keep the champion moving backward. Judges and spectators alike considered the fight to be more of a brawl than a professional-level bout, but the fight did solidify Santos's reputation as a powerhouse opponent.

10. WANDERLEI "THE AXE MURDERER" SILVA

A graduate of the famed Chute Boxe Academy in Brazil, Silva has a long fighting history that goes all the way back to 1996 when he fought in the brutal *vale tudo* (no rules) competitions of Brazil. During this period Silva gained a reputation for being a master of dirty tricks who specialized in headbutting. In fact, some argue that the more restrictive rules of his later Pride and UFC matches resulted in a slump in his career. However, with a 2010 victory over a game Michael Bisping, Silva has again shown himself to be in proper form as a top fighter. Regardless of his future record, Silva will go down as one of MMA's most accomplished and respected combatants.

15

Dominating Dutchmen

The Best from the Netherlands

The Netherlands has produced some of the world's best competitors in combat sports. Many great kickboxers have come from the Netherlands, including Ernesto Hoost and Remy Bonjasky. Many exceptional mixed martial artists also are native Dutchmen. The following are ten of the most famous.

1. BAS RUTTEN

Bas "el Guapo" Rutten is one of the most recognizable names in the history of mixed martial arts. In his heyday in the early 1990s, he was also one of the finest fighters in the world. Born in Tilburg, the Netherlands, in 1965, Rutten initially began his foray in combat sports with Muay Thai kickboxing. He later transitioned into mixed martial arts, dominating Pancrase. He defeated the likes of Frank Shamrock, Maurice Smith, Guy Mezger, and Kevin Randleman in his illustrious career. Rutten had incredible flexibility and used a variety of impressive leg kicks. He also loved to punish opponents with his patented liver shot. After seven years away from fighting, Rutten won his last match in the first round in July of 2006.

2. GEGARD MOUSASI

Gegard Mousasi is one of the world's best light heavyweights in mixed martial arts. Born in Iran in 1985, his family moved to Leiden, the Netherlands, when he was a young boy. There he learned several fighting sports, including judo and boxing. He began his professional MMA career in 2003 and, as of this writing, has compiled an outstanding record of 31-3-2. The former Strikeforce light heavyweight champion, Mousasi has defeated Melvin Manhoef, Mark Hunt, Denis Kang, and Renato Sobral in his career. He remains one of the sports' top fighters.

3. MELVIN MANHOEF

Melvin Manhoef is one of the dangerous strikers in the world of mixed martial arts. Born in 1976 in Suriname, his family moved to Rotterdam, the Netherlands, when he was three years old. He learned Muay Thai kickboxing as a teenager and showed great aptitude. As with so many of his country-men, he has excelled professionally as both a kickboxer and a mixed martial artist. He won the Cage Rage light heavy-weight title in 2005. Of his twenty-four wins, he has won twenty-three of them by knockout or technical knockout.

4. ALISTAIR OVEREEM

The current Strikeforce heavyweight champion, the Nether-lands' Alistair Overeem is one of the sport's most entertain-ing strikers. Born in 1980 in England, Overeem moved to the Netherlands with his Dutch mother and his brother when he was six years old. He trains in Amsterdam with his older brother Valentijn. Overeem turned professional in kickbox-ing and mixed martial arts in 1999. Known as the Demoli-tion Man, Overeem became Strikeforce's first heavyweight champion by stopping Paul Buentello in November 2007.

He recently crushed Brett Rogers in 2010 to retain his title and then won the Dream Interim Heavyweight Championship fight in December 2010 with a nineteen-second destruction of Todd Duffee. Alistair then avenged an earlier loss in his career by defeating Fabricio Werdum in June 2011 in the Strikeforce Grand Prix Heavyweight tournament. He has not lost a fight since September 2007.

5. SEMMY SCHILT

Semmy Schilt is a mixed martial artist and kickboxer known for his intimidating height and powerful strikes. Born in Rotterdam, the Netherlands, in 1973, Schilt began his professional MMA career in 1996. He has won more than twenty-five professional fights and has faced Fedor Emelianenko, Josh Barnett, and Antônio Rodrigo Nogueira in his career. He has reached the pinnacle in the sport of kickboxing, winning major, international K-1 competitions.

6. BOB SCHRIJBER

Bob Schrijber is a former mixed martial artist who competed professionally in MMA from 1995 to 2008. Born in Alkmaar, the Netherlands, in 1965, Schrijber won twenty bouts and lost seventeen in his career. In 2003, he stopped countryman Melvin Manhoef for perhaps his best career win. He currently coaches Dutch mixed martial artists and UFC fighter Stefan "Skyscraper" Struve.

7. GERARD GORDEAU

Gerard Gordeau is a former Dutch mixed martial artist best known for making the finals of the first UFC tournament in 1993, where he lost by submission to the Brazilian Royce Gracie. To reach the finals, Gordeau defeated Teila Tuli and Kevin Rosier in successive bouts that each lasted less than a minute. Born in 1959 in Den Haag, the Netherlands, Gordeau was known in fighting circles as a world champion in savate, a form of kickboxing that is most popular in France. Gordeau was known for employing anything-goes tactics, including biting and eye gouging.

8. ANTONI HARDONK

Antoni Hardonk, like many other Dutch fighters, is one of the sport's better strikers. Currently in the UFC, Hardonk's heavy hands and powerful leg kicks led him to a successful kickboxing career. Born in 1976 in Weesp, the Netherlands, Hardonk turned pro in mixed martial arts in 2001. He has fought eight of his fourteen career MMA bouts on the sport's highest stage in the UFC.

9. GILBERT "THE HURRICANE" YVEL

Gilbert Yvel is a heavyweight mixed martial artist who currently competes in the UFC. Born in 1976 in Amsterdam, the Netherlands, Yvel began his professional MMA career at age twenty-one in 1997. He has won more than thirty-five professional MMA bouts in his career. His flying knee strikes and reputation for controversy still make him a compelling figure in mixed martial arts.

10. VALENTIJN OVEREEM

The older brother of Alistair, Valentijn was born in Amersfoort, the Netherlands, in 1976. He has fought more than fifty professional mixed martial arts bouts in a career that began in 1996. He submitted Randy Couture in February 2001, with a guillotine choke in a Rings promotion. He also defeated Renato Sobral with a toehold submission in October 2000.

16

Japanese Juggernauts

The Best Fighters from Japan

Many of the world's top mixed martial artists have come from Japan, the country known for such fighting organizations as Pride Fighting Championships, Pancrase, and Shooto. Founded in 1997, Pride for a time was arguably the greatest MMA organization in the world, rivaling and for a while exceeding the current top brand in MMA, the Ultimate Fighting Championships.

Pro wrestling is very popular in Japan. Many of the great early Japanese mixed martial artists had made the transition from pro wrestling to mixed martial artists. The following men are ten of the greatest Japanese mixed martial artists.

1. KAZUSHI SAKURABA

Kazushi Sakuraba is arguably the most famous Japanese mixed martial artist of all time. In the early days of Pride Fighting Championships, Sakuraba was the most popular fighter in the organization. Born in Katagami, Japan, Sakuraba was known as the Gracie Hunter for his successive victories over several members of the vaunted Brazilian family. He defeated Royler, Royce, Renzo, and Ryan Gracie in his career. He also successfully submitted Quinton "Rampage" Jackson at Pride 15 in July 2001.

2. TAKANORI "FIREBALL KID" GOMI

Takanori Gomi possesses dynamite in his powerful left hand. Born in Kanagawa, Japan, Gomi turned pro in mixed martial arts in November 1998. He has wrestling and submissions skills but is best known for his devastating power. A southpaw, Gomi has knocked out Hayato Sakurai, Tyson Griffin, and Jens Pulver in his professional MMA career. From 1998 to 2003, he won fourteen straight bouts, and had a 14-1 record between 2004 and 2006. At the time of this writing, he currently competes in the UFC.

3. MASAKATSU FUNAKI

Masakatsu Funaki was a skilled submission specialist who dominated Pancrase with his exceptional skill set. Formerly a pro wrestler, Funaki cofounded Pancrase with Minoru Suzuki. He frequently fought in Pancrase, defeating Bas Rutten, Ken Shamrock, Frank Shamrock, and Guy Mezger in his celebrated career. He also tangled with the legendary Rickson Gracie and countryman Kazushi Sakuraba during his storied career. He is best known for his advanced submission skills during an era when many of his fellow competitors were struggling to keep up with his advanced moves.

4. YUSHIN "THUNDER" OKAMI

Yushin Okami, one of the top middleweights in the world, currently competes in the UFC. Born in Kanagawa, Okami made his professional debut in September 2002 and won his first six fights. In August 2006, he made his UFC debut with a victory over Alan "the Talent" Belcher. He has gone 10-3 in the octagon with victories over Mark Muñoz, Evan Tanner, and Mike Swick. Earlier in his career, he held a disqualification victory over the great Anderson Silva after the Brazilian, who was on the ground, nailed Okami with a kick while Thunder was on his knees. Okami lost a rematch to Silva in August 2011.

5. NORIFUMI "KID" YAMAMOTO

Norifumi Yamamoto is a skilled mixed martial artist who competes in the featherweight and lightweight divisions. Born in Kawasaki, Yamamoto was educated in Arizona in the United States. Dangerous with his strikes, Yamamoto has defeated an array of well-known opponents, including Genki Sudo, Caol Uno, and Royler Gracie. He stopped Kazuyuki Miyata with a four-second knockout in a K-1 Hero bout in 2005. He has lost four times in his professional MMA career, with the last three by decision.

6. SHINYA AOKI

Shinya Aoki is one of the most unusual mixed martial artists in the world, using an intriguing array of submission moves in his repertoire. During his career, he has been called the Master of Flying Submissions for his unusual attempts at scoring victories. He submitted rival Joachim Hansen with a gogoplata in December 2006 at a Pride event. Earlier that year he had won the Shooto middleweight title with a win over Akira Kikuchi. Currently, he competes in the 155-pound lightweight division.

7. YOSHIHIRO AKIYAMA

Yoshihiro Akiyama is a Japanese mixed martial artist who currently competes in the UFC's light heavyweight (185-pound) division. The muscular Akiyama made his professional debut in December 2004 after a successful judo career. Aggressive Akiyama makes for exciting fights, as he often presses the attack against his opponents. He owns

Japanese fighters and promotions are known for their showmanship.
Here we see a typical Japanese production. *Reith52*

victories over Denis Kang, Melvin Manhoef, and Alan Belcher
in his career. Even his losses are exciting, as his knockout
loss to Chris Leben in July 2010—a fight that Akiyama was
winning at the time of the stoppage—won Fight of the Night
honors.

8. HAYATO SAKURAI

Hayato Sakurai is a Japanese mixed martial artist who
competes in the 170-pound welterweight division. Born in
the Ibaraki Prefecture, Sakurai turned professional in MMA
in 1996 with a submission victory over Caol Uno. He did
not lose a professional fight for five years until he dropped
a decision to Anderson Silva in August 2001 and lost his
Shooto championship. He owns victories over Shinya Aoki,
Mac Danzig, Joachim Hansen, and Jens Pulver.

9. CAOL UNO

Caol Uno is a gifted mixed martial artist who was born in Yokosuka, Japan. A gifted submission specialist and wrestler, Uno has uncanny balance and the ability to confuse his opponents. He turned pro in 1996 with a loss to fellow future great Hayato Sakurai. He has defeated many name fighters in his career, including Dennis Hallman, Rumina Sato, Din Thomas, and Mitsuhiro Ishida. In 2003, he fought a draw with B. J. Penn at UFC 41 in a bout for the UFC lightweight world championship.

10. MITSUHIRO ISHIDA

Mitsuhiro Ishida is a Japanese mixed martial artist known for his wrestling prowess and excellent cardio. The fighter nicknamed the Endless Fighter made his professional MMA debut in July 2001, losing to Daisuke Sugie. He did not lose again for three years. He owns victories over Gilbert Melendez, Marcus Aurelio, and Christiano Marcello.

Fighting Occupations

17
Fighting Fires
They Put Out Fires outside the Cage

Mixed martial artists are of all ages and races and come from all countries and professions. Many mixed martial artists have served in the military and worked in law enforcement. Others have fought fires for a living. The following ten mixed martial artists have faced dangers both in the cage and in society at large fighting fires. They all either currently work as firefighters or have done so earlier in their careers.

1. CHRIS "LIGHTS OUT" LYTLE
Chris Lytle is one of the most popular fighters in mixed martial arts. He competes for the Ultimate Fighting Championship in the welterweight division and frequently garners Fight of the Night or other bonus awards for his aggressive fighting style. He nearly won *The Ultimate Fighter* season 4, losing a disputed decision to Matt Serra in the finals. A former pro boxer, Lytle possesses an incredible defense and has never submitted to his opponents. He also works for the Indianapolis Fire Department, which he greatly enjoys.

2. DON "THE PREDATOR" FRYE
Don Frye is a living legend in the sport of mixed martial arts. Frye had a storied career fighting in the UFC, Pride, and other

fighting organizations. He made his professional debut in MMA at UFC 8, where he won the tournament by stopping Thomas Ramirez, Sam Adkins, and Gary "Big Daddy" Goodridge all in the same night. He then won the Ultimate Ultimate 96 tournament with a finals victory over David "Tank" Abbott. Frye also worked for years as a firefighter and an emergency medical technician in New Mexico and Arizona. According to his website, he began his career as a firefighter in Santa Fe, New Mexico, and then at Bisbee, Arizona.

3. CHAD "THE GRAVE DIGGER" GRIGGS

In August 2010 Chad Griggs shocked the mixed martial arts world by pounding out heavyweight prospect and former pro wrestling superstar Bobby Lashley at a Strikeforce event in Houston, Texas. Brought in as an underdog opponent, Griggs showed endurance, defensive skills, and the ability to time his punches effectively in defeating Lashley. Griggs works for the Tucson Fire Department in Tucson, Arizona, both as a firefighter and a paramedic in addition to fighting professionally.

4. JAMES "SLEDGE" HAMMORTREE

Since 2008, James Hammortree has worked for the Marion County Fire Rescue in Ocala, Florida. He also competed on season 11 of *The Ultimate Fighter*, losing by decision to Brad Tavares in episode 3. He did receive another shot from the UFC and faced Chris Camozzi at *The Ultimate Fighter*'s finale event in his official debut in the octagon. Unfortunately, he lost another unanimous decision.

5. JOHN KELLY

John Kelly is a professional mixed martial artist who competes in the 170-pound division. A former walk-on linebacker for Florida International University, Kelly does not shrink away from challenges. He has compiled a professional MMA record of 5-2, losing only to Edson Diniz in a Bellator Fighting Championships event and Ailton Barbosa in a Scorpius Fighting Championship so far. Kelly also faces challenges as a firefighter in Miami-Dade County, Florida.

6. DAVID BARON
David Baron is a French mixed martial artist who has faced the likes of Takanori Gomi, Dan Hardy, and Hayato Sakurai in his professional career. Since his debut in November 1999, he has compiled an impressive record of 17-3-1. He has been fighting fires even longer than he has been fighting professionally, having worked as a firefighter since 1994.

7. SHAMAR BAILEY
Like the more famous Chris Lytle, Shamar Bailey doubles as a professional mixed martial artist and an employee with the Indianapolis Fire Department. Bailey, who wrestled in college, made his professional MMA debut in October 2006. He currently competes for Strikeforce and has compiled an impressive record of 12-4.

8. DAN BARRERA
Dan Barrera left his firefighting job in Fort Knox, Kentucky, to take his shot at the big time with the UFC. Now a professional mixed martial artist, he is best known for his participation on *The Ultimate Fighter*'s season 6. Though Barrera lost a split decision to Ben Saunders in the season finale, UFC president Dana White awarded each fighter $5,000 extra for the great fight. Barrera now fights fires in Hawaii and trains at B. J. Penn's fighting academy in Hilo.

9. LYLE STEFFENS

Lyle Steffens is a professional mixed martial artist who earned an invitation to *The Ultimate Fighter*'s season 11. In the opening episode, he lost a decision to Rich Attonito and did not last past the first episode. Steffens has compiled a professional MMA record of 5-3, fighting in Rage in the Cage and other events. He also works as a firefighter with the Tucson Fire Department in Tucson, Arizona.

10. IMAN "THE PREDATOR" ACHHAL

Iman Achhal is a female professional mixed martial artist. She escaped Morocco and an arranged marriage, fleeing to the United States in hopes of finding a better life. Though she was homeless for a time, her life turned around when she landed a job with the Fairfax County, Virginia, Fire Department. After more than twenty weeks of training, she became a firefighter. She also has competed professionally in MMA since 2009. At the time of this writing, she is 2-1.

18
Law Dawgs
They Serve the People

Mixed martial arts is a dangerous business, and fighters must be able to deal with skilled opponents who are looking to put them to sleep with knockouts or submissions. Law enforcement presents similar challenges, as officers are charged with preserving order and peace in an often violent world. These ten special mixed martial artists have dealt with violence both in and out of the cage, while their careers have led them to fight opponents for sport and as a vocation.

1. MIRKO "CRO COP" FILIPOVIĆ
Mirko Filipović, better known as Mirko Cro Cop, acquired his nickname for his years of law enforcement service in his native Croatia. Cro Cop, or Croatian cop, served several years in an antiterrorist special forces unit. He later was a member of the Croatian Parliament from 2003 to 2007. Cro Cop is best known for his devastating knockouts in Pride, though he currently competes in the UFC. He is well known for his famous saying about the power of his tremendous leg strikes: "Right leg, hospital; left leg, cemetery."

2. PAULO THIAGO
Paulo Thiago is a Brazilian mixed martial artist who com-

petes in the UFC's 170-pound division. He has knocked out top contender Josh Koscheck and submitted the tough Mike Swick in his MMA career. He also doubles as a member of an elite Brazilian special police force known as Batalhão de Operações Policiais Especiais (BOPE). Thiago began his professional MMA career in 2005 and hopes to secure a title shot in the near future.

3. FORREST GRIFFIN

Forrest Griffin, the former UFC light heavyweight champion, is one of the most popular mixed martial artists of recent memory. Fans appreciate his aggressive style and never-say-die attitude. He became famous for brawling his way to a win over Stephan Bonnar in the finale of *The Ultimate Fighter* in August 2006. He first became interested in MMA while watching a video at the police academy. He served several years with the Athens, Georgia, Police Department before becoming a full-time mixed martial artist.

4. "BIG" JOHN MCCARTHY

John McCarthy is considered the best referee in the history of mixed martial arts. For years he was the leading third man in the octagon for the UFC, and still referees many major MMA events. He also served as a police officer for the Los Angeles Police Department for twenty-two years (1985–2007). His official website, bigjohnmccarthy.com, reports, "In his 22 years on the force, McCarthy instructed over 10,000 recruits in Arrest and Control procedures and survival tactics."

5. MIKE RUSSOW

Mike Russow is a heavyweight mixed martial artist who currently competes in the UFC. He surprised observers by absorbing significant punishment before delivering a comeback knockout punch over hyped prospect Todd Duffee. Perhaps Russow obtained his toughness from working as one of Chicago's finest. Russow worked many years in the Englewood community of the Windy City. "Being a police officer, I've pretty much seen every horrible thing you could think of," Russow told Michael Huang of *FIGHT!* magazine.

6. ROBERT "MAXIMUS" MACDONALD

Robert MacDonald is a professional mixed martial artist who formerly worked as a cop in Toronto, Canada. MacDonald left the police force as his mixed martial arts career progressed. MacDonald participated in season 2 of *The Ultimate Fighter* in the light heavyweight division. He later received a contract with the UFC, where he fought three times in 2006. In August 2006, he lost by submission in the first round to Eric Schafer in what was his last UFC bout. In 2008, he handed in his badge at the Toronto Police Department and moved to Utah to continue his pursuit of professional mixed martial arts.

7. CHRIS BATEN

Chris Baten works as a sheriff's deputy for Hillsborough County, Florida, but he moonlights as a professional mixed martial artist. He started training in karate at age four and in his mid-twenties turned his attention to mixed martial arts. He also had a lifelong goal for a career in law enforcement. After majoring in criminal justice at the University of South Carolina, Baten worked as a correctional officer at a maximum security prison in South Carolina. He now protects, serves, and fights in Tampa, Florida.

8. SEAN "THE CANNON" GANNON

Sean Gannon is a Boston police officer who is best known for his underground brawl with street-fighting legend Kevin

"Kimbo Slice" Ferguson in 2004. The brawl, which can be viewed on the Internet, was one of the most downloaded videos in YouTube history. Gannon defeated Slice, though some suggested that his victory was tainted by the use of knee strikes. Gannon parlayed the win over Slice into a UFC contract to fight Branden Lee Hinkle. Unfortunately for Gannon, Hinkle stopped him in the first round.

9. RICHARD ODOMS

Richard Odoms is a veteran police officer with more than a dozen years' service with the San Antonio Police Department. He's also a former professional boxer, having retired in 2003 with a 5-0 record after suffering an eye injury. He underwent successful eye surgery in 2006 and made him yearn to return to combat sports. This time he chose mixed martial arts. In July 2010, Odoms made his professional MMA debut against Lucas Gomez at an ABG Promotions event billed as the Alamo Showdown. Odoms stopped Gomez in the second round.

10. JOE DeMORE

Joe DeMore is a captain at the Allegheny County Jail in Pittsburgh, Pennsylvania. After graduating with a degree in political science from Slippery Rock University, he initially intended to become a police officer; however, he landed a job as a corrections officer first. He began fighting in amateur MMA events in 2007, compiling a 6-3 record. He turned professional as a mixed martial artist in 2009 but has found it more difficult. His current professional MMA record is 1-4.

19

GI Fighters

Soldiers in the Octagon

Militaries throughout the world have been quick to capitalize on the popularity of mixed martial arts by recruiting as many top-tier athletes as possible. Not only do these athletes pass on their fighting knowledge to other soldiers, but they also give the military plenty of press coverage in a sport that caters to their prime recruiting demographic. Although many fighters in MMA have military backgrounds, the ones below are known for being respected both in and out of the ring.

1. BRIAN "ALL AMERICAN" STANN

Before defeating all comers to score the World Extreme Cagefighting light heavyweight championship, Brian Stann was busy fighting Iraqi insurgents. Perhaps the most courageous man to ever step into the cage, Stann graduated from the U.S. Naval Academy and was commissioned as a second lieutenant in the Marine Corps. While serving in Iraq he commanded a platoon that took part in Operation Matador and earned a silver star after he and his men were ambushed while attempting to secure a bridge in Karabilah.

Although often considered a one-dimensional fighter with limited grappling ability, Stann brings to the ring a level of intensity and professionalism that, when combined with his solid boxing skills, often makes up for his lack of a solid ground game. Unfortunately for him, Krzysztof Soszynski capitalized on this deficiency during Stann's Ultimate Fighting Championship debut and secured a Kimura armlock during the first round for the win. Having previously bounced from one training facility to the next, Stann now trains out of the famed Jackson's Gym in Albuquerque, where he finally has access to top training partners.

2. JOE "THE HYBRID" DUARTE

Born in Guam and having dabbled in mixed martial arts since he was a teenager, Duarte moved to Texas in 2002 to further his fighting career. Totally broke and unable to get a solid foothold in the sport, he soon enlisted in the U.S. Army. There he met Pat Tillman, formerly of the Arizona Cardinals. Together they went through basic training and airborne school, eventually earning the right to be called army rangers.

A combat veteran who ended up losing his best friend during a vicious gun battle in Iraq, Duarte left military service in 2006 to continue his MMA career. He won a few minor fights and was recruited for the 2008 season of *The Ultimate Fighter* television series. When filming was completed, he began training at the Arena in San Diego, winning a fight against David Gardner. His current record is 10-2.

3. JOHN "THE SAINT" RENKEN

Another ranger turned fighter, Renken has had a long career in MMA, having fought more than sixty professional bouts since 1997. While most MMA fighters are content to simply hone their own skills, Renken has gone on to achieve instructor-level status in many martial arts, including sambo, judo, combat submission wrestling, and U.S. Army Combatives. Owning and operating the Clarksville Mixed Martial Arts Academy in Tennessee, Renken has held several championship titles, including the International Fighting Championship (IFC) lightweight title, the HooknShoot middleweight belt, and the Submission Fighting Championship (SFC) cruiserweight title.

Not only does Renken continue to develop his own martial arts game, the U.S. Army also has employed him as a chief hand-to-hand instructor at Fort Campbell, Kentucky. On top of all of these accomplishments, Renken is also a highly respected preacher and uses his physical prowess and fighting knowledge to appeal to youth who might otherwise stray from the Christian path.

John "the Saint" Renken, professional MMA fighter and soldier. *Courtesy of John Renken*

4. TIM KENNEDY

Beginning with his Chuck Norris obsession, Tim Kennedy's entire life has been about fighting. While serving as a Green Beret in the U.S. Army, Tim fought opponents on battlefields all over the globe and in the ring. He had postponed a full-time fighting career to fulfill his commitment to his nation, but he recently made the difficult decision not to reenlist and instead focus on his MMA career.

Tim originally trained with Chuck Liddell out of the Pit in San Luis Obispo and went on to fight under the now defunct International Fight League. As an amateur fighter, he had a 30-1 record. After his last deployment, Tim returned to the United States to defeat Nick Thompson handily during the Strikeforce Challengers event in June 2009. Three weeks later the Texas Army National Guard offered him a position as a spokesman for the organization, a job that allows the full-time MMA fighter to maintain an association with the military.

5. RANDY "THE NATURAL" COUTURE

After finding out that his high school sweetheart was pregnant, Randy Couture immediately proposed marriage and turned to the U.S. Army for support, enlisting in 1982. While Randy served as an air traffic controller in Germany, a fellow soldier discovered that Randy had been a successful high school wrestler and suggested that they go to the local wrestling club. From that point Randy spent more time wrestling than he did guiding airplanes. He won several competitions, earned a spot on the All-Army Team, and became a full-time wrestler.

Randy spent the rest of his army career traveling the world, wrestling, and waiting for the Olympic tryouts, which come around only once every four years. Meanwhile, he filled his time by competing in MMA, eventually dethroning Maurice Smith as UFC heavyweight champion in 1997. Following a fourth failure to place on the Olympic wrestling team (and then thirty-six years old), Randy finally decided to give up on his Olympic quest and made MMA his full-time job.

6. FRANKLIN ROBERTO "BOBBY" LASHLEY

A successful amateur wrestler, Bobby Lashley graduated from Missouri Valley College and quickly discovered that having a college education didn't mean that he could pay the bills. Enlisting in the U.S. Army through its World Class Athletes Program (WCAP), Lashley went on to infantry school and then reported to the WCAP, where he continued to train as a wrestler and twice won the Armed Forces Championship. After being discharged from the army, Lashley was recruited into the World Wrestling Entertainment (formerly the World Wrestling Federation), put on more than fifty pounds of muscle, and eventually competed in the famed Royal Rumble.

Lashley moved into MMA in 2008, defeating Joshua Franklin in a small venue on a lesser-known ticket. Six months later he defeated the legendary Bob Sapp in front of a sold-out crowd at Ultimate Chaos in Biloxi, Mississippi. Although not the fight of the century, Lashley regards such fights as learning experiences and fully expects to move into the primetime as he becomes a better-rounded fighter.

7. JAMES DAMIEN STELLY

Enlisting in the army just before 9/11, James Stelly went into an Airborne Division as soon as he could. He eventually graduated from the famed Ranger School and quickly found himself at the forefront of the war on terrorism. A skilled grappler and All-American wrestler, Stelly was asked

to become one of the first instructors of U.S. Army Combatives. A well-versed fighter by anyone's standards, Stelly has
been both a World FIAS (Federation International Amateur
Sambo) champion and an amateur freestyle wrestling national champion.

8. MIRKO "CRO COP" FILIPOVIĆ

Although his nom de guerre identifies him as a police officer,
as most men living in Eastern Europe, Mirko was drafted
into the army at a young age. While serving in the Croatian
military, he applied for police training and was accepted into
the academy. From there he found his way into the elite ATJ
Lučko, a group similar to an American special weapons and
tactics (SWAT) team but much more militarized. Splitting the
difference between a military special operations unit and a
civilian assault team, ATJ Lučko is one of Croatia's premier
counterterrorist units. Even though he continues to fight
all over the world and has even taken time off to serve in
Croatia's Parliament, Mirko is still dedicated to the unit and
continues to train with its members.

9. FRANK "THE TANK" LESTER

It was always expected that Lester, the son of a U.S. Army
colonel, would eventually join the service. The tragic events
of 9/11 helped make his decision easier, and after com-
pleting advanced infantry training, Lester was sent to Iraq.
Although unwilling to talk about many of his combat experiences, Lester credits his military service with helping him in
his MMA career. Upon his return to the United States, Lester
took part in *The Ultimate Fighter: United States vs. United
Kingdom* show, where he won a slot on the American team as
a replacement fighter. Eventually eliminated halfway through
the season, he returned once again as a replacement and

defeated his opponent. The only return fighter ever to win his bout, Lester trained with Team Quest out of Temecula, California and has since move on to train with Greg Jackson in New Mexico.

10. ANDREW "THE POWERHOUSE" CHAPPELLE

Following one of his fights, Chappelle decided to join the military after talking to the founder of the U.S. Army Combatives Program. With eleven years of martial arts training under his belt and a work ethic second to none, Chappelle immediately sought the distinction of becoming an airborne ranger and was quickly promoted to noncommissioned officer. He transferred to the Army Combatives School at Fort Benning, Georgia, where he currently serves as an instructor. Although not fighting as often as he did before enlisting, Chappelle's record has improved. It is expected that once Chappelle's enlistment is up, he'll go on to establish himself as a dominant fighter.

Not Your Average Fighter

20

Age Is Nothing but a Number

Defying Father Time

Many sports icons have continued to perform at a high level in their respective fields at what many consider an advanced age from an athletic standpoint. Archie Moore won a boxing world championship in his forties, and "Big" George Foreman captured the world heavyweight title in November 1994 at age forty-five with a stunning knockout of Michael Moorer. Bernard Hopkins Jr. won a piece of the world light heavyweight title in 2011 at the age of forty-six. Gordie Howe played professional hockey in his fifties, while Martina Navratilova, the tennis player who's in her fifties, still competes in mixed doubles. The following ten mixed martial artists have shown that they have stared down Father Time.

1. DAN "THE BEAST" SEVERN

A former Ultimate Fighting Championship tournament champion, Dan Severn amazingly still competes as a professional in his early fifties. Born in 1958, Severn first turned professional in MMA in 1994 at UFC 4, where he manhandled his first few opponents before falling to Brazilian jiu-jitsu master Royce Gracie in the finals. Severn later won the UFC 5 and Ultimate Ultimate 1995 tournaments, defeating the likes of

Dan Severn in his wrestling days. *Courtesy of ASU Media Relations*

Oleg Taktarov, David "Tank" Abbott, and Dave Beneteau. Severn's last winning streak went ten bouts from May 2009 to April 2011.

2. RANDY COUTURE

Randy Couture competed in the UFC until the age of forty-seven, having beaten former world champion boxer James Toney in August 2010. Couture pulled an array of upsets against younger opponents in his Hall of Fame career. He became the first person ever to hold titles in two different UFC weight divisions, as he won both the UFC light heavyweight and heavyweight championships when he was in his forties. He defied Father Time by taking care of his body and showing incredible training and lifestyle discipline. In his autobiography *Becoming the Natural*, Couture writes:

"For most of my life, I've eaten healthfully and taken care of my body as best I could." In August 2010, Couture looked as fit as ever while he easily submitted boxer James Toney. He retired following a loss in April 2011 to Lyoto Machida.

3. RON "BLACK DRAGON" VAN CLIEF

Ron van Clief is a highly respected karate champion who crossed over into movies during his heyday in the 1970s. He founded his own martial arts style, which he called Chinese Goju. In 1994, the fifty-one-year-old van Clief entered the fourth UFC tournament. In the first round, he squared off against two-time champion and Brazilian jiu-jitsu expert Royce Gracie. Van Clief acquitted himself reasonably well and showed good strength, but he succumbed to a rear naked choke hold four minutes into the bout. A Vietnam veteran (United States Marine Corps), he remains the oldest person ever to have fought in the UFC.

4. HELIO GRACIE

Helio Gracie, the legendary Brazilian jiu-jitsu master, is best known for teaching his sons Royce, Rickson, Rorion, and Royler the family art. But Helio, who passed away in 2009 at the age of ninety-five, was a formidable fighter in his own right. He learned the art firsthand from his older brother Carlos Gracie. Helio submitted numerous combatants in a career that spanned more than forty years. In 1967, at the age of fifty-five, Helio submitted Valdomiro dos Santos Ferreira.

5. JOHN WILLIAMS

John Williams entered into the *Guinness Book of World Records* by competing and winning a mixed martial arts event at the age of seventy in July 2010. Williams, who has trained in martial arts since 1947, defeated forty-nine-year-old Larry

Brubaker at the Wild Card event for Elite 1 MMA Productions in New Brunswick, Canada. Williams submitted Brubaker with an ankle lock in the second round. Williams told columnist James Ryan in an interview for *Bleacher Report* that "for me, it's too soon to give up on life like a lot of others my age and younger have already." He proved his point with his recent victory in actual competition.

6. SKIP HALL

At sixty-three years old, Skip Hall fought as a professional mixed martial artist in March 2008 at the Dixie Throwdown V in Irondale, Alabama. A former amateur boxer, military veteran, and power lifter, he turned professional at age fifty-seven and fought at least nine times as a professional. In his article for MSNBC.com, writer Mike Chiappetta referred to Hall as the "baddest grandfather on the planet."

7. MARK "THE HAMMER" COLEMAN

Mark Coleman is often referred to as the godfather of the ground and pound. He used his strong wrestling skills to force his opponents down on the mat and then literally pounded them into submission. He won his first six fights in the UFC, capturing the UFC 10 and UFC 11 tournaments and the first-ever UFC heavyweight championship. Coleman still competes at the highest level of mixed martial arts, defeating Stephan Bonnar at a UFC event in 2009 at the age of forty-four. He later lost to Randy Couture in a battle of legends at age forty-five.

8. ANTONIO MCKEE

Antonio "Mr. Decision" McKee continues to ply his trade at forty years of age in professional mixed martial arts. McKee always comes to fight in excellent shape with superb cardio conditioning. Perhaps that is why he has built up a record of 26-4-2. While some criticize his style as "lay and pray," he is a technician who knows how to win fights and often against much younger men. In October 2010, McKee finally received a shot at the big time with a bout in the UFC. He lost a split decision to Jacob Volkmann and is no longer with the UFC.

9. BOBBY SOUTHWORTH

Bobby Southworth is the former Strikeforce light heavyweight champion who still competes in mixed martial arts even though he has passed the age of forty. He turned professional in 1999 and has competed in both Pride and the UFC. In July 2010, he recently notched another win on his belt by defeating Aaron Boyes in a professional MMA event in Australia.

10. PATRICK SMITH

Patrick Smith is a former kickboxer who fought in the UFC tournament events in the early 1990s. His powerful strikes carried him to several victories over the years. During his career, he has tangled with such legends of the sport as Ken Shamrock and Royce Gracie, who defeated him in the finals of UFC 2. At age forty-six, Smith fought three times in 2009 and won two of those fights.

21
Fighting Phenoms
Bursting on the Scene at a Young Age

Athletes peak at different ages in their careers. Randy Couture showed that a fighter in his forties can compete at the highest levels of the sport. Other fighters progress at a much earlier age. The following ten fighters began their professional careers early and earned the title of phenom.

1. B. J. PENN
There is a reason why B. J. Penn is called the Prodigy. He first learned Brazilian jiu-jitsu at age seventeen, and a few years later he won a world championship in Brazilian jiu-jitsu. He earned his black belt in Brazilian jiu-jitsu in only three years. He signed his Ultimate Fighting Championship contract at age twenty-two, and his first professional fight was in the octagon. He swept through Joey Gilbert, Din Thomas, and Caol Uno in his first three bouts. The rest, as they say, is history, as the Prodigy remains a top contender in the light-weight division.

2. JOSÉ ALDO
José Aldo, the current World Extreme Cagefighting's feath-erweight champion, made his professional debut at age

seventeen in August 2004, knocking out his opponent in less than twenty seconds with a head kick. He made his WEC debut in June 2008 and won nine straight bouts. He has a professional record of 20-1 and is listed as one of the sport's top pound-for-pound fighters. He may only get better, as he is only twenty-four years of age at the time of this writing.

3. **MARCIN HELD**

Polish prodigy Marcin Held discovered Brazilian jiu-jitsu at age nine and turned professional in mixed martial arts at the tender age of seventeen. At the time of this writing, the nineteen-year-old Held has compiled a professional record of 11-2. Various MMA publications, including *FIGHT!* and *Sherdog*, have listed him as one of the sport's top young prospects. Some have predicted he will be a future world champion.

4. **DAN LAUZON**

In 2006 Dan Lauzon was the youngest fighter to earn a UFC contract, at eighteen years and seven months old. Lauzon had made his professional debut only two days after his eighteenth birthday earlier that year. He won his first four pro fights before his UFC debut against the tough Spencer Fisher, which he lost. At the time of this writing, Lauzon is only twenty-three years old and has the talent to return to the UFC. Only time will tell if he lives up to his vast potential.

5. **NICK DIAZ**

Bad boy Nick Diaz of Stockton, California, is one of the sport's top pound-for-pound fighters. He is also one of its most impressive phenoms. He became a professional right after he turned eighteen in August 2001 with a win over Mike

Wick. While still a teenager, he won the WEC's welterweight championship with a win over Joe Hurley. Diaz has fought all over the world for various top promotional companies, including the UFC, Pride, and Strikeforce.

6. VITOR BELFORT

Vitor Belfort earned his nickname the Phenom with his early prowess in mixed martial arts. He made his professional MMA debut at age nineteen at a SuperBrawl event, where he knocked out Jon Hess in twelve seconds. While still nineteen, he fought in the UFC 12 tournament, stopping Tra Telligman and Scott Ferrozzo in the first round of successive bouts to win the heavyweight tournament. Later that year, he also blitzed David "Tank" Abbott in the first round. He remains a top-level MMA fighter and again competes in the UFC.

7. "BAD" BRAD MCDONALD

Brad McDonald made his professional debut in mixed martial arts in 2008, at age fifteen. He fights in Gladiator Challenge events in California, compiling a record of 7-1 according to *Sherdog*. He has two older brothers who also complete in professional mixed martial arts bouts.

8. JON JONES

Jon Jones is well on his way to becoming the UFC's next superstar. The talented, six-foot-four, light heavyweight has decimated foes since his first appearance in the octagon in August 2008, as a twenty-one-year-old. Jones turned pro at age twenty in April 2008 and won six fights before signing a UFC contract. To date his only loss has been via disqualification for illegal elbow strikes against Matt Hamill. This phenom became a UFC champion in March 2011 with a technical knockout win over Mauricio Rua.

9. RORY MacDONALD

Canadian fighter Rory MacDonald turned professional in mixed martial arts at age sixteen with a win over Terry Thiara at an Extreme Fighting Challenge event. He is one of the UFC's youngest fighters at only twenty-one years of age. This skilled fighter has a record of 12-1 and hopes to climb the ladder and gain a shot at a UFC title in the next few years.

10. STEFAN "SKYSCRAPER" STRUVE

Stefan Struve began his professional mixed martial arts career in March 2005 at age seventeen. He defeated John De Wilde at the Gentlemen Fight Night. In February 2009, he made his UFC debut, losing to the powerful Junior dos Santos. At the time of this writing, the twenty-three-year-old Struve remains a heavyweight prospect and phenom.

22

Extra Large

Human Anomalies

Fighters come in all shapes and sizes, and often the small-est fighters put on the best shows. Despite this fact the heavyweight division draws the most spectators, mainly because the less knowledgeable fight fans generally think that the biggest and strongest fighters are naturally capable of dominating their smaller and weaker opponents, regardless of skill level. When promotions have had unlimited weight classes, such as in the early Ultimate Fighting Championship, this belief was consistently proven not to be the case, but the myth still persists and the heavyweights remain the top draws. This list highlights heavyweights who push the size envelope—that is, men who are too big even for the modern UFC's heavyweight division.

1. CHAD "AKEBONO" ROWAN

Nothing says "big" more than a giant, half-naked man running around in a thong. Chad Rowan, also known as Akebono to his Japanese fans, is one of the tallest and heaviest fighters ever to enter the cage. At six foot eight and weighing more than five hundred pounds, Akebono was, and still is, the epitome of the ideal sumo wrestler. Unfortunately for him, sumo is currently much more of a ritual than it is a fighting art, and the former grand champion was soundly trounced in all of his MMA matches. One of his more interesting bouts was against MMA legend Royce Gracie, where, before succumbing to a shoulder lock, he threw his 180-pound competitor the entire length of the ring. Akebono went on to fight other no-holds-barred legends, such as Don Frye and Giant Silva, but was defeated in every match.

2. EMMANUEL YARBOROUGH

Two of the more interesting aspects of the early UFC were that there were no weight classes and fights between dwarfs and giants were widely promoted. Perhaps the most memorable such fight occurred in UFC 3, where Keith Hackney, weighing in at about two hundred pounds, fought Emmanuel Yarborough, who weighed roughly *three times* as much. The lighter man used his superior speed to dodge the giant's lumbering punches while occasionally ducking into the pocket to throw a few shots of his own. Not being the best boxer in the world, Hackney occasionally slowed down long enough to fall into Yarborough's clutches, and at one point Yarborough smashed him into the cage so hard that the metal door broke open, flinging him into the audience. As luck would have it, Yarborough's footwork and conditioning were less than optimal, and an accidental slip landed him on his back. Once on the ground Yarborough flailed like a beached whale, giving Hackney the opportunity to land a stream of hard shots that ended the match.

3. HONG MAN "TECHNO GOLIATH" CHOI

An Internet legend in his own right, Choi is a Korean MMA fighter who has what most other giants lack—muscles and skill. Standing taller than seven foot two and weighing more than three hundred pounds, Choi was a kickboxer before he entered the cage and even boasts alternative careers as a pop singer and soldier. Though he moves slowly, Choi is considered a dangerous fighter because his size allows him to clear large amounts of canvas in single steps while consistently generating tremendous power in all of his shots. Choi's most notable MMA win was against former American baseball star José Canseco during a brief, lopsided fight. His most notable (and entertaining) losses occurred to Fedor Emelianenko via armbar and then to Mirko Filipović, who chopped the larger man down with a series of devastating leg kicks.

4. PAUL VARELANS

A freestyle fighter out of California with a black belt in something called trap fighting, Varelans had a number of well-publicized MMA fights during the mid- to late 1990s. Although he fought some of the best fighters of the decade, his most memorable fight was a loss in 1997 to Mark Kerr, who at the time was making his MMA debut in Brazil. The fight started with Kerr throwing a number of illegal kicks that forced the referee to issue a warning and separate the fighters. When the fight recommenced, Kerr rushed Varelans, taking his 330-pound opponent to the ground and achieving a side mount. Kerr followed up with a series of knees and punches that turned Valerans's face into a bloody mess, forcing a stoppage when blood began gushing from the big man's hairline.

5. RICARDO "THE MUTANT" MORAIS

A six-foot-six Brazilian fighter who specializes in boxing and Brazilian jiu-jitsu, Morais was expected to become a dominating force in the heavyweight division. With a long reach and spindly legs, Morais has an imposing physical presence and is respected as a tough and resilient opponent. With a host of early wins under his belt, many assumed that Morais would eventually work his way up the championship ladder, but it was never meant to be. Once knocked off balance, the big Brazilian never seemed to get his legs back under him. His problem was exemplified in his dramatic knockout loss to Aleksander Emelianenko, which effectively halted his upward momentum in the heavyweight division.

6. BOB "THE BEAST" SAPP

Perhaps one of the most beloved giant men in all of Japanese history, Sapp was a former professional football player turned professional wrestler who took up real fighting when he agreed to a match against William "the Refrigerator" Perry in a televised Toughman competition. Standing six foot five, weighing 330 pounds, and having a neck that's thicker than most men's waists, Sapp soon found his way to Japan's unique professional wrestling circuit. With a fighting style that more resembles a video game caricature than an actual system, Sapp went on to compete in Pride, where he lost to Antônio Rodrigo Nogueira. He fared somewhat better in K-1, twice defeating an aging Ernesto Hoost. Since that time Sapp has had a number of fights but none of particular note.

7. SEMMY "THE DUTCH DESTROYER" SCHILT

Standing nearly seven feet tall and weighing almost three hundred pounds, Schilt is a Dutch kickboxer who cut his teeth in MMA. The ninth king of Pancrase, Schilt has also held seven world kickboxing titles. Notwithstanding his size, power, and kickboxing ability, Schilt has had great difficulty when confronted with elite MMA fighters. Between 2002 and 2003 he lost three consecutive fights to Fedor Emelianenko,

Antônio Rodrigo Nogueira, and Josh Barnett. Despite these losses Schilt has shown an increasing ability on the ground and continues to improve his game. Having also defeated "Mighty Mo" Siliga by triangle choke, Schilt's most notable MMA win to date was over former UFC champion Pete Williams, whom he defeated by strikes back in 2001.

8. PAULO "GIANT" CÉSAR DA SILVA

A former professional basketball player turned MMA fighter, Silva is another massive human being who found fame competing in Japan. Standing seven foot two and often weighing more than four hundred pounds, the Giant makes his living more by being a human anomaly than he does as a fighter. Throwing punches more as if he were an angry third grader than as a schooled pugilist, Silva regularly finds his way to the ground during his MMA fights but rarely gets back up. Known for his strange, overhand slaps, which he uses to bat opponents on top of the head, Silva's best win was against fellow giant Chad Akebono Rowan, whom he defeated via standing armlock.

9. STEFAN "GIANT" GAMLIN

Comparable to Bob Sapp in fighting style but two inches taller and twenty pounds heavier, Gamlin's short MMA career was typified by bull-rushing his opponents with a flurry of poorly aimed punches. When they failed to connect (which has always happened so far), Gamlin immediately tried to take his opponent to the ground, but that tactic generally didn't work too well for him either. His most notable fights so far were a short striking contest against Bob Sapp (who dominated him) and an even quicker loss by submission to Jason "Mayhem" Miller. At this point Gamlin hasn't gotten out of the first round unscathed and appears to have gone into early retirement.

10. ROSS "THE GRIZZLY BEAR" CLIFTON

The only deceased member of this list, Clifton stood six foot eight and weighed 360 pounds. His career began in 2001 and lasted until 2009 when he died of a heart attack at age thirty-two. Along the way he entertained audiences with strange facial expressions and a primitive beard that no doubt added to his intimidating ring persona. Surprisingly nimble for a big man, Clifton was always a game fighter, but he had a weak chin. His most notable and penultimate opponent was Ken Shamrock, who connected early in their fight with an overhand right and followed up with an armbar for the win.

It's All Showbiz

23

Best Nicknames

Most Interesting Appellations

One of the most fun aspects of sports is nicknames, or monikers we attribute or attach to our favorite athletes. Mixed martial arts is no exception, as fight fans love to talk about the "Iceman" Chuck Liddell or Quinton "Rampage" Jackson. Some nicknames become so ingrained that they replace the fighters' given first name. The following are ten of our favorite nicknames in the sport.

1. THE KOREAN ZOMBIE
Chan Sung Jung is known as the Korean Zombie, an un-usual nickname for a warrior. Jung simply fights his heart out, coming forward with a relentless assault of kicks and punches. His featherweight war with Leonard Garcia in a World Extreme Cagefighting bout in 2010 has earned rave reviews as one of the best fights of all time. Jung says the Korean Top Team gave him his colorful nickname because like a zombie he walked through punches and kicks but kept moving forward without getting knocked down.

2. THE LAST EMPEROR
Fedor Emelianenko, in the eyes of many MMA experts and fellow combatants, is the greatest fighter of all time. It is

fitting then that this great fighter carries the epic moniker of the Last Emperor. Many concluded that since winning the Pride heavyweight championship from Antônio Rodrigo Nogueira in March 2003, Emelianenko reigned as the best heavyweight in the world. For nine and a half years he was considered undefeated, as his only "loss" occurred in a December 2000 bout after an illegal strike against Tsuyoshi Kohsaksa opened a cut. Because the bout was part of a tournament format, Emelianenko technically had a loss, one that he avenged convincingly in April 2005. Thus, from December 2000 until June 2010 when he lost to Fabricio Werdum, Emelianko lorded over mixed martial arts as its Last Emperor.

3. THE ARM COLLECTOR

Brazil's Givanildo Santana is one of the best submission specialists in mixed martial arts. His favorite move is the classic armbar submission, which explains why his nickname the Arm Collector is apropos. From July 2005 through April 2008, Santana won eleven straight professional MMA bouts— all via armbar submissions. Of his sixteen career victories, twelve have come via armbars.

4. THE DEAN OF MEAN

Everyone loves a good rhyming moniker, and Keith "the Dean of Mean" Jardine possesses one of the best. Jardine's appearance is fearsome, with his bald head, long goatee, and ferocious scowl. Jardine can also fight, as he showed in defeating the likes of Forrest Griffin, Chuck Liddell, and Brandon Vera in his MMA career.

5. THE AXE MURDERER

Wanderlei Silva may be the most exciting fighter in the history of mixed martial arts. This former Pride superstar and current Ultimate Fighting Championship fighter thrills audiences worldwide with his no-holds-barred assaults on his opponents. Silva constantly takes the role of aggressor, seeking to punish his opponents with knees, kicks, and punches. His brutal knockouts of Quinton "Rampage" Jackson with his Muay Thai knee strikes are legendary. He earned his memorable nickname after defeating Eugene Jackson in 1999. Silva's ultra-aggressive style not only made him one of the sport's favorite fighters but also earned him one of the sport's greatest nicknames.

6. ICE COLD
The legendary Russian kickboxer Igor Vovchanchyn was known as Ice Cold. His devastating power in his legs and hands enabled him to knock out a slew of opponents "ice cold" in his career: Gary Goodridge, Enson Inoue, Nobuhiku Takada, Dan Bobish, and Francisco Bueno. He had submission skills as well, as Gilbert Yvel and Valentijn Overeem could attest. For a period in the late 1990s and early 2000s, he was one of the most feared mixed martial artists on the planet.

7. THE PRODIGY
B. J. Penn is a true prodigy in the sport of mixed martial arts. He first learned Brazilian jiu-jitsu at age seventeen and three years later won a world jiu-jitsu championship in Brazil in 2000. The next year, he made his professional MMA debut in the octagon by stopping Joey Gilbert in the first round. He followed that win up with first-round stoppages of reputable veterans Din Thomas and Caol Uno. A prodigy was born. He remains one of the sport's best pound-for-pound fighters.

8. KRAZY HORSE

Charles "Krazy Horse" Bennett's nickname fits him perfectly because he fights in an unpredictable fashion. This talented puncher lives a chaotic life marked by highs and lows. When avoiding arrests and getting in proper condition, he can provide solid competition for fellow lightweights. He also entertains fans by mugging for the cameras, pulling off back flips, and acting a little crazy. Bennett can fight, too, as he showed by knocking out K. J. Noons in the first round in an upset of an Elite XC card.

9. THE CRIPPLER

Chris Leben is a fight fan's dream, as he wades into the octagon throwing bombs in an ultra-aggressive style. For a time, Leben was known for his rowdy and unusual behavior—he urinated on a fellow contestant's pillow during season 1 of *The Ultimate Fighter*—but now he is recognized for his devastating power, which can "cripple" an opponent. For example, he flattened Jorge Santiago and Terry Martin in UFC bouts. He also recently overcame what appeared to be a sure defeat to stop Yoshihiro Akiyama at the end of the third and final round. He added to his kayo ledger in the summer of 2011 with a devastating kayo of the legendary Wanderlei Silva.

10. CYBORG

Cristiane Santos arguably is the most fearsome female mixed martial artist in the world. Since losing her pro debut in May 2005, she has dominated all her opponents. In August 2009, she crushed the popular Gina Carano to win the Strikeforce middleweight championship. The Cyborg shows no mercy in pounding her opponents into submission with superior strength and power. Sometimes her overwhelmed opponents may feel that she is indeed more machine than human.

24

Wannabes

Celebrities Who Cross Train

Let's face it; every male in the world, including the pretty boys of Hollywood, wants to be considered tough. When the svelte Royce Gracie stepped into the cage and started dismantling opponents three times his size, the TV tough guys started paying attention and began wondering if they had finally found their ticket to street credibility. Whether everyone on this list took martial arts to toughen up is a matter of conjecture, but what isn't up for debate is that none of these folks have gone out of their way to hide their pursuits, with the sole exception of the one legitimate tough guy on the list, Steve "the Crocodile Hunter" Irwin.

1. STEVE IRWIN

Few would suspect that the beloved Crocodile Hunter was also a martial arts enthusiast. It should come as no surprise, though, that years of wrestling wildlife gave Irwin incredible strength and stamina, which proved to be equally effective on human beings. When these attributes were coupled with his large, robust frame, Steve Irwin had everything it takes to be a grappling powerhouse. A huge fan of mixed martial arts since the sport's well-publicized beginning, Irwin specifically sought out bodyguards with MMA backgrounds. He regularly trained with his bodyguards in boxing and Brazilian jiu-jitsu, even going so far as to inquire about having a professional bout before his untimely death in 2006.

2. NICOLAS CAGE

There aren't many A-list actors who put much effort into anything other than looking good and maybe pumping iron. As one of the more eccentric personalities in Hollywood whose spending habits would have put Michael Jackson to shame, Cage has actually made time throughout his life to pursue a variety of martial arts. Having displayed his faux fighting prowess in a number of films, Cage showcased his exceptional Wing Chun abilities in *Bangkok Dangerous,* which debuted in 2008. Reputed to be a black belt in jiu-jitsu under Royce Gracie, Cage makes no bones about his interest in the Asian arts and actively seeks to add a martial flare to many of his acting roles.

3. VIN DIESEL

As a famous Hollywood tough guy who for years has been rubbing elbows with famous MMA personalities, Diesel can be expected to have picked up at least a few tricks along the way. Vin Diesel also claims to have studied a number of martial arts for movie roles, including Kali and Muay Thai, although his knowledge of both seems to be cursory at best. His tough guy persona is such that he has been credited with a wide range of fictitious fighting exploits, from vicious knife fights to illegal, underground vale tudo matches in Brazil. Most of those stories are pure fantasy, but it is widely accepted that Diesel is a talented Brazilian jiu-jitsu practitioner who trains under one of the Gracies.

4. **ED O'NEILL**

Ed O'Neill gained fame by bringing low-class, suburban machismo to new heights with his portrayal of Al Bundy in *Married . . . with Children.* Unlike most seasoned actors, Ed O'Neill had an athletic background as a football player, and before cutting his teeth in the movies was a draft pick for the Pittsburgh Steelers. Another celebrity who found BJJ to his liking, O'Neill persevered in the martial art for nearly fifteen years under the tutelage of Rorion Gracie before being awarded his black belt in 2007.

5. **SEAN PATRICK FLANNERY**

A quality actor who is best known for his role in *The Boondock Saints*, Flannery hasn't found as much success in Hollywood as some of the other stars on this list. He has had, however, more success in the martial arts arena and teaches classes throughout the Hollywood area. Originally an accomplished student of Tae Kwon Do, Flannery went on to study Brazilian jiu-jitsu under Rickson Gracie and was eventually awarded his black belt from Shawn Williams. Not only has Flannery been seen in grappling competitions but he also went on to acquire another black belt—this one in karate—and has since opened up a successful martial arts school.

6. **KEVIN JAMES**

The star of the hit show *King of Queens*, Kevin James is about as unlikely a fighter as one can imagine. With full-on comedic sensibilities and a stomach that rivals John Belushi's, James has been in a host of television shows and several feature-length films, including *Paul Blart: Mall Cop*, which defied expectations by grossing nearly $150 million dollars domestically. In the martial arts world James is known for training at Xtreme Couture, a fact that came to light when a video of him sparring with Randy Couture was released on the Internet. The video quickly went viral, leading many martial arts enthusiasts to wonder how it is that a man so seemingly out of shape can move so quickly. James currently has a movie in postproduction, *Here Comes the Boom*, in which he plays a science teacher who moonlights as an MMA fighter to save the school's music program. Joe Rogan and Bas Rutten are among his costars.

7. MILLA JOVOVICH

Everyone who likes science fiction movies knows of the beautiful Milla Jovovich and her exceptional athletic abilities. Having dabbled in various martial arts for film roles, Jovovich has even gone through hard-core firearms training on several occasions. With exceptional kicking skills, Jovovich bucks the Hollywood stereotype and uses martial arts instead of the gym to stay in shape. Her martial arts prowess is on view in several films, with some of her more recent roles displaying the whirling movements of a dedicated Wushu practitioner. In interviews Jovovich often talks about her love of all things fighting but concedes that the only martial art she has continually stuck with through the years is Brazilian jiu-jitsu.

8. WESLEY SNIPES

Some actors have entire careers that are devoted to action, and Wesley Snipes is one of them. Snipes has had a wide range of roles, and almost all of them involve either beating people up or killing them. He has studied many martial arts for their theatrical value, has showcased his technical fighting abilities in film, and is especially noted for his exceptional kung fu weapons skills in the *Blade* trilogy. Unfortunately, as of late Snipes has been in the news more often for his legal problems than for his movie roles. In the martial arts community, however, Snipes is best known for a supposed feud with Joe Rogan (most likely a publicity stunt) that was supposed to end in an MMA bout between the two stars. Other than launching heated debates in Internet chat rooms, the feud has so far led nowhere, and with Snipes serving a three-year stint in federal prison for tax issues, the match is unlikely to happen.

9. JOE ROGAN

Joe Rogan may be the star of *Fear Factor*, but to many sports fans he is best known as the voice of the Ultimate Fighting Championship. In that respect Rogan has an advantage over everyone else on this list, because his primary career revolves around hobnobbing with the best fighters in the world. Not only does he frequent more matches than just about anybody else on the planet, he also trains with some of the best instructors in the business, including Eddie Bravo. Unlike other stars who have jumped on the BJJ bandwagon, Rogan is also a black belt in Tae Kwon Do, meaning that he has some stand-up skills to back up his submission talent.

10. JASON STATHAM

Statham is one of the few action superstars to have surfaced since the late 1990s, a feat he accomplished by virtue of his British accent and sheer athleticism. A former member of the British Olympic diving team, Statham differs from other Hollywood types in that he is an honest-to-goodness lifelong athlete. Because of his many action roles, Statham has practiced all sorts of fighting disciplines and has shown off his Chinese weapons skills during his films. He has also repeatedly discussed an obsession with MMA training techniques in interviews and is known to be an excellent kickboxer. Couple that experience with having Bas Rutten as a close friend and there can be little doubt that Statham has the conditioning and skills to handle himself outside the movie studio.

25

Fake Wrestlers Fighting for Real

Professional Wrestlers in MMA

With the exception of a handful of American elementary school students, just about everyone on the face of the earth knows that professional wrestling is fake. Vince McMahon's denials aside, professional wrestling exists because it passes for family entertainment, something that couldn't be done if the canvas was covered with blood and teeth at the end of every event. Professional wrestling also features some of the biggest, strongest, and most athletic people on the planet. It is only natural that professional wrestling fans should wonder how these specimens would fare in a real fight and that MMA promotions around the world, seeing these fans as an untapped demographic, would seek out game professional wrestlers for combat in the cage. Following are the best-known and most talented professional wrestlers who have left their mark on mixed martial arts.

1. BROCK LESNAR

One of the most maligned fighters in MMA, Brock Lesnar began his athletic career as an amateur wrestler and eventually pulled a National Collegiate Athletic Association (NCAA) championship win. After college he moved on to professional wrestling and was a mainstay for World Wrestling Entertainment. Despite having many "wrastling" successes, Lesnar soon tired of the business and ventured into football, where he briefly played for the Minnesota Vikings before being cut. After losing his job Lesnar made his way across the globe to take part in the Japanese pro wrestling circuit. In 2006 Lesnar began mixed martial arts training and had his first professional fight in 2007. Even though he lost his second fight to Frank Mir, Lesnar was soon given a title shot against Randy Couture, whom he defeated to become the Ultimate Fighting Champion heavyweight champion. Lesnar went on to defend his title a single time before being sidelined for a year because of illness. Upon his return to the UFC, Lesnar once again reaffirmed his fighting prowess by defeating Shane Carwin at UFC 116, only to be defeated three months later by Cain Velasquez.

2. BOB "THE BEAST" SAPP

Known as much for his unique look as his fighting ability, Sapp was a standout college football player and spent four years playing for the National Football League (NFL). He then went on to work as wrestler for World Championship Wrestling (WCW) and World Wrestling Federation (WWF) before moving into Japanese professional wrestling. He also took part in various MMA and kickboxing competitions while in Japan, where his size contributed to his initial success. Never considered a real contender for any MMA belts, Sapp is still one of the most recognized figures in international MMA competition, largely because of his gigantic proportions and countless cameos on Japanese television shows.

3. KAZUSHI "GRACIE HUNTER" SAKURABA

The man known as the Gracie Hunter needs no introduction to MMA fans who are old enough to have been following the sport since the late 1990s. Sakuraba started as a successful college wrestler before moving on to Japanese professional wrestling. He entered MMA competition to gain publicity for the wrestling league he was working for and to prove that Japanese professional wrestlers were just as tough as any other fighters. In his first fight tournament Sakuraba defeated a Brazilian jiu-jitsu black belt and went on to defeat a number of others, including Vitor Belfort. He gained the nickname Gracie Hunter after defeating Royler, Royce, Renzo, and Ryan Gracie in what became one of MMA's most well-known feuds.

4. SCOTT "BAM BAM" BIGELOW

With a flaming tattoo covering most of his bald head, Bigelow had few career paths left to him other than professional wrestling. As luck would have it, Bigelow also stood six foot four and weighed more than four hundred pounds, so he fit the other criteria of professional wrestling as well. For a giant of a man, Bigelow was deceptively quick, a talent he used to ingratiate himself with wrestling audiences in both the United States and Japan for almost ten years. His one and only venture into MMA occurred during 1996, but powerhouse Kimo Leopoldo quickly defeated him. Bigelow's wrestling star began to fade in the late 1990s, but he once again made headlines in 2000 by rescuing several children from a burning house and suffering significant burns over a large portion of his body. Bigelow died in 2007 of a drug overdose.

5. FRANKLIN ROBERTO "BOBBY" LASHLEY

A phenomenal college wrestler who was expected to represent the United States in international competition, Lashley decided to enlist in the U.S. Army after graduating from Missouri Valley College in order to prepare for Olympic glory. Unfortunately his Olympic dreams were cut short after he injured a knee while diving for cover when a bank he was in was suddenly robbed. In 2004 he tried his hand at professional wrestling and became a mainstay of the WWE. When his contract with the wrestling promotion was finished, Lashley began his MMA career, defeating all of his early opponents. To date his most noteworthy bout was against Bob Sapp, whom he defeated by ground and pound during the first round.

6. PAULO "THE GIANT" CÉSAR DA SILVA

A former basketball player who made a name for himself as an oddity in Japanese wrestling promotions, Silva stands out from the crowd by being seven foot two and weighing more than four hundred pounds. Originating from Brazil, where his height landed him on the Brazilian Olympic basketball team, Silva eventually discovered that his gigantic proportions made him a professional wrestling draw, and he began working for the WWF. It wasn't until 2003, however, that Silva decided to enter no-hold-barred competition. He was unlucky enough to have as his first opponent Heath Herring, who defeated him by a rear choke. Silva went on to have eight fights, winning only two. His last fight was against sumo superstar Chad Akebono Rowan, whom he defeated by standing Kimura.

7. MICHAL BURTON POLCHLOPEK JR.

Better known as Bart Gunn and Bodacious Bart, Polchlopek was a professional wrestling star who specialized in tag team matches and won the WWF tag team championship on three different occasions. When his WWF contract came to an end, he began competing in various wrestling venues around the globe and even tried his hand in MMA. To date his only win was against Wesley "Cabbage" Correira via doctor stoppage due to a cut. Polchlopek has since fallen out of the limelight except for the occasional professional wrestling appearance. He did make national news in 2007, however, when his son died of an accidental gunshot wound.

8. CRAIG "THE PITBULL" PITTMAN

Pittman began his professional wrestling career rather late in life after retiring from the Marine Corps, where he had been a successful amateur wrestler. He is best known for his mid-1990s appearances in the WCW where he played a not-so-patriotic former sergeant who supposedly liked nothing better than to terrorize former military comrades. Pittman fought in Vale Tudo Japan in 1998. He defeated his first opponent by triangle choke but lost his second fight via armbar. Since then he has moved on to smaller professional wrestling venues and has never stepped back into the cage.

9. SYLVESTER "THE PREDATOR" TERKAY

Terkay is a seasoned amateur wrestler who lost the 1992 NCAA championship to Kurt Angle only to win the same championship in 1993. He took up professional wrestling soon afterward and spent a year working for the WWE, eventually moving to Japanese promotions. During the same period he began training in MMA and eventually fought several matches. He also fought in K-1, losing decisions to Hong Man Choi and Remy Bonjasky. Terkay has since gone back into professional wrestling. He spent 2006–2007 with the WWE and made himself available to other promotions after his contract expired.

10. TONY "THE VIKING" HALME

Much has been said and written about Tony Halme, and not all of it is been good. Halme began his athletic career as a boxer and used that association to land a professional wrestling contract in the early 1990s. With his outspoken personality and Nordic appearance, Halme used his roguish attitude to land gigs wrestling in Japan and the United States, eventually earning a WWF contract and a slot on the Finnish game show *Gladiaattorit*. From 1995 to 2002 he was also an active boxer, winning both the World Boxing Federation (WBF) and Finnish titles. Later he fought in the early UFC, losing a match to Randy Couture. In later life Halme went on to become a member of the Finnish Parliament, where his hardened appearance and brash speeches made him a hero of the Far Right and nativist movements. Halme was found dead of a self-inflicted gunshot wound in January 2010.

26

MMA on the Big Screen

The Best and Worst MMA Movies

On the one hand, a good Hollywood movie has a way of making real life look much more appealing than it really is. A bad movie, on the other hand, can make reality look downright pathetic and certainly has the ability to paint its subject in a negative light. In that regard, the movie industry has not been particularly kind to mixed martial arts. Maybe the screenplays are all terrible or maybe there are no decent directors left in Hollywood, but either way there just aren't many good movies about MMA. The exception is the occasional documentary that at least tries to do the sport justice. Taste being a subjective thing, following is a list of the best of the best, and it isn't pretty.

1. REDBELT

Perhaps the finest movie ever made about mixed martial arts, *Redbelt* has an actual story line, dialogue, and even two legitimate actors playing the lead characters. The story revolves around a Brazilian jiu-jitsu instructor whose business partner has hatched a scheme to steal the dojo out from under him. In order to fulfill his financial obligations the lead character, played by Chiwetel Ejiofor, enters the competitive fighting circuit only to discover that the sport is marked by corruption and bitter rivalries. Even though the movie lacks many of the over-the-top fight scenes that we've come to expect, the human interest is compelling enough to keep audiences riveted to their seats. Unfortunately for MMA fans, the movie lost more money than it made, so a second installment is unlikely.

2. THE SMASHING MACHINE: THE LIFE AND TIMES OF EXTREME FIGHTER MARK KERR

Regarded as the best documentary ever made about mixed martial arts, *The Smashing Machine* focuses on the two no-hold-barred stalwarts Mark Kerr and his friend Mark Coleman, who for a time were the most controversial duo in MMA. A championship wrestler known for his extreme strength and speed, Kerr made short work of his early MMA opponents and took the Ultimate Fighting Championship 14 and 15 heavyweight titles. Along the way Kerr decided that there was more money to be made in Japan and moved to Pride, where he had an initial string of victories but quickly encountered more experienced competition. *The Smashing Machine* shows plenty of fighting and details the true NHB nature of early MMA, but it does so by focusing on the physical and mental trials that Kerr endures as he competes. Not exactly an outstanding propaganda piece for the sport, *The Smashing Machine* is nonetheless an important and worthwhile film that gives audiences and fans a better idea of what being a professional fighter is all about.

3. NEVER BACK DOWN

More a cliché than a movie, *Never Back Down*'s cast of attractive young people is obviously intended to capture the hormone-filled teenage market. As with most movies of this type, *Never Back Down* begins with a local bully kicking the hero's butt in front of a crowd. Humiliated and disgusted with himself, the hero talks to one of his friends, who introduces him to the mysterious science of mixed martial arts. Our hero then goes under the tutelage of a mixed martial arts "master" (not that MMA has any masters).

4. THE ELIMINATOR

This movie is tough to characterize because it's chock-full of Bas Rutten goodness but suffers from many of the basic filming issues that afflict many straight-to-video movies. The story has been told a million times before. Contestants are kidnapped and dropped off on a remote island, where they are hunted for sport, and the last man standing will win a substantial cash prize. The characters are one dimensional, and the only person who does any real acting is Paul Logan, who teams up with Rutten's character. Rutten acts like Rutten throughout the film. That is a good thing, because he ends up doing what he does best, fighting. One of the film's more amusing aspects is that during several fight sequences, Rutten ends up moving around as Bruce Lee did, going to show that Lee really was ahead of his time.

5. TOKYO ZOMBIE

Calling this one a straight-up mixed martial arts film may be a bit of a stretch, but any movie that combines multiple, unique fighting sequences with a zombie invasion gets a thumbs-up in my book. Basically the movie begins as a buddy flick, with one man teaching jiu-jitsu to a friend who has cancer. Naturally, when zombies begin to populate the city, the two decide to use their jiu-jitsu skills on the living dead. Without going into too much detail, this movie presents a great deal of weirdness combined with Japanese humor and a massive dose of violence. If that mix sounds enjoyable

to you, then certainly watch it, but just don't expect it to be
a traditional martial arts film.

6. PIT FIGHTER

This entry is one of those movies that you watch when
you can't sleep with the expectation that it will knock you
out within five minutes. With a reported budget of around
$500,000, this movie at first appears to be another low-
budget, straight-to-video movie. The story line—a guy wakes
up from a coma and competes in the pit fighting circuit to
get revenge on his enemies—is fairly similar to others from
this genre. The concept may be ho-hum, but the acting is
gritty, the fight sequences are good, and the shoot-outs are
even better. Not your typical MMA movie, *Pit Fighter* delivers
all the violence one expects but does it at the behest of an
exceptional director, Jesse Johnson.

7. CONFESSION OF A PIT FIGHTER

This movie is strange. It is probably the best film that Art Comacho has ever made and contains a bit of decent acting by
B-level professionals, including Quinton Jackson. The plot is
another one that has been done a million times and involves
an ex-con who has to fight his way up the social ladder to
avenge his brother's murder. For a movie that uses experienced MMA fighters and a plot that revolves around—you
guessed it—fighting, the action sequences are comparatively
dull and unrealistic. But if that kind of fighting is to your
liking, you are in luck, because Art Camacho is willing to
personally teach you the art of film fighting. Full details can
be found at his website, www.artcamachostunts.com.

8. BLOODSPORT

No list of martial arts movies would be complete without

Bloodsport. Even though some people will certainly choose to disagree with its inclusion on a list devoted to mixed martial arts movies, the whole premise behind *Bloodsport* is that of an illegal, NHB competition, where anything, even grappling, is allowed. Featuring Jean-Claude Van Damme at his finest along with the big Asian guy from *Enter the Dragon* (1973) and Ogre from *Revenge of the Nerds* (actor Donald Gibb) in supporting roles, *Bloodsport* revolves around the legendary underground Kumite competitions that were supposed to have taken place during the 1970s. Although no reasonable records of such competitions exist, their legend and the tales of Frank Dux still inspired what many consider to be the most influential martial arts fantasy movie of all time.

9. ONG-BAK

Not a mixed martial arts movie in the strictest sense, *Ong-Bak* is without a doubt the best Muay Thai and street-fighting movie ever made. Showcasing both traditional and sportive Muay Thai techniques, *Ong-Bak* sets a new standard for martial arts action films. Through a series of street battles and competitive bouts, a Muay Thai expert attempts to retrieve the head of an ancient Buddha statue that has been stolen from his destitute village. Filled with fast-paced action sequences, superb technique, and awesome running stunt work, *Ong-Bak*'s lead actor, Tony Jaa, betters Jackie Chan in everything but humor. It's a modern classic.

10. FIGHT CLUB

The best movie ever made that involves full-contact fighting, *Fight Club* is less about violence than it is about the deeply disturbed people who take part in it. Capitalizing on a generation of disgruntled office workers who seek real meaning in their lives, *Fight Club* appealed to a wide swath of the American middle class and spawned any number of local fight clubs throughout the nation. Originally written as a short story by Chuck Palahniuk, the movie brought an unconventional book into the lives of a mainstream audience. *Fight Club* is not strictly about martial arts, but there can be little doubt that the movie greatly influenced the eventual acceptance of the real-life sport.

27

MMA Actors

Fighters Who Have Made the Great Leap

It seems as if every sports figure in the world wants to land an acting gig, yet there are only a handful of world-class athletes who have ever managed really to make it in Hollywood. Recent examples include Jason Statham and Vinnie Jones, both of whom have solid athletic backgrounds and still managed to land leading roles in big-budget films. But for every Vinnie Jones there are a dozen or more Dennis Rodmans, athletes turned actors who are so bad that they kill the careers of their costars. With that issue in mind we offer this list of mixed martial arts fighters who have managed to land movie roles but who are probably best served by not quitting their day jobs.

1. BAS "EL GUAPO" RUTTEN

One of the great things about Rutten is that his personality needs no polishing, and when he winds up in a movie, his fans know exactly what to expect. In that sense Rutten isn't really an actor so much as he is a caricature of himself, and it just so happens that his caricature works well on the big screen. As of late he has had small roles in a half-dozen films and even managed to overshadow the star in the low-budget film *The Eliminator*. Like many MMA personalities,

Rutten has been featured on television and portrayed in video games, with his televised appearances being more acclaimed than his film roles.

2. RANDY "CAPTAIN AMERICA" COUTURE

Randy Couture has appeared in video games and movies and has had recurring cameos on several television shows. His good looks, clean-cut personality, and friendly demeanor make him one of the few MMA athletes who has a real chance of having a Hollywood career once his fighting days come to an end. By some accounts he already has the most successful movie career of any MMA figure, culminating with his role in *The Expendables*. Couture might not have many lines and his character doesn't show much development in the film, but he certainly looks good kicking the living crap out of people. Before showing up in *The Expendables*, Couture played Sargon in *The Scorpion King 2: Rise of the Warrior*. Aside from some poorly done computer-generated imagery and hokey lines, the film was actually pretty good.

3. KEN SHAMROCK

One of the most maligned and yet still loved fighters in mixed martial arts, Ken Shamrock has put in a number of guest appearances on television shows and in the movies. Known as the Most Dangerous Man in the World to his World Wrestling Federation fans, he is also known within the WWF community as being difficult to work with. Once expected to have a substantial movie career because of his looks, notoriety, and presence, Shamrock's future on the big screen has not looked promising. Although he has been in several low-budget films, including the little-known *Scarecrow Gone Wild,* it seems that Shamrock's film career, much like his fighting career, is slowly sputtering out.

4. FORREST GRIFFIN

Respected as being an all-around funny guy, Forrest Griffin also has potential as an actor, mainly because he doesn't take himself too seriously. To date he has had a few cameo roles and has appeared (along with many of his MMA co-horts) in at least one straight-to-video release. Griffin, a former police officer, also played a cop in the movie *I Hope They Serve Beer in Hell*. His appearance may have been brief, but some strange element of his performance made the scene surprisingly memorable, an attribute that will likely aid him in acquiring more substantial acting jobs.

5. QUINTON "RAMPAGE" JACKSON

Unlike many of his contemporaries, Jackson seems to be making headway in the movie industry. With a dozen or so cameos under his belt and a few more substantial roles, Jackson finally broke out of the "real fighter turned movie fighter" realm and landed an actual role as B. A. Baracus in the new *A-Team* movie. And it isn't a cameo role, either. Jackson appears in the entire film and has quite a bit of dialogue, which he pulls off reasonably well. One can only hope that he does well enough in order to pave the way for more fighters to make it on the big screen.

6. KEVIN "KIMBO SLICE" FERGUSON

Once Kimbo found his way into televised fighting, nobody had any doubts that he would eventually be given a few film roles, if only because of his unique look. So far Kimbo has had a few mainstream roles but nothing that really sets him apart from other fighters. That is, unless one takes into account his appearances in a number of pornographic films. Not exactly sporting a clean-cut image, Kimbo used to be employed by a porn company as a bodyguard, and he apparently still maintains those connections. His most recent pornographic cameo was in a movie called *Farold and Fumar Escape to the Bottomless Party*. There's really no telling how these appearances will impact Kimbo's career, but nobody ever expected the guy to be squeaky clean anyway.

7. DON "THE PREDATOR" FRYE

Anyone who has followed MMA since the 1990s knows who Don Frye is. He is a feared wrestler who fought and defeated some of the best in the business at a time when MMA was an even more brutal sport than it is today. Since those glorious days Frye's fighting career has slowed down, but he has still managed to land a few movie gigs. His most noteworthy movie appearance is in *Public Enemies*. While Frye's role wasn't huge, his presence was felt, and with his great mustache, he appeared even more menacing. With any luck the same mustache that landed him this role will land him many more, and MMA fans will finally be able to call a real Hollywood star one of their own.

8. BOB "THE BEAST" SAPP

Practically a legend in Japan, Bob Sapp is regarded as more of a brand at this point than he is a real person. Not known for complex dialogue or sharp wit, Sapp nonetheless brings a hulking, powerful presence to the screen that no respectable actor in the world can possibly hope to emulate. With a host of small roles and walk-ons under his belt, Sapp's most notable performance to date was portraying Switowski in the remake of *The Longest Yard*. He got to rub shoulders with real stars such as Burt Reynolds and Adam Sandler while playing on the convicts' football team.

9. GEORGES "RUSH" ST-PIERRE

There simply aren't many MMA fighters who sport the qualities of St-Pierre. He's ruggedly handsome, charming, well spoken, and fairly witty. He isn't nearly as intimidating as many less genteel fighters and, if rumors can be believed, has a decent-size female fan base. Despite his endearing attributes, St-Pierre has only appeared in a few films, all of which fall strictly in the "meathead" category of movies. Most of these movies are particularly bad because they cast professional fighters as the main characters and leave the supporting roles to the professional actors. The worst of these films, *Death Warrior,* is practically unwatchable. It seems that St-Pierre's fighting prowess has done nothing to help him pick good acting jobs.

10. HEATH "THE TEXAS CRAZY HORSE" HERRING

Remembered by many for his strange hairstyles, his outlandish behavior, and his calling out Dana White, Herring is a veteran of the Japanese fighting circuit. Sporting a substantial international fan base, it is somewhat surprising that Herring hasn't picked up more roles in overseas films. That being said, he landed a small role in the film *Salt* starring Angelina Jolie, and that move is certainly a step in the right direction.

28

MMA Goes Global

MMA Promotions and Bodies throughout the World

Citizens of the United States generally consider North American mixed martial arts promotions to be the most prestigious in the world, and a good number of American fans don't even know that other fighting venues exist. Not only is MMA a worldwide phenomenon, however; in many cases these other organizations have longer and more dynamic histories than their more media-savvy North American counterparts do. The following list contains ten international promotions that have heavily influenced the sport of mixed martial arts.

1. INTERNATIONAL VALE TUDO CHAMPIONSHIPS (IVC)

The IVC is often called the last, true, no-holds-barred fighting promotion on the planet and is prohibited from holding shows in most locations. Originally out of Brazil, the promotion marketed itself as a more realistic version of the Ultimate Fighting Championship. Early fights saw many dirty tactics used, and it was mostly left to the opponents to develop gentlemen's agreements about what they would and would not do to each other. While the IVC originally *had* no rules, it has since banned the use of eye gouges, fish hooking, and biting. Numerous well-known fighters gained fame from competing in the IVC, including Wanderlei Silva. Though the IVC has been defunct for a number of years, it is expected that another tournament will be held sometime in 2011.

2. SHOOTO
Developed in Japan during the mid-1980s as a way to make professional wrestling more realistic, Shooto was originally a hybrid grappling promotion that limited striking to standing only. This rule changed as Shooto began to draw more international competitors and the organization sought more exciting bouts. Shooto officially became a combat sport when the original organization dissolved into several divergent bodies. Differing from most other MMA promotions in various ways, for many years Shooto organizations had a standing eight count rule and also allowed shots to the back of the head. These regulations changed in 2009 as the sport sought legitimacy in the North American market.

3. COMBATE EXTREMO
The United States is such a media powerhouse that citizens often forget about the sporting traditions of our neighbors. A nation long dominated by the sports of boxing and professional wrestling, Mexico has been much slower to adopt MMA than their more fickle northern neighbors have. Combate Extremo is currently the longest-running Mexican mixed martial arts promotion and has been in business since 2000. Featuring fighters such as Jesus Torres, Ricardo Arreola, and Shannon Ritch, the promotion is quickly growing in popularity, and fights are beginning to draw crowds that rival the smaller boxing tickets.

4. THE ART OF WAR FIGHTING (AOW) CHAMPIONSHIP
Many consider China to be the birthplace of martial arts.

Whether this assertion is true is a moot point, as for the last twenty years the nation has been behind the curve in adopting MMA as a legitimate sport. In 2005, however, well-connected Chinese American brothers Andrew and Konrad Pi contacted the Chinese government and received permission to organize an MMA body. Billed as an international operation, the AOW showcases a large number of unknown or barely known fighters and appeals primarily to the Chinese market.

5. FREE FIGHT ASSOCIATION (FFA)

Like many nations, Germany has always had progressive fighters who wanted to try their skills at "real" fighting. And, again as in most nations, these fighters sought ways to test their skills regardless of the legality of their actions. Developing out of these early NHB-type fights, the Free Fight Association was created in 1994 to sanction MMA events. It remained a fairly obscure and sporadic affair during the late 1990s, but by 2000 the organization had pulled itself together and adopted the Unified Rules of MMA. Since 2002 the FFA has been promoting yearly regional championships, giving the worldwide MMA community a few notable fighters in the process.

6. ELITE FIGHTING CHAMPIONSHIP (EFC)

Citizens of the United States often look surprised when they find out that an accomplished actor or star athlete hails from Canada. MMA has seen several notable Canadian fighters—Georges St-Pierre being the best known—but most Americans have heard little about Canadian promotions. Originating in Vancouver, the Elite Fighting Championship has been in business for more than twelve years and is one of the larger promotions in Canada. EFC has so far produced

With the success of the UFC, local fight promotions have popped up all over the United States. Here a battle rages between two fighters in a *Total Combat* match at the Cocopah Casino in Somerton, Arizona. *United States Marine Corps*

few fighters of note, although in February of 2007 the EFC's Marvin Eastman was defeated by Quinton Jackson in a widely publicized UFC bout.

7. UNIVERSAL REALITY COMBAT CHAMPIONSHIP (URCC)

Every country on earth has some sort of martial arts heritage, but the Philippines stands out from the rest in the diversity and effectiveness of the artists' traditional fighting styles. The nation has produced a host of champions, including "Manny" Pacquiao, who is arguably the best welterweight boxer ever. However, to date we have seen few Filipino fighters in MMA, and the URCC is seeking to rectify that. Created by Alvin Aguilar from the underground fight scene in Manila, the URCC opened its doors in 2002 and has become the most important MMA promotion in the islands. The organization holds two annual events in Manila and since 2009 has broadened its reach outside the capital.

8. CAGE RAGE CHAMPIONSHIPS (CRC)

It was expected that MMA would be an overnight success in the United Kingdom, and Cage Rage was developed to take advantage of this potential. Created as a small competition to raise funds to purchase new mats for a martial arts school, the event was such a success that other fights were conducted and the organization grew to meet the needs of its fan base. Eventually purchased by ProElite, Cage Rage was marked by controversy, not the least of which was caused by Bob Sapp's last-minute withdrawal from a televised title match. The promotion filled the main event with an aged and slow David "Tank" Abbott, disappointing viewers. The television provider Sky eventually stopped airing the promotion's shows. Cage Rage has been relegated to the dustbin, although its early reputation suggests that it may again appear under a different guise.

9. M-1 GLOBAL

Headquartered in Holland, M-1 is co-owned by Fedor Emelianenko, although Vadim Finkelstein handles the day-to-day operations. With a competitive framework that was based primarily on national MMA teams and has recently switched to single fighters, M-1 became a major player in MMA as soon as it started promoting events and has since hosted a slew of the world's best fighters. Gaining ground quickly on the international market, M-1 has worked closely with Strikeforce in order to compete directly with the groups' powerful rival, the UFC. Unlike the UFC, however, M-1 gives lesser-known fighters a chance to compete internationally by emphasizing technique and fighting prowess over celebrity and sensationalism.

10. FINNFIGHT

While most MMA promotions are inclined to add more and more rules to their events in order to make their fights more palatable to the general public, the good folks at FinnFight haven't adopted any of their suggestions. Tracing its heritage back to 1998, FinnFight was originally known for its exceptionally violent bouts, where fighters tended to rely heavily on unconventional techniques such as headbutts, stomps, and grounded knees to defeat opponents. Years later Shooto rules were introduced, but they are still less restrictive than those found in the bigger promotions. An annual competition, FinnFight has a solid fan base that tends to eschew other MMA events in preference of the more realistic FinnFight bouts.

29

not Quite Boxing

Biggest MMA Paychecks

It is very difficult to determine exactly how much money good mixed martial artists are paid for their performances. Even though promotions release payout numbers after the events have concluded, they never tell us exactly what deals they worked out with fighters concerning other sources of revenue. Rest assured that when lesser-name fighters seem to command bigger purses than their more noteworthy opponents that the better-known fighter has likely worked out an agreement for a percentage of the ticket sales instead of a direct paycheck. While the following list contains ten of the biggest payouts in MMA history, undoubtedly much more money has changed hands under the table.

1. ANDREI "THE PIT BULL" ARLOVSKI VS. FEDOR "THE LAST EMPEROR" EMELIANENKO

Without a doubt the largest officially recognized payout ever went to Andrei Arlovski in Affliction: Day of Reckoning in January 2009. The fight began with Arlovski keeping his opponent moving backward by throwing highly effective low leg kicks interspersed with the occasional knee. As the first round progressed, Arlovski complemented his advantage with an excellent display of pugilism (thanks to his new coach Freddie Roach) and backed Fedor into a corner. As the fight continued and the commentators gushed about Arlovski's precise striking skills against the world's greatest fighter, Arlovski grew overconfident and tried to land a flying knee against his cornered opponent. Fedor immediately retaliated with a trademark looping right hook that knocked Arlovski out cold, ending the match at three minutes and fourteen seconds in the first round. Arlovski was paid approximately $7,732 per second for his performance.

2. TIM "THE MAINE-IAC" SYLVIA VS. FEDOR "THE LAST EMPEROR" EMELIANENKO

For good reason, fighters who take on Fedor Emelianenko command high salaries. Tim Sylvia, the former Ultimate Fighting Championship heavyweight champion, earned a cool $800,000 when he took on the erstwhile champion in mid-2008 on the Affliction: Banned ticket. At the time of the fight, Sylvia had recently been dethroned by Randy Couture and was coming off a loss against Antônio Rodrigo Nogueira. Intent on regaining his reputation as one of the best heavyweight fighters around, Sylvia looked to dominate his smaller opponent with his ever-improving striking skills. Unfortunately for Sylvia that opponent just happened to be Fedor, who derailed Sylvia's plans by opening up the fight with a hard combination that dropped Sylvia on the mat. Twenty seconds after the drop, Fedor secured a rear naked choke, and Sylvia was out of the fight for good.

3. ANDREI "THE PIT BULL" ARLOVSKI VS. ROY "BIG COUNTRY" NELSON

There can be little doubt that Andrei Arlovski has good management. Not only did he pull in $1.5 million when he fought Fedor Emelianenko, he managed to pocket $750,000 when he took on Roy "Big Country" Nelson. Touted as an exceptional jiu-jitsu practitioner whose pudgy appearance and heavy weight disguise good endurance and ballistic movement, Nelson expected to use his excellent grappling skills to beat his more experienced opponent. Unfortunately Nelson made the cardinal mistake of many Brazilian jiu-jitsu fighters in believing that theirs is the only effective grappling art. Being a seasoned sambo player, Arlovski fought off Nelson's ground attacks. He then put Big Country down for the count after connecting with an inside leg kick followed by a straight right hand in the second round.

4. KEVIN "KIMBO SLICE" FERGUSON VS. SETH "THE SILVERBACK" PETRUZELLI

Not many fighters can command $500,000 for a single match, and all of them have much more extensive experience than does former street fighter Kimbo Slice. When he stepped into the ring against Seth Petruzelli, his only claims to fame were three professional bouts, an exhibition match under MMA rules, and a loyal Internet following. After Ken Shamrock backed out at the last minute, Petruzelli had taken the fight on short notice and, despite his decent record, was somehow considered an underdog. Apparently nobody had mentioned this status to Petruzelli, who started the fight with a front kick followed by a stiff jab that knocked Kimbo to the matt. Petruzelli followed with a quick beat down. The fight was over in a staggering fourteen seconds and permanently destroyed Slice's fearsome reputation.

5. BROCK LESNAR VS. MIN "MR. SHARK" SOO KIM

Commanding large purses from the beginning of his MMA career, Brock Lesnar was the first fighter to bring legions of professional wrestling fans to the sport. His first fight was against journeyman fighter Min Soo Kim and was intended to see if Lesnar had the aggressiveness and tenacity to use his immense physical power to dominate and hurt resisting opponents. The expectations were well founded. Lesnar came into the ring hyped up and immediately took Kim down. Caught in Kim's half guard, Lesnar began throwing short punches to his opponent's head and soon took the full mount. From this position he landed a few punches, and his opponent tapped out. For this quick performance Lesnar earned a cool $500,000 and soon found himself under contract with the UFC.

6. CHUCK "THE ICEMAN" LIDDELL VS. RICH "ACE" FRANKLIN

Every time a former champion loses a fight, detractors come out of the woodwork claiming that the new generation of fighters are somehow better and that the old should make way for the new. As one of the biggest names in MMA for more than a decade, Chuck Liddell has certainly had his fair share of critics, including his boss, Dana White. But Chuck was able to silence those critics with a long list of victories spanning nearly five years. Unfortunately for Chuck, since 2007 he has had only had one win, and by the time his fight with Rich Franklin rolled around, everyone in MMA seemed to be screaming for his retirement.

To everyone's surprise the fight started with a reinvigorated Liddell bullying Franklin around the ring, using his superior striking skills to keep his opponent backpedaling. Liddell was active on all levels, throwing low kicks and punches and even taking Franklin to the ground. One of Liddell's kicks broke Franklin's arm, and it appeared that the fight was going to be a short one. At the end of the first round with Franklin backed up against the ropes, Liddell began to throw wild punches in anticipation of a knockout.

Franklin fired back awkwardly but still managed to catch Liddell clean on the button, knocking him out for the win. Liddell was paid $500,000 for what many expect was the last fight of his career.

7. JOSH "THE BABYFACED ASSASSIN" BARNETT VS. GILBERT "THE HURRICANE" YVEL

Among the many grapplers in MMA Josh Barnett has made a name for himself as one of the best by using a unique style that he simply refers to as professional wrestling. With a career that goes all the way back to 1997, Barnett has fought in just about every promotion imaginable and has won three world championships, including being crowned the UFC heavyweight champion in 2002, but the title was stripped after he tested positive for steroids. His association with the UFC may be dissolved, but he has continually proven himself to be one of the top grapplers in the world. In 2009 he fought Gilbert Yvel in a lively match that seesawed back and forth from the start. Yvel, a feared striker in his own right, sought to stay on his feet, but Barnett continually took him down and managed to mount him during the fight. Yvel tried to fight from his back but eventually succumbed to a series of strikes, earning Barnett a $500,000 payday.

8. ANTÔNIO "MINOTAURO" RODRIGO NOGUEIRA VS. RANDY "CAPTAIN AMERICA" COUTURE

The limelight has always shone on the UFC, and in recent years the promotion has managed to attract—and keep—many top fighters. One of these fighters is Antônio Nogueira, a man who made a name for himself by continually fighting difficult opponents. Acknowledged as one of the foremost submission grapplers in the world, Nogueira finally earned the money he has long deserved when he took on former champion Randy Couture at UFC 102. In what turned out to be an extremely entertaining fight, both contestants showcased a wide range of striking and grappling ability combined with a composure that only true warriors bring to the ring. Although both fighters were in trouble at various times during the fight, Nogueira grew more active as the fight progressed, using his superior striking to put Couture on the mat. When the bell rang at the end of the third round, Nogueira had pulled off a decision victory and earned every cent of his $460,000 payout.

9. BROCK LESNAR VS. RANDY "CAPTAIN AMERICA" COUTURE

Everyone watching MMA knows that the biggest draw in the North American market is Brock Lesnar, and when he fought MMA legend Randy Couture, the entire fighting world tuned in. The fight was controversial because Lesnar had virtually no professional fighting experience yet was already being given a title shot. Regardless of the criticism the fight took place as planned, with the two wrestlers locking up early in a stalemate that turned into a brief striking match. Using his immense weight advantage, Lesnar repeatedly tried to keep his smaller opponent on the ground, but Couture used his superior wrestling skills to get back to his feet. As the second round progressed, Couture consistently outpunched Lesnar until he walked into a right hand that sent him straight down. Lesnar immediately jumped on Couture, forcing a referee stoppage that gave him the UFC heavyweight belt and a $450,000 paycheck.

10. GEORGES "RUSH" ST-PIERRE VS. B. J. "THE PRODIGY" PENN

Most smaller fighters cannot command the same payments that the heavyweights do. Georges St-Pierre managed to climb into the heavyweight payout division with help from a win bonus that doubled the $200,000 he made for stepping into the octagon against B. J. Penn in UFC 94. The two had met once before, and Penn was looking to avenge his earlier loss. In what turned out to be a classic grappler versus wrestler match, St-Pierre used his superior strength and conditioning to keep the smaller Penn on the defensive. As the fight continued and Penn tired, St-Pierre managed to escape Penn's guard and grind his opponent through superior positioning. In between the fourth and fifth rounds, Penn's corner threw in the towel, giving St-Pierre the victory and a $400,000 purse.

Competitive Cousins:
Boxing and MMA

30

Boxers' Biggest Failures in MMA

Should Have Stayed in the Sweet Science

Boxing great Floyd Mayweather Jr. disdainfully dismissed mixed martial artists as "guys who couldn't do boxing." Legendary boxing promoter Bob Arum once said that to him MMA features "two guys who can't throw punches . . . [and] . . . if they get hit, can't take a punch." However, MMA enthusiasts counter that boxers are one dimensional and wouldn't stand a chance against decent mixed martial artists when fights hit the ground. Some boxers have attempted the transition to MMA. Most famously, boxing champion James "Lights Out" Toney attempted the transition in August 2010, months after he brashly proclaimed that he could knock out the great Randy Couture. Instead, Couture showed how woefully one dimensional Toney was and took him to the ground. It was over in the first round. A sign at the arena said it best: "Lights Out for James Phony." Here are some other boxers who did not fare very well in mixed martial arts.

1. ART JIMMERSON

Art Jimmerson was a former cruiserweight boxing contender who had the misfortune of accepting an invitation to something called the Ultimate Fighting Championships in Colorado in 1993. "I punch hard, I'm fast and I'm quick and you can't hit what you can't see," explained Jimmerson in the promo clip that ran before his ill-fated bout with an unimposing-looking Brazilian named Royce Gracie. Jimmerson sauntered into the ring, looking ridiculous with one boxing glove. Gracie took Jimmerson down by tackling him low. Then Gracie mounted him and quickly tired the bigger man. Jimmerson actually tapped out before Gracie attempted any submissions, much to the amazement of even the Brazilian. It was a most ignoble effort from a practitioner of "the noble art."

2. RUBIN "MR. HOLLYWOOD" WILLIAMS

This 2009 Dream 11 matchup between professional boxer Rubin Williams and legendary Japanese mixed martial artist Kazushi Sakuraba was a mismatch of epic proportions. Rubin Williams was a talented amateur boxer who started quickly in his professional boxing career but could not prevail when he stepped up to face quality competition. For some reason, he attempted the transition to MMA against living legend and Pride great Kazushi Sakuraba, who needed a win after a couple straight losses.

In the opening minute, it was apparent Williams was not prepared for Sakuraba's leg strikes. Then, when Sakuraba shot low for a takedown, Williams showed gaping holes in his ground game. In fact, he had no game on the ground. Sakuraba did what he wanted and eventually won via Kimura in the first round.

3. RAY MERCER

Former world heavyweight champion and Olympic gold medalist Ray Mercer assumed he would knock out some guy named Kimbo Slice, who had achieved notoriety off the Internet by beating a few bums in backyard brawls. Instead, in their June 2007 bout, which was officially an exhibition, Mercer showed nothing other than the ability to eat a few knees, elbows, and punches. Slice pressed Mercer, landing some Muay Thai knees and elbow strikes. Slice actually showed some grappling skills or at least more than Mercer had. Mercer couldn't create enough distance to land any punches. Slice submitted Mercer with a guillotine choke in a minute and twelve seconds. Mercer did redeem himself two years later by knocking out former two-time UFC heavyweight champion Tim Sylvia in only nine seconds.

4. FRANCOIS "THE WHITE BUFFALO" BOTHA

Francois Botha was a top heavyweight contender who faced six world champions during his career, including Mike Tyson and Lennox Lewis. He later transitioned to kickboxing and mixed martial arts. In December 2004, he faced Japanese judo star Yoshihiro Akiyama, who was making his professional MMA debut. Botha had two advantages—his size and Akiyama's inexperience. It didn't matter, though, as Botha had no skills beyond his hands. Akiyama threw him to the ground and submitted the White Buffalo in the first round.

5. MELTON "THE PUNISHER" BOWEN

After Art Jimmerson the next boxer to appear at a UFC event was former fringe heavyweight boxer contender Melton Bowen. At UFC 4 in December 1994, he faced surprise UFC 3 winner Steve Jennum, a Nebraska-based police officer who is well versed in Taijitsu, in the first round. Unlike Jimmerson, Bowen threw and landed a few punches, particularly when Jennum grabbed him and pushed him up against the fence. The Punisher managed to get back to his feet, and then Jennum submitted him via an armbar before the bell, or at four minutes and forty-seven seconds into the first round.

6. MICHAEL "THE BODY SNATCHER" LERMA

Michael Lerma boxed professionally from 1995 until 2004. He was a fringe middleweight contender who fought several times on ESPN against such name fighters as Alex Bunema, J. C. Candelo, and Wilfredo Rivera. In October 2005, he tried his hands—and other body parts—in mixed martial arts against the skilled Yoshihiro Akiyama. Lerma, known for his durability in boxing, could not make it out of the first round against Akiyama. He never fought again in MMA.

7. ERIC "BUTTERBEAN" ESCH

Eric Esch is better known to the world as Butterbean, the former Toughman Contest participant turned professional boxer turned mixed martial artist. Butterbean became an interesting show in boxing, billed as the King of the Four Rounders. The rotund pugilist won nearly eighty professional boxing matches, often against marginal competition, in a career that began in 1994. In 2003, he tried his hand at mixed martial arts against the much smaller Japanese fighter Genki Sudo, who submitted him with a heel hook in the second round. Bean's punching power has lifted him to some impressive victories in his MMA career, including wins over Wesley Correira and James Thompson, but his debut was less than inspiring.

8. JULIUS FRANCIS

Julius Francis is a former journeyman heavyweight from Great Britain who is best known for losing to Mike Tyson in the second round of their 2000 bout. He did defeat Danny Williams, who was best known for beating Tyson, over twelve rounds in 1999. After a long losing streak, Francis ended his boxing career in 2006 and turned to mixed martial arts. In September 2007, he fought in a Cage Rage event in London and lost to Gary Turner in the second round. It was his only MMA fight.

9. YURI VAULIN

Yuri Vaulin is a tough Latvian boxer who compiled a 13-3 record in professional boxing. Two of his three losses were to champions Tommy "the Duke" Morrison and Arthur Williams. Vaulin did not fare nearly as well in professional mixed martial arts. He made his debut at UFC 14 against Joe Moreira in July 1997. Moreira took Vaulin to the ground, and the ex-boxer simply had neither the ground game nor the skills to get to this feet. The tough Vaulin went the distance, though, and lost a unanimous decision.

10. SAM "THE EXPERIENCE" ADKINS

Sam Adkins, a journeyman professional boxer, ended his boxing career in 1993 after consecutive losses to Lionel Butler, Rocky Pepeli, and King Ipitan. Adkins then made a career for himself in mixed martial arts beginning in 1996 at UFC 8. He won his first bout over Keith Mielke but then lost badly to Don Frye. In his MMA career, the Experience has a career record of 7 wins and 20 losses.

31

Mixed Martial Artists Who Boxed Professionally

Trying the Sweet Science

Some established mixed martial artists also tried their hands in the sweet science of boxing. These MMA fighters figured that professional boxing would give them a chance to test their striking skills, improve their hand and foot coordination, and otherwise provide another test for their athletic mettle. Unlike the list in chapter 30, this one focuses on guys who transitioned from mixed martial arts to boxing but are still primarily known as mixed martial artists.

1. JENS PULVER

Jens Pulver was one of the greatest little fighters in the Ultimate Fighting Championship. He defeated B. J. Penn over five rounds in January 2002 to defend his UFC world lightweight championship. In 2004, Pulver tried his hand at professional boxing, winning all four bouts. His closest test came in his second boxing match against then undefeated Steve Vincent (3-0). The two engaged in a seesaw affair that saw Pulver score two knockdowns and Vincent one. Pulver garnered a four-round, split decision victory.

2. KEITH "THE DEAN OF MEAN" JARDINE

Keith Jardine is an accomplished mixed martial artist best known for his victories over former UFC light heavyweight champions Chuck Liddell and Forrest Griffin. In his career, Jardine has tangled with the best of the best, including Quinton Jackson, Brandon Vera, and Ryan Bader. In 2003, Jardine tried his hands at professional boxing. He compiled a record of 3-0-1. In his last bout he fought a six-round draw with Jason Cordova.

3. CHRIS "LIGHTS OUT" LYTLE

Chris Lytle is one of the most crowd-pleasing fighters in the history of mixed martial arts. Fighting in the UFC welterweight division, Lytle frequently garners Fight of the Night honors with his nonstop, aggressive style of fighting. He began his professional MMA career in February 1999. Several years later in 2002, Lytle also plied his hands at professional boxing. Over several years, Lytle compiled a 13-1-1 boxing record. He even won a match over a talented Philadelphia fighter named Omar Pittman in his last bout in 2005. His only loss in pro boxing was an eight-round decision loss to Shay Mobley.

4. ANTÔNIO ROGERIO NOGUEIRA

The twin brother of Antônio Rodrigo Nogueira, Rogerio is an accomplished mixed martial artist in his own right. He owns victories over Alistair Overeem (twice), Dan Henderson, Kazushi Sakuraba, and Guy Mezger in his professional MMA career, which began in 2001. A veteran of Pride, he began fighting in the UFC in 2010. Rogerio is also an accomplished amateur boxer, winning national competitions in his native Brazil in 2006 and 2007. He also won a bronze medal at the 2007 Pan American Games.

5. K. J. noons

K. J. Noons is a mixed martial artist who fights under the Strikeforce banner. He is probably best known for his bouts with Nick Diaz. His quick hands and sharp mind enable him to be effective in all aspects of combat sports. Noons began his professional mixed martial arts career in 2002. Two years later Noons made his professional boxing debut. Unlike most fighters, he fights steadily in both sports. Noons boasts an 11-2 record as a pro boxer with both of his losses coming by decision.

6. TRA TELLIGMAN

Tra Telligman is an accomplished mixed martial artist who has battled the likes of Tim Sylvia, Pedro Rizzo, and Vitor Belfort in a career that began in September 1995. In March 2001, he defeated the highly favored Igor Vovchanchyn at Pride 13 by unanimous decision. Later that year he made his professional boxing debut against Walter Wiggins in Tunica, Mississippi. Telligman won his first four bouts before losing two consecutive fights via first-round knockouts. He finished his pro boxing career with a mark of 4-2.

7. NICK DIAZ

Nick Diaz is a talented mixed martial artist who currently competes for Strikeforce. He is considered one of the top fighters in the world and has defeated a whole host of excellent competitors, including Frank Shamrock, Hayato Sakurai, and Scott Smith. Diaz shows excellent striking ability in his fights, and in 2005, he took that ability to professional boxing. In Sacramento, California, he defeated Alfonso Rocha after four rounds.

8. NICK "THE PROMISE" RING

Nick Ring is an undefeated mixed martial artist from Canada

who had to leave the eleventh season of *The Ultimate Fighter* because of a knee injury. Ring began his professional MMA career in 2002 and has never tasted defeat. While recovering from a previous knee injury in 2007, Ring tried his hands at professional boxing. He compiled a marker of 4-1 in the ring, losing only one fight by decision to Kevin Reynolds, a fighter with a 9-1 record.

9. VITOR "THE PHENOM" BELFORT

Vitor Belfort is an explosive, dynamic mixed martial artist best known for his rivalry with Randy Couture in the UFC and his devastating knockout of the rugged Matt Lindland. Belfort began his professional mixed martial arts career in 1996. Ten years later he made his pro debut in professional boxing. He knocked out Josemario Neves in the third round in his native Brazil for the victory. His quick hands and power would serve him well in professional boxing, but so far Belfort has focused solely on mixed martial arts.

10. ANDERSON "THE SPIDER" SILVA

Many experts and fans consider Anderson Silva as the top pound-for-pound mixed martial artist in the world. He has dominated the UFC middleweight division and has had no problems when he stepped up to face light heavyweights, either. In 2005, Silva stepped into the ring for a professional boxing match. He stopped a fighter named Julio Cesar De Jesus in the second round.

32

Same Nickname Game—Mixed Martial Artists and Boxers

Sharing Nicknames with Famous Boxers

Many mixed martial artists have catchy nicknames that describe their fighting prowess, their aggressive style, or their particular skill set. Many of these MMA fighters have the same nicknames as famous boxers who preceded them. The following are ten nicknames used by current mixed martial artists and boxing greats.

1. HANDS OF STONE

Canadian Sam Stout competes in the Ultimate Fighting Championship lightweight division and thrills fans with his willingness to engage in stand-up wars. During his career, Stout has frequently won Fight of the Night bonuses for his aggression. He is known as Hands of Stone for his fistic powers. The great Panamanian warrior Roberto Durán carried the same moniker during a Hall of Fame boxing career that lifted him to numerous world titles. Many consider Durán to be the greatest lightweight in boxing history. He is known for handing "Sugar" Ray Leonard his first professional defeat.

2. **THE REAL DEAL**

Ross Pearson is a tough lightweight who competes in the UFC and is a former winner of the *The Ultimate Fighter* competition. Known as the Real Deal, Pearson has lost only once in the octagon at the time of this writing. Evander Holyfield was the Real Deal during his lengthy boxing career, which saw him capture the world cruiserweight boxing title and then the heavyweight championship. He owns two victories over Mike Tyson, including the infamous "Bite Fight" in 1997.

3. **THE HITMAN**

UFC light heavyweight fighter Jason Brilz sports the nickname of the Hitman. He earned legions of fans for his performance against Antônio Rogerio Nogueira. Even though he dropped a controversial decision, he gained fans by taking the fight on short notice and pressing the action against his more experienced opponent. The Hitman was also the nickname of legendary boxing champion Thomas Hearns, who is best known for his fights against "Sugar" Ray Leonard, Marvin Hagler, Roberto Durán, and Wilfred Benítez. Hearns won world championships in six different divisions.

4. **THE DRAGON**

Lyoto "the Dragon" Machida has used his brand of karate to win the UFC light heavyweight championship by stopping previously unbeaten Rashad Evans. Though he lost his title to Mauricio "Shogun" Rua, Machida remains one of the sport's top light heavyweights. Wilfred Benítez called himself Dragon during a Hall of Fame boxing career that saw him set a world record by winning a world championship at age seventeen in the light welterweight division. He later won titles in the welterweight and the light middleweight divisions.

5. LIGHTS OUT

Scott "Lights Out" Lighty is a former professional kickboxer and current mixed martial artist who competes in the light heavyweight division for Strikeforce. He has a professional MMA record of 6-2. James Toney, who debuted in mixed martial arts against Randy Couture in August 2010, is one of the best boxers of his generation. He has won world titles in numerous divisions, starting with his come-from-behind knockout of Michael Nunn in 1991 for the middleweight championship. He also owns victories over Evander Holyfield, Mike McCallum, and "Prince" Charles Williams.

6. THUNDER

Japanese mixed martial artist Yushin "Thunder" Okami currently thrills MMA fans in the UFC's middleweight division. He has defeated Mike Swick, Alan Belcher, and Mark Muñoz in his UFC career. The late boxing warrior Arturo "Thunder" Gatti also thrilled boxing fans with his no-holds-barred attacking style. He was best known for his exciting trilogy with Micky Ward and two wars with Ivan Robinson.

7. RAGING BULL

Rich "the Raging Bull" Attonito competes in the UFC's middleweight division. A competitor on *The Ultimate Fighter*, Attonito won his official debut in the octagon in June 2010. He shares his nickname with the legendary "Bronx Bull" Jake LaMotta, whose life story was told in the famous movie *Raging Bull*. Robert De Niro won an Academy Award for his portrayal of LaMotta.

8. THE HURRICANE

Gilbert Yvel and Gerald Harris are two mixed martial artists who compete in the UFC. Yvel is a heavyweight veteran who has squared off against some of the biggest names in his division in Pride, Affliction, and other promotions. Harris competes as a middleweight and has yet to lose in the octagon. Yvel and Harris share the Hurricane nickname with former middleweight boxing contender Rubin Carter, who is best known for serving years in prison for a crime he did not commit.

9. SMOKIN'
Joey Villaseñor pulls no punches when he squares off in mixed martial arts bouts. In his career, this middleweight has fought in Pride, Elite XC, and Strikeforce. He owns victories over Tim Credeur, Ryan Jensen, and Phil Baroni. He shares the nickname with former heavyweight boxing champion "Smokin" Joe Frazier, who is best known for his trilogy of epic battles with the great Muhammad Ali.

10. RAZOR
Benji Radach possesses excellent all-around skills as a mixed martial artist. He currently competes in the Strikeforce middleweight division. He has fought in the UFC in his professional career, which began in 2001. Donovan "Razor" Ruddock, a former tough heavyweight contender, is known for his bouts with former heavyweight champions Mike Tyson, Greg Page, and Lennox Lewis.

Somebody Usually Wins

33

Stunning Surprises

The Greatest Upsets in MMA History

One of the greatest aspects of sports is that the favored team or individual does not always win. In 1919, Man o' War—arguably the greatest racehorse of all time—lost the only race of his career to a horse named Upset. Seventy years later, Mike "the Baddest Man on the Planet" Tyson lost his undisputed world heavyweight boxing crown to 42-1 underdog James "Buster" Douglas. Many great upsets have likewise occurred in the history of mixed martial arts.

1. FEDOR EMELIANENKO VS. FABRICIO WERDUM

In June 2010, Fedor Emelianenko, generally regarded as the sport's top pound-for-pound great, faced off against Brazilian jiu-jitsu expert Fabricio Werdum. Most expected that Fedor's superior striking ability would overwhelm the Brazilian, who had lost bouts in the Ultimate Fighting Championship to strikers Junior dos Santos and Andrei Arlovski. Dos Santos had pounded out Werdum in less than a minute and a half. However, in this Strikeforce main attraction, Fedor perhaps entered the cage overconfident. In the opening seconds of the fight, he threw a couple of his trademark winging bombs, and Werdum went down, maybe from simply a glancing blow. Fedor went in to finish the Brazilian, who grabbed onto Fedor's arm. Instead of immediately pulling out, Fedor moved into the Brazilian's dangerous limbs even more, enabling the Brazilian to put his legs on Emelianenko and lock in a body triangle with the armbar. Fedor's face started to turn purple, and to the amazement of the MMA world, Fedor tapped out at only one minute and nine seconds into the first round.

2. GEORGES ST-PIERRE VS. MATT "THE TERROR" SERRA

In April 2007, Georges St-Pierre, one of the most athletic fighters in the history of MMA, defended his title against Matt Serra. St-Pierre, known as GSP, was supposed to make relatively quick work of Serra, who had barely won *The Ultimate Fighter*'s season 4 with a disputed decision win over Chris Lytle. However, a big punch to the head can change anything, and it happened at UFC 69 in April 2007. A confident Serra entered the octagon and threw his right hand with abandon. To his credit, when he connected, he pounced on St-Pierre and threw a dozen more right hands, forcing the referee to stop the contest in the first round. St-Pierre did gain revenge a year later by dominating Serra in April 2008, but he can never undo the upset that Serra pulled at UFC 69.

3. FORREST GRIFFIN VS. MAURICIO "SHOGUN" RUA

For several years, many considered former Pride champion Mauricio Rua as the top light heavyweight in the world. In Pride, he had used brutal stomps and soccer head kicks to devastating effect in Japan, defeating Antônio Rogerio Nogueira, Quinton "Rampage" Jackson, Ricardo Arona, and Alistair Overeem. In September 2007, Rua made his long-awaited debut in the UFC against the former winner of *The Ultimate Fighter*'s season 1, Forrest Griffin. People loved Griffin's heart, but few gave him a chance against the quicker, more dangerous Rua. To the surprise of many, Griffin's superior conditioning made the difference, and he submitted Rua in the third and final round. Rua exacted revenge in August 2011 and stopped Griffin in the first round.

4. SETH PETRUZELLI VS. KIMBO SLICE

Kevin Ferguson—better known to the world as Kimbo Slice—was marketed as Elite XC's top attraction. His popularity had skyrocketed because of Internet videos of several underground fights against various inept opponents. Further, Slice has good power in his hands and looks fearsome. He made the official transition to mixed martial arts with wins over former boxing champion Ray Mercer in a bout that was officially listed as an exhibition. He then blasted out MMA veterans Bo Cantrell and David "Tank" Abbott in the first round in Elite XC fights. In his third Elite XC bout, he managed to eke out a victory over James "the Colossus" Thompson. That win set the stage for a bout with an over-the-hill Ken Shamrock. The night of the fight, Shamrock pulled out because of a cut. Seth Petruzelli, who usually fought at light heavyweight, accepted the fight as a replacement. Petruzelli had fought in the UFC and had much more martial arts experience than Slice had; however, observers assumed that Slice would knock out Petruzelli with his superior power before the fight ever hit the ground. Stunningly, Petruzelli hurt Slice with a jab and then followed with a few more strikes. Petruzelli stopped Slice only fourteen seconds into the fight. CBS commentator Gus Johnson overstated the bout when he called it the "greatest upset in MMA history," but it was an upset.

5. MAURICE SMITH VS. MARK COLEMAN

In July 1997, Mark Coleman faced kickboxer Maurice Smith for the UFC heavyweight title. Coleman, the godfather of the ground and pound, had dominated the UFC 10 and 11 tournaments and then defeated Dan Severn at UFC 12 to become the organization's first heavyweight champion. He outweighed Smith by more than twenty-five pounds. Prevailing opinion was that Smith would be dangerous on his feet, but when the fight hit the ground, Smith would be toast. Meanwhile, Smith trained hard with Frank Shamrock for the fight. His superior striking and takedown defense enabled him to score points, and his superior cardio carried the night against the gassed Coleman. Smith captured a well-deserved unanimous decision victory and a place in mixed martial arts history.

6. RANDY COUTURE VS. TIM SYLVIA

Randy Couture surprised the world when he came out of retirement in 2007, at age forty-three, to face UFC heavyweight champion Tim Sylvia—a man who dwarfed him in height, reach, and weight and was ten years younger. Most people thought it would be an easy night for Sylvia, but Couture saw something when he served as a guest commentator for Sylvia's successful title defense against Jeff Monson. Couture proved prescient, as he effectively used head movements to avoid Sylvia's jab and cross and managed to land his own strikes before moving in to control Sylvia with his grappling skills. In the opening seconds of the fight, Couture landed a low, inside left kick followed by an overhand right. He dropped Sylvia and nearly finished him. Couture didn't finish Sylvia, but he won every round en route to a convincing unanimous decision and the respect of the MMA world.

7. MATT HUGHES VS. B. J. PENN I

In January 2004, UFC welterweight champion Matt Hughes looked to be a relatively safe bet to make the sixth successful defense of his crown. Hughes had not lost a fight in nearly three years and was well on his way to cleaning out the division. Additionally, his highly skilled opponent, B. J. Penn, normally fought in the lightweight division. Most expected the naturally bigger man to win the bout. Things didn't turn out that way, as the man known as the Prodigy showed his excellent striking and submission skills. He defeated Hughes by a rear naked choke near the end of the first round. Hughes would avenge the defeat more than two and a half years later.

8. RANDY COUTURE VS. CHUCK "THE ICEMAN" LIDDELL

When Randy Couture faced Chuck Liddell for the first time in June 2003 for the interim UFC light heavyweight crown, observers had many reasons to favor Liddell. Couture was rusty, as he had not fought in nearly nine months. Couture was coming off back-to-back losses in the heavyweight division and had dropped to the light heavyweight ranks. Additionally, Liddell had won ten straight bouts, including impressive stoppages of Vitor Belfort and Renato Sobral. Finally, the Iceman was considered the most dangerous striker in MMA at that time. Randy Couture, however, has proven many times that he is never to be counted out. Couture beat Liddell at his own striking game before taking him to the mat and pounding out a victory. Liddell would come back, though, to win two more bouts in this famous rivalry.

9. GABRIEL GONZAGA VS. MIRKO "CRO COP" FILIPOVIĆ

In April 2007, former Pride legend Mirko Cro Cop Filipović entered the octagon for the second time in what was supposed to be another stepping-stone toward an eventual shot at the UFC heavyweight crown. Cro Cop had already defeated Eddie Sanchez in his first UFC bout, and his next bout was against a relatively untested Brazilian named Gabriel Gonzaga. Though Gonzaga had won three straight in the

UFC, he had never faced a fighter with Cro Cop's credentials. Most expected that Cro Cop would use his explosive strikes, particularly his devastating leg kicks, to win by knockout. Instead, the opposite happened. Gonzaga unloaded with a right head kick that decimated the Croatian. Gonzaga not only won Knockout of the Night honors but also completed one of the most spectacular knockouts in MMA history.

10. CHAD GRIGGS VS. BOBBY LASHLEY

Bobby Lashley entered his August 2010 bout for Strikeforce as the future of the heavyweight division. The former collegiate and pro wrestling star had made a seamless transition to MMA in his first several bouts. His next opponent was a guy named Chad Griggs, who worked as a part-time firefighter. Griggs, however, entered the cage confident and not intimated by the muscular Lashley. While Lashley controlled much of the early action with his takedowns and ground and pound, Griggs showed excellent defense in his guard and the ability to take a good punch. He also landed an effective uppercut as Lashley was moving in for a takedown. The punch opened a serious cut over Lashley's eye that seemed to bother him more as the fight progressed. Gradually, Lashley began to tire, and Griggs began to land more punches. Toward the end of the second round, he caught Lashley with another solid punch and then hit him with hammer fists and other blows until the referee stopped the contest.

34
Winning on Points
They Get Decisions

Fans love to watch fighters who end fights, particularly by a devastating knockout or the slick submission. But not all mixed martial arts fighters possess incredible power or excellent jiu-jitsu to end bouts early. These fighters have to grind it out by any means necessary. The following ten fighters win most of their fights the hard way, by going the distance and besting their opponents over three or five rounds.

1. ANTONIO McKEE
When it comes to decisions, Antonio McKee may be the king. Any fighter nicknamed Mr. Decision wins the majority of his fights taking the long route. McKee has compiled an enviable professional MMA record of 26-4-2, but he has not endeared himself to the fans or developed mass fan appeal. Eighteen of his twenty-five career wins have come by decision. He uses his speed and superior wrestling ability to take guys down, lay on them, and do enough to earn the judges' nod. His method may not be exciting, but it has been effective.

2. YASUKO TAMADA
Yasuko Tamada is a Japanese female fighter who currently competes in Greatest Common Multiple (GCM) events in

her home country, and she has fought in Deep, Shooto, and other organizations. The 100-pound fighter has compiled a professional record of 12-6-3. Eleven of her twelve victories have come by decision. Her only non-decision win was by submission in 2007. All five of her losses have been by decision too.

3. HISAKI HIRAISHI

Hisaki Hiraishi is a Japanese mixed martial artist who competes professionally in Shooto events in his native country. Since turning pro in 2003, he has compiled a record of 10-5-4. All of his wins have been by decision, with eight of the nine wins being traditional points wins. The other was a technical decision win over Komei Okada, as the referee determined that both fighters were too injured—a hematoma over Okada's left eye and a nasty cut on Hiraishi's head—to continue. All four of Hiraishi's losses have been by decision as well.

4. HAYATE USUI

Hayate Usui is a tough fighter who competes in Shooto events in his native Japan. While his journeyman-like record is 10-8-1, he always brings his wild punches mixed with a solid work ethic. Nine of his ten career wins have come by decision as well as five of his eight losses. He also lost his last two bouts on points.

5. JON FITCH

Jon Fitch is one of the top Ultimate Fighting Championship welterweights in the world. He possesses a 25-3-1 record (including two amateur matches) and has won thirteen of fourteen fights in the octagon. The only fighters he could not defeat in the biggest stage are the great champions Georges

St-Pierre (loss) and B. J. Penn (draw). Fitch has won thirteen fights by decision, including his last five in the UFC over Akihiro Gono, Paulo Thiago, Mike Pierce, Ben Saunders, and Thiago Alves. The former Purdue All-American wrestler and Olympic alternative simply takes fighters down to the mat and wears them out.

6. BRADLEY GRAY "THE BULLY" MAYNARD

Gray Maynard is a contender in the UFC's lightweight (155-pound limit) division. A former collegiate wrestler at Michigan State University, Maynard has used his superior wrestling skills to control his opponents on the mat. In his career, Maynard has compiled a 10-0-1 record with one no contest. He has not finished off many opponents, however, scoring only two knockouts. Eight of his ten victories have been decisions, including his last seven wins.

7. KAZUHIRO NAKAMURA

This Japanese light heavyweight fighter has fought professionally in MMA since a 2003 debut against the great Brazilian Antônio Rogerio Nogueira. Nakamura has won fifteen professional MMA bouts, eleven of them on the judges' scorecards. During his career, he has outpointed Yuki Kondo, Kevin Randleman, Igor Vovchanchyn, and Murilo Bustamante.

8. KEIICHIRO YAMAMIYA

Japanese mixed martial artist Keiichiro Yamamiya has had forty professional MMA fights go to decision. Fortunately for him, he has won twice as many of those fights as he has lost, with twenty-six wins and thirteen losses from the judges. Overall, this veteran of DEEP and Pancrase has won thirty-nine bouts in his professional MMA career.

9. YUKI KONDO

Yuki Kondo is a longtime veteran of mixed martial arts with more than eighty professional bouts in his distinguished career. This veteran of the UFC, Pride, Pancrase, and Sengoku has won more than fifty fights. Many of his victories have come by decision, as he uses his quickness and wrestling ability to score takedowns. While he has won his share of fights by knockout and submission, his most frequent form of victory is grounding out a decision, with his last two victories coming by decision. Over the course of his career, he has outpointed such notables as Pete Williams, Semmy Schilt, and Guy Mezger.

10. MARVIN "THE BEASTMAN" EASTMAN

Marvin Eastman is a former kickboxer and mixed martial artist who has fought under the King of the Cage, World Extreme Fighting, and UFC banners. He has won seventeen professional mixed martial arts bouts with more than half of them (nine) coming by decision. In his pro MMA debut, he outpointed Quinton "Rampage" Jackson. He also holds points wins over Jason MacDonald and Alan Belcher in his career.

35

Captivating Comebacks

They Pulled It Out from Behind

One of the greatest aspects of combat sports is that a fighter always has a chance to turn the tide by pulling out a submission or landing a knockout punch. In other words, the famous saying attributed to former National Basketball Association coach Dick Motta—"The opera ain't over till the fat lady sings"—applies with full force in mixed martial arts. The following ten mixed martial artists proved this saying apropos by landing a knockout punch or sinking in a submission while trailing badly in the bouts.

1. ANTÔNIO RODRIGO "BIG NOG" NOGUEIRA

Brazilian legend Antônio Rodrigo Nogueira deserves his place at the top of this list because of his uncanny ability to pull submissions that snatch victory from the jaws of defeat time after time. In August 2002 at a Pride event, Nogueira squared off against the behemoth Bob Sapp, a man who outweighed him by more than 150 pounds. The powerful Sapp threw Big Nog around as if he were a rag doll for the first round and some of the second. Nogueira showed an inhuman ability to absorb punishment and then came back to submit Sapp with an armbar.

In February 2008, Nogueira struck again and rallied with a submission win, this time over former two-time Ultimate Fighting Championship titleholder Tim Sylvia. The much taller Sylvia used his longer reach to control the first two rounds, winning them handily. He was winning the third round too, until Nogueira managed to pull out another submission victory via the guillotine choke. Afterward, Sylvia could only express admiration, saying that it was a typical Nogueira come-from-behind victory.

2. SCOTT "HANDS OF STEEL" SMITH

Scott Smith deserves to be listed second on this list of captivating comebacks because he has pulled victory from the jaws of defeat with his patented right-hand bombs in several fights. In April 2009, he ate leather for most of three rounds against the slightly quicker Benji Radach. However, in the final round Smith landed a right-hand punch, forcing the referee to stop the contest.

Even more dramatically in December 2009, Smith pulled the biggest upset in Strikeforce history by defeating the previously unbeaten Cung Le. For two and a half rounds, Le executed his unorthodox kicking and punching style to great effect, battering Smith about the cage. Smith then landed a right-hand bomb that changed the complexion of the fight. Smith followed up quickly and pounded Le to earn the victory.

3. ANDERSON "THE SPIDER" SILVA VS. CHAEL SONNEN

At UFC 117, UFC middleweight champion Anderson Silva looked to make another successful title defense against skilled wrestler Chael Sonnen. Silva seemed invincible to some observers given his flashy striking skills. But Sonnen, a master of trash talking, had the bravado to insist that he had the style, game plan, and skill set to pull off the upset. For more than four rounds, Sonnen proved true to his word. He managed to land the first significant blow in the initial round and then took Silva down. He won the first four rounds by taking Silva down every round and occasionally putting the Brazilian in serious trouble.

But the champion showed incredible heart and resolve in surviving. He turned the tables in the fifth round, as Silva has always proved dangerous on his back from his guard. He managed to submit Sonnen with an arm triangle with three minutes and twenty-two seconds gone in the final round.

4. MIKE RUSSOW VS. TODD DUFFEE

At UFC 114, Mike Russow entered the octagon as the heavy underdog against the hyped and Herculean prospect Todd Duffee. The favored Duffee had won all of his bouts by knockout and owned the quickest knockout in UFC history by stopping Tim Hague in seven seconds in his octagon debut. Most expected Russow to be similar fodder for Duffee's meteoric rise up the heavyweight ladder.

For the first two and a half rounds, the pundits were proved correct, as Duffee landed quick and powerful punches. The much slower Russow only showed courage and the ability to take a heavy punch. Out of nowhere in the third round, Russow landed a straight right hand, and as Duffee fell, Russow quickly landed another right hand, which knocked his opponent out cold. UFC announcer Joe Rogan called it the most amazing comeback knockout in mixed martial arts history. Even Russow admitted in his post-fight interview that he was surprised.

5. SHANE CARWIN VS. BROCK LESNAR

At UFC 116, heavyweight champion Brock Lesnar faced off

against another giant in the division, power-punching Shane Carwin. The challenger had won all of his previous UFC fights by knockout in the first round, and he nearly pulled it off again in the biggest fight of his life. He nailed Lesnar with a series of power punches that had Lesnar ducking for cover and running backward. Carwin grounded and pounded Lesnar to the point where it appeared Referee Jake Rosenthal was about to stop the fight. Fortunately for Lesnar, Rosenthal gave him every benefit of the doubt, and he managed to survive a nightmarish first round. In the second round, Carwin appeared totally gassed. Lesnar managed to score a takedown, worked his way into side control position, and submitted Carwin with an arm-triangle choke.

6. SHONIE CARTER VS. MATT SERRA

At UFC 31, the colorful and charismatic Shonie Carter squared off against another brash, young fighter named Matt Serra. For much of the bout, Serra's more multifaceted skill set proved superior. Serra took Carter down only fifteen seconds into the fight. He nearly armbarred Carter and even landed a right high kick during the first round. Near the end of the first round, Carter landed a spinning elbow on Serra with only five seconds left; however, Serra dominated the first round.

The second round was close, with not nearly as much action as the first. In the third round, though, Serra had more submission attempts and looked to be on his way to winning a decision. Then Carter landed one of the most improbable knockouts in UFC history, a thrilling, spinning back fist that stopped Serra with only about fifteen seconds left in the bout. The referee stopped the bout with only nine seconds remaining. Serra was out cold.

7. JORGE SANTIAGO VS. KAZUO MISAKI I AND II

Excuse Kazuo Misaki if he feels as if he is cursed when he fights Jorge Santiago. These two warriors met twice—once in 2009 and once in 2010—for the Sengoku middleweight championship. In each bout, the athletic Misaki won most of the early rounds with more takedowns and strikes. In the fifth round of each bout, though, Santiago pulled out a near-miraculous victory. In the first bout, Santiago had sunk in a rear naked choke to win by submission with only a minute and a half remaining in the fight. In their second bout, Misaki's corner threw in the towel with only twenty-nine seconds remaining in the bout. At the time of these fifth-round endings, Misaki was ahead on the judges' scorecards in both bouts.

8. YOSHIHIRO AKIYAMA VS. CHRIS "THE CRIPPLER" LEBEN

At UFC 116, Chris Leben returned to the octagon only two weeks after his last fight, which was a win over Aaron Simpson. This time Leben faced the powerful Japanese fighter Yoshihiro Akiyama, a skilled striker with excellent wrestling skills. Akiyama and Leben engaged in a classic brawl, but Akiyama appeared to be comfortably ahead going into and then even near the end of the third round because he had scored many more takedowns during the fight. Leben landed some trademark bombs, however, and with only twenty seconds left in the round won by a triangle choke submission.

9. PETE WILLIAMS VS. MARK "THE HAMMER" COLEMAN

Pete Williams entered the octagon for the first time at UFC 17 in May 1998 against former champion Mark Coleman. Most expected that Coleman would rebound after a disappointing loss to Maurice Smith a few months earlier. Coleman took Williams to the canvas with only thirty-seven seconds into the first round. Williams attempted an armbar submission, but Coleman controlled the action with his solid wrestling base and ground-and-pound attack. He kept Williams on his back for more than five minutes. When referee "Big" John McCarthy stood the fighters up, Coleman landed a couple of good right hands. Coleman and Williams finished the twelve-minute regulation period. Then, the fighters had a rest before a three-minute overtime period.

During the rest period, Williams's cornerman, Jerry Bohlander, was brutally honest: "You're behind on points." When the action resumed, Williams heeded his corner's advice and went on the attack. Thirty-eight seconds into the overtime period, he landed a right kick to Coleman's head that knocked the Hammer out cold.

10. STEFAN STRUVE VS. CHRISTIAN MORECRAFT

Heavyweights Stefan Struve and Christian Morecraft squared off at UFC 117 on the undercard of the Anderson Silva versus Chael Sonnen card. In the first round, Morecraft used his superior strength to maul Struve, pounding him to such an extent that it appeared the referee was on the verge of stopping the fight on multiple occasions. Somehow, Struve survived the first round and then came back to knock out Morecraft in the second.

36

Quickest Knockouts

These Fights Ended Early

A primary reason for the public's fascination with mixed martial arts concerns the numerous ways that one combatant can defeat another. One mixed martial artist can use any number of submissions or stop his opponent by striking with his hands, feet, elbows, or knees. Many fans enjoy mixed martial artists for the ultimate knockouts. Sometimes one fighter will land a knockout blow early in a bout. These ten bouts featured strikes that ended the night quite early for their opponents.

1. DON FRYE VS. THOMAS RAMIREZ

Instead of the promised "David versus Goliath" battle, the Ultimate Fighting Championship 8 in February 1996 presented a battle of "Don versus Goliath," as Don Frye faced off against four-hundred-pound Thomas Ramirez in the tournament's opening round. Frye, a distinguished wrestler with professional boxing experience, proved to be too fast and powerful for the behemoth Ramirez. Frye advanced swiftly in the southpaw stance, landed a quick, powerful right, and followed with a more powerful right hook to the head of Ramirez, who fell like a sack of potatoes. Frye landed one more punch before Referee "Big" John McCarthy stopped the bout a mere eight seconds into the contest. Frye set a mark for one of the quickest knockous in UFC history, one that still stands. The same evening, Frye stopped opponents Sam Adkins and Gary "Big Daddy" Goodridge in the first round and captured the tournament championship.

2. JAMES "THE SANDMAN" IRVIN VS. HOUSTON "THE ASSASSIN" ALEXANDER

In April 2008, Houston Alexander looked to rebound from his first loss in the UFC when he squared off against fellow power puncher James Irvin at UFC Fight Night 13. Many pundits predicted that Alexander would return to the winning ways that led to his first-round destructions of Keith Jardine and Alessio Sakara. James Irvin, however, had a different idea. The two met and traded right-hand bombs. Alexander missed, Irvin connected, and the rest was history, as Irvin's punch knocked Alexander out cold. The fight was over in eight seconds, tying the Frye-Ramirez fight for the quickest knockout in UFC history.

3. SETH PETRUZELLI VS. KEVIN "KIMBO SLICE" FERGUSON

Kevin Ferguson, also known as Kimbo Slice, became a sensation after videos showed him defeating people in bare-knuckle brawls. This Internet sensation later turned pro in mixed martial arts, after Elite XC sought to capitalize on his popularity and make a profit. Slice delivered in violent fashion, as he stopped Bo Cantrell, David "Tank" Abbott, and James Thompson. Slice looked to continue his winning ways in October 2008 when he was scheduled to face the legendary veteran Ken Shamrock. But a bizarre chain of events unfolded, and Shamrock, who suffered a cut, was forced to withdraw from the bout.

Former WEC champ Brian Stann made a name for himself with his heavy hands and holds the record for the fastest knockout in WEC history at sixteen seconds. *United States Marine Corps*

In his place entered Seth Petruzelli, a fighter who had competed in the UFC but who was not expected to present a great challenge given Slice's size and supposed edge in punching power. Meanwhile, Petruzelli, who had trained in full-contact karate for years, had other ideas. At the start of the bell, Slice advanced in his typical, aggressive fashion.

Petruzelli backpedaled and threw a short, straight right hand that dropped Slice. Petruzelli immediately pounced and delivered several more punches before the referee stopped the fight. The CBS announcers proclaimed, "Rocky is here!" They hyperbolically called the fourteen-second knockout "the most incredible victory in mixed martial arts."

4. B. J. "THE PRODIGY" PENN VS. CAOL UNO

UFC 34: High Voltage featured an intriguing matchup between distinguished MMA veteran Caol Uno of Japan and newcomer B. J. Penn of the United States in November 2001. Uno had fought about twenty professional MMA bouts while the talented Penn had only two fights under his belt, though he had looked impressive in both. Uno came charging out of the gates with a flying leg kick. The elusive Penn avoided the quick attack and countered with several quick punches—a straight left followed by two right uppercuts. The referee wisely halted the contest after only eleven seconds. It was a stunning victory for such a young fighter over such a seasoned foe. Uno was out cold, and the Prodigy had served notice that he was a force to be reckoned with for years to come. Uno gained a measure of respect, but no revenge, at UFC 41 in 2003 when he fought Penn to a five-round draw.

5. DAVID "TANK" ABBOTT VS. JOHN MATUA

The Ultimate Fighting Championships billed its sixth tournament as the Clash of the Titans. The first round of the July 1995 event fit the billing, as it featured 265-pound "pit fighter" David Abbott against 400-pound John Matua, a practitioner of the art of Kuialua, or bone breaking. Abbott didn't back down from the larger man; instead, he did what he did best, throw right-hand bombs. Abbott landed a couple of his vicious bombs, which felled Matua and caused his body to contort in a scary fashion. Referee McCarthy had to dive in to save Matua from Tank. Abbott entered UFC lore with this eighteen-second knockout in his octagon debut and his subsequent mocking of the prone Matua, as his opponent lay unconscious. There was no doubting Abbott when he told announcer Jeff Blatnick, a former Olympic gold medal wrestler, that the fight was a "cakewalk, baby."

6. STEVE RAMIREZ VS. DARVIN WATTREE

Most professional mixed martial arts fights take place with smaller promotions and outside of the public spotlight given to premier promotions such as the UFC, Strikeforce, and Dream. Now, in the age of the Internet and YouTube, fight fans can see many other fights. A notable example was a bout at Pure Combat 9: Home Turf in July 2009 between Steve Ramirez and Darvin Wattree, both of whom sported mediocre records. The fight was literally a one-punch knockout. Ramirez connected with the first punch he threw, a right hand, and Wattree immediately checked out. The referee properly halted the contest after a mere three seconds. It is believed to be the quickest knockout in professional mixed martial arts history.

7. FEDOR "THE LAST EMPEROR" EMELIANENKO VS. HIROYA TAKADA

Many people believe that the greatest mixed martial artist of all time is none other than Russian sambo expert Fedor Emelianenko. During his illustrious career, he captured the Pride heavyweight championship from the vaunted Antônio Rodrigo Nogueira and has defeated a host of other top contenders and former champions. In his third professional bout in Rings, he squared off against Hiroya Takada. Emelianenko quickly sized up his opponent and threw two left hooks that knocked Takada silly. The referee stopped the bout after only twelve seconds.

8. ALEKSANDER EMELIANENKO VS. JAMES "THE COLOSSUS" THOMPSON

Fedor's younger brother Aleksander Emelianenko bested Fedor's quick knockout record by one second when he tangled with James Thompson at Pride 28: High Octane in October 2004. Like a caged bull, Thompson charged across the ring and actually hit Emelianenko with a glancing blow that dropped the Russian. Emelianenko rose quickly and proceeded to pound Thompson with a powerful flurry of punches. After only eleven seconds, the referee mercifully saved Thompson from further punishment.

9. VITOR "THE PHENOM" BELFORT VS. "BIG" JON HESS

In October 1996, Vitor Belfort made his professional mixed martial arts debut against the much larger Jon Hess at SuperBrawl 2. Hess charged his smaller opponent, but Belfort deftly moved aside and then took Hess down to the ground. Belfort then unloaded a barrage of quick punches, knocking Hess senseless. The referee stopped the contest after only twelve seconds. Belfort earned his first victory, while Hess received only a concussion.

10. MIRKO "CRO COP" FILIPOVIĆ VS. YUJI "THE REVOLUTIONIST" NAGATA

One of the most feared strikers in mixed martial arts history is Croatian sensation Mirko Filipović, better known as Cro Cop because of his career as a law enforcement official in his native country. Cro Cop honed his deadly leg kicks during his days as a professional kickboxer. In December 2001, Japanese professional wrestler Yuji Nagata learned firsthand how deadly Cro Cop's legs can be. After a few moments of feeling each other out, Cro Cop landed his first kick, a left roundhouse kick that felled Nagata. The referee stopped the bout after only twenty-one seconds. This fight may have been one of the reasons Nagata had only one other professional MMA bout in his career. Afterward, he wisely stuck to professional wrestling.

37

Controversial Decisions

The Wrong Fighter Won

Fighters often like to say that they want their fists, legs, or other body parts to be their judges and to finish off their opponents. Otherwise, the three judges sitting at the cage or ring will render their verdict. And, as the saying goes, you never know what the judges are going to see or how the judges are going to score a fight. In mixed martial arts, one judge may prefer superior striking while another judge will focus more on effective aggression and control of the cage. Still, another judge may be more impressed with takedowns and submission attempts. The following ten decisions created some controversy in mixed martial arts.

1. BAS RUTTEN VS. KEVIN RANDLEMAN

At the Ultimate Fighting Championship 20: Battle for the Gold in 1999, Rutten of Pancrase fame battled the ridiculously athletic Randleman. A minute into the fight, Randleman's Ohio State wrestling pedigree showed as he easily took Rutten down and proceeded to pound him with punches. At one point Referee "Big" John McCarthy even had the doctor examine Rutten's bloody face. While Randleman tired during the later stages of the fight, he still inflicted far more damage and had Rutten on his back for nearly the entire fight, which went into overtime. Rutten managed little offense. The fight was scored before the adoption of the ten-point must scoring system, and somehow two judges scored the bout for Rutten in a disgraceful decision.

2. QUINTON "RAMPAGE" JACKSON VS. MURILO "NINJA" RUA

At Pride 29: Ring of Fire in 2005, Jackson faced Rua in an intriguing matchup. Rua's greater versatility showed throughout much of the bout. He attempted many more submissions, appeared to land more strikes, and dominated much of the action. Jackson had his moments, particularly at the first part of the third round, but it was clear to ringside observers that Ninja had won the bout. The judges, however, awarded a split decision victory to Jackson. It was such a bad decision that Jackson told Rua's corner that Ninja had won the fight. He even tried to hand his trophy to Ninja as the Brazilian left the ring area. Unfortunately for Jackson, Ninja's younger brother Mauricio exacted his revenge two months later by breaking Jackson's rib and smashing his face with a series of kicks.

3. MICHIHIRO OMIGAWA VS. HATSU HIOKI

At Sengoku 11 in 2009, Omigawa clearly lost the first two rounds of his three-round bout with Hatsu Hioki. To his credit, Omigawa picked up the pace and fought better in the final round, but he should have lost by a unanimous decision. Instead, to the amazement of everyone in attendance—including Omigawa—he captured a split decision. Omigawa, with microphone in hand, apologized in the ring to his opponent.

4. LYOTO MACHIDA VS. MAURICIO "SHOGUN" RUA I

Machida entered his first title defense undefeated after devastating Rashad Evans for the UFC light heavyweight title.

Most expected Machida to defeat Rua, who seemingly had declined in the octagon since his dominant days in Pride, but Rua pressed the action for much of the five-round bout in October 2009. While Machida had his moments, Rua won at least three of the five rounds on nearly everyone's scorecard, except for the three scorecards that mattered. The three judges somehow gave Machida the three rounds.

Rua exacted revenge in the May 2010 rematch. This time Shogun let his fists and legs be the judges, stopping Machida and handing the Brazilian the first loss of his career.

5. RANDY "THE NATURAL" COUTURE VS. PEDRO RIZZO I

At UFC 31, Couture and Rizzo battled for the UFC heavyweight championship. Couture dominated the first round, but Rizzo rebounded and nearly knocked out the Natural in the second. Rizzo appeared to win two of the remaining three rounds and, in many viewers' eyes, should have earned the victory, but the judges handed Couture a unanimous decision. Even Couture looked surprised that he had won unanimously.

6. MICHAEL "THE COUNT" BISPING VS. MATT HAMILL

This battle between two former contestants of *The Ultimate Fighter*'s season 3 was part of the UFC 75 fight card held in England in September 2007. Michael Bisping, who had won *The Ultimate Fighter* competition, squared off against rival and powerful wrestler Matt Hamill. It appeared to most observers that Hamill was the more aggressive fighter and scored more takedowns and landed the more damaging blows. Bisping had his moments, particularly in the third and final rounds, but it was hard to see Bisping winning more than one round. Still, two of the three judges scored the bout for Bisping, creating an uproar in the MMA community.

7. LEONARD GARCIA VS. CHAN SUNG "THE KOREAN ZOMBIE" JUNG

The incredible battle between these two featherweight warriors in the World Extreme Cagefighting tournament in April 2010 is best known for its nonstop action. The two men literally waged war for the entire three rounds. Most observers felt that Jung won at least two of the three rounds. He landed more than a hundred strikes in the bout and clearly hurt Garcia on numerous occasions. While Garcia landed his far share of strikes, Jung seemingly inflicted much more damage during the bout. FightMetric had Jung as the clear winner of this bout. Yet, the judges still gave the nod to Garcia.

8. MIKE EASTON VS. CHASE BEEBE

Chase Beebe and Mike Easton faced off in October 2009 in Fairfax, Virginia, for the Ultimate Warrior Challenge's bantamweight title. Beebe, a decorated wrestler, was on Easton's back for much of the five rounds. He also attempted more submissions and appeared to inflict more damage. Yet, two of the three Virginian judges scored the bout for Easton. *Sherdog* labeled the decision "Robbery of the Year" for 2009.

9. ANTÔNIO ROGERIO NOGUEIRA VS. JASON BRILZ

Antônio Rogerio Nogueira was slated to face Forrest Griffin at UFC 114 in May 2010. After Griffin had to bow out with an injury, the UFC scrambled for a replacement. The unheralded Jason Brilz accepted the challenge and took the fight to Nogueira. An effective wrestler, Brilz took Nogueira down and nearly finished him with a guillotine choke in the second round. Brilz appeared to control and win the first two rounds. While Nogueira came out in the third round, many observers felt Brilz deserved the nod. FightMetric scored the fight for Brilz. Two of the three judges, however, scored the bout for Nogueira and awarded him a controversial split-decision victory.

10. FRANKIE EDGAR VS. B. J. PENN

Frankie Edgar shocked the MMA community at UFC 112 in April 2010 by defeating the vaunted B. J. Penn for the UFC lightweight championship. The judges scored the five-round bout by scores of 50–45, 49–46, and 48–47. According to FightMetric's fight report, Penn landed more strikes than Edgar did and should have earned the judges' nod. The fight was close, but two judges ostensibly seemed way off the mark. It is hard to justify Edgar winning all five rounds or even four of the five rounds in that fight. Later, Edgar did dominate the fighters' August 2010 rematch and won a lop-sided unanimous decision by justifiable 50–45 scorecards.

38

Biggest Losers

Fighters on a Perpetual Losing Streak

Fighting is not for the tenderhearted. Every bout has a winner and a loser. The winners go on to pursue their dreams while the losers start looking for new careers. But some people fight just to fight, regardless of the humiliation or personal and physical consequences. Though the new media often lampoon these underdogs, they still represent a uniquely American phenomenon—namely, the competitor who refuses to give up even when he has absolutely no chance of winning. These ten mixed martial arts fighters have been through the school of hard knocks and then some.

1. STACY "HAMMERING" HAKES
MMA is similar to boxing in that some fighters are convinced that their next fight is always going to be the one that starts a winning streak. With a fight record of 4-16-0, Stacy Hakes actually did have a three-fight winning streak early in his career, but he lost all but one of his next seventeen fights. Hakes won his eighth fight by a surprise armbar (surprising because he had never won by submission before). Looking more like a barroom brawler than a trained athlete, Hakes's MMA career spanned from 2003 until 2007, and he hasn't fought professionally since.

2. KENNETH ALLEN

Sporting a record of one win and twenty-eight losses, Kenneth Allen is the epitome of a fighter on a perpetual losing streak. In fact, his record is so bad that there seems to be a discrepancy among the authoritative sources as to how many fights he's actually lost. Allen is one of those naturally athletic fighters who tries and tries but gets continually taken out of his game plan. He spends the first ten seconds of every fight in offensive mode and the rest of it entirely on defense. At least Allen has gone the distance a few times, and that is more than can be said for many of the other fighters on this list.

3. MIKE SUTTLES

A man who has made a career out of never throwing a straight punch, Mike Suttles uses his unorthodox fighting style to confound his opponents into effective action. With limited striking ability and poor defensive skills, Suttles has managed to rack up an impressive record of thirty-three defeats and only three wins in a career that spans just longer than five years. Besides never having sustained permanent damage, Suttles also has the miraculous ability never to get in an underhook even when they're practically given to him.

4. STEVE HORTON

Strong as a bull and willing to fight anybody, Steve Horton is a wrestler with a proclivity to take his opponents to the ground, where his inactivity eventually leads to defeat. With a career spanning longer than a decade and a record of 1-17, Horton rarely makes it out of the first round unscathed. During what was turning out to be a fine performance against an inexperienced competitor, Horton made the mistake of changing his normal strategy of inaction to throwing a single roundhouse kick. He promptly dropped to the floor, writhing in pain from a blown-out knee. Robbed of his victory by doing something slightly different, Horton has since racked up four more losses and has now become inactive.

5. JOSH PANKEY

Another fighter with a questionable record, there is little doubt that Pankey has at least been in a lot of brawls, if nothing else. Unfortunately for him, out of eighteen matches, he only carried a victory in a single bout. In his career Pankey made it into the second round once, but he was defeated by a guillotine choke. Surely his inability to survive long was made considerably worse by his consistent rushing at his opponents at the beginning of every match while throwing wild punches. More often than not, these wild charges ended up with Pankey face down on the ground, where his more skilled opponents dominated him.

6. SCOTT "LIONHEART" BLEVINS

Sporting the prerequisite illegible tattoos and ears that would make our president proud, Scott Blevins has an abysmal record of seventeen fights without a single win. Not only does Blevins consistently lose, he also does so in a manner that makes the audience cringe. Perpetually uncoordinated and prone to throwing the worst kicks ever seen in MMA, Blevins's actions leave viewers questioning why he continues to use the same ineffective tactics in every fight. Never having seen a second round as most of his fights last less than a minute, Blevins still manages to look the part of a badass, probably because people confuse him with Matt Lindland.

7. JOSEPH "THE HO BAG" BOCHENEK

While he might not own the worst record in MMA, Bochenek

certainly sports the worst nickname. Often confused as an Internet legend, Bochenek—whose name many people do not believe is real—is, in fact, a real fighter who actually lands the occasional good strike. With a 0-10 record that shows him to be a less-than-ideal candidate for a top matchup, Bochenek's supporters have suggested that many of his defeats were from fixed fights or other abnormalities that didn't allow him to compete at the top of his game. Whether any of these arguments is true, one thing is for sure: Bochenek has found a permanent place in Internet lore and will continue to be suggested as the ideal opponent for the less-than-savory characters who try to make a name for themselves in mixed martial arts.

8. SHAWN NOLAN

With a career spanning a decade and more than forty losses on his record, Shawn Nolan is one of those competitors whose name makes him sound as if he's famous, but he isn't. Turning pro in 2001 after an amateur career that was also filled with losses, Nolan is listed on several official MMA websites as sporting the worst record in mixed martial arts. Despite his reputation for losing, Nolan does have the occasional win, but all of his "fans" tend to forget this fact and consistently idolize him as the man who just keeps fighting to lose. This assumed fatalism has brought him some hard-earned respect from other fighters who have used him as a human punching bag.

9. DAVID "THE FURY" DAVIS

A fighter who is on a seventeen-fight losing streak, Davis still continues to take on all comers. Known for his dedication to the ground and pound, Davis has four wins to his record, but all of them came early in his career. Lacking technical stand-up ability and possessing only rudimentary ground work, his early victories came as a result of his using brute strength to overcome skill. Unfortunately his most recent opponents have been strong, in comparatively good shape, and well trained, pretty much negating his primary advantages.

10. **ADAM JOHNSON**

Sporting a bald head and goatee long before they were even popular, Adam Johnson enters every fight with a tremendous amount of energy only to have it dissipated by more polished opponents. Beginning his career in 1998, Johnson continues to accept—and lose—fights. With three wins and fourteen losses to his record, Johnson never got beyond his general lukewarm enthusiasm for the sport in order to become a multidimensional fighter. With decent wrestling skills and a never-say-die attitude, Johnson could have had a much better career if he had worked on his technical efficiency.

39

Debut
Disappointments

They Lost Their First Fight

Most top-level fighters dominate their early opponents and showcase their prodigious skill sets over lesser opponents. However, sometimes a top-level fighter faces a tough opponent in his or her first bout or simply has a hard time early in his or her career. It is not that unusual in combat sports for even world champions to lose their pro debuts. In the sport of boxing, middleweight great Bernard Hopkins Jr. lost his professional boxing debut. The following ten, top-level mixed martial artists lost their initial professional bouts.

1. ANDERSON "THE SPIDER" SILVA

Many MMA pundits consider Anderson Silva to be the greatest striker in the history of the sport and one of the sport's all-time greats. His devastating combination of speed and power has led to his domination over the Ultimate Fighting Championship middleweight division. He has destroyed the likes of Rich Franklin (twice), Nate Marquardt, Dan Henderson, Forrest Griffin, and a host of other contenders. But Silva lost his pro debut at Mecca: World Vale Tude 1 in May 2000 in his native Brazil. He dropped a decision to Luiz Azeredo.

2. KAZUSHI SAKURABA

Kazushi Sakuraba is one of the true legends in the mixed martial arts world. The veteran of Pride, Dream, and Shooto thrilled audiences with his leg kicks, unusual strikes, and grappling prowess—all skills that he first used as a professional wrestler. During his illustrious career, he submitted Quinton "Rampage" Jackson, Kevin Randleman, and Carlos Newton. He became known as the Gracie Hunter for his successful wins over numerous members of the Brazilian fighting family. In his 1996 MMA debut, though, Sakuraba lost to the much bigger Kimo Leopoldo at a shoot boxing event.

3. FORREST GRIFFIN

Forrest Griffin became the darling of many mixed martial arts fans for his incredible brawl with Stephan Bonnar to win *The Ultimate Fighter* competition in 2005. He later cemented his legacy in mixed martial arts by upsetting Quinton "Rampage" Jackson to capture the UFC light heavyweight title in 2008. In his career, he's also defeated former champions Tito Ortiz and Mauricio "Shogun" Rua. But in his pro debut in 2001 Griffin faced a much more experienced foe, forty-three-year-old octagon veteran Dan Severn. Severn outpointed Griffin over three rounds in a Reality Submission Fighting event.

4. THIAGO "PITBULL" ALVES

Thiago Alves wreaks havoc in the UFC welterweight division with his devastating punches and kicks. He has stopped the likes of Karo Parisyan and Matt Hughes with his trademark power. He also defeated the tough Josh Koscheck over three grueling rounds. But Alves did not begin his professional career with devastating wins. In fact, he lost his first two pro fights. In his debut, he lost to Gleison Tibau in a champions' night event in Brazil in June 2001.

5. ANDREI "THE PIT BULL" ARLOVSKI

Andrei Arlovski has been a top-ten heavyweight in mixed martial arts for many years. In 2005, he captured the UFC interim heavyweight championship with a submission win over Tim Sylvia in the first minute of the first round. He defended that title twice against Justin Eilers and Paul Buentello with first-round knockouts. Arlovski was on top of the MMA world. Unfortunately, he fell off that top perch with two consecutive losses to Sylvia. Later, his chin has been called into question with knockout losses to the great Fedor Emelianenko, Brett Rogers, and Sergei Kharitonov. Ironically, Arlovski suffered his first knockout loss in his first pro bout in April 1999 to Viacheslav Datsik.

6. CLAY "THE CARPENTER" GUIDA

Clay Guida is known for his exceptional cardio and physical strength, which he uses literally to maul and brawl his opponents. He has captured more than twenty-five wins in his professional mixed martial arts career, including the Strikeforce world lightweight championship in 2006 with a win over Josh Thomson. Guida has garnered three Fight of the Night bonus awards for his ferocious fights with Tyson Griffin, Diego Sanchez, and Nate Diaz in the UFC. However, in July 2003 at a smaller event called the Silverback Classic in Ottawa, Illinois, Guida lost his first fight via submission to a fighter named Adam Copenhaver.

7. AKIHIRO "THE MAGIC MAN" GONO

Akihiro Gono has thrilled audiences in his native Japan and around the world with his colorful ring entrances, his unexpected submissions, and his innovative fighting style. He submitted Gegard Mousasi in 2006 and holds victories over Yuki Kondo, Hayato Sakurai, and Dae Won Kim. Gono had some difficulty, however, early in his career. In fact, he lost five of his first nine bouts, including a submission loss to Yasunori Okuda in his pro debut in 1994 at the Lumax Cup: Tournament of Japan.

8. CAOL UNO

Japan's Caol Uno is a mixed martial arts legend known for his unorthodox style, submissions, and fancy leg takedowns. He has faced a veritable who's who in the sport's lighter weight divisions, defeating the likes of Hermes Franca, Din Thomas, Rich Clementi, and Yves Edwards. He once battled the great B. J. Penn to a draw in a UFC bout. Though he has won twenty-six professional MMA bouts, Uno lost in his pro debut in 1996 in a Shooto event. The loss is more understandable when considering the opponent, Hayato Sakurai, was considered in his prime one of the sport's pound-for-pound greats. Sakurai secured an armbar and submitted Uno in the first round of their encounter.

9. ROB "THE SAINT" EMERSON

Rob Emerson is a rough-and-tumble lightweight who has fought in DEEP, Shooto, Pancrase, and the UFC in his professional career. He has fought more than twenty times in his professional career with a record of 11-10 with one no contest. He knocked out Manvel Gamburyan in only twelve seconds and holds a decision win over Phillipe Nover. But Emerson's career began rather slowly. He lost his first four bouts. In his pro debut in 2002, he faced former UFC world champion Jens Pulver, losing by decision.

10. SHONIE CARTER

The charismatic Shonie Carter has won nearly fifty professional bouts in his mixed martial arts career. He is best known for his devastating, spinning back fists, which he used to garner a highlight-reel knockout over Matt Serra in May 2001 in a UFC fight. In 2003, he captured the World Extreme Cagefighting world lightweight title with a win over J. T. Taylor. In his pro debut at a February 1997 Extreme Challenge event, however, Carter quickly dropped to LaVerne Clark. Clark punched Carter out in only nine seconds.

Fighters Have to Start Somewhere

40

It Takes More than a Singlet

Collegiate Wrestlers

Wrestling is one of the few combat sports that has been widely accepted at the collegiate level. Perhaps wrestling reminds professors of the glory days of Greece, or maybe the sport simply gives universities another road to Olympic glory. Whatever the case, numerous college wrestlers have successfully made the jump into mixed martial arts. This list features some of the most recognizable college wrestlers to compete in MMA.

1. CHUCK "THE ICEMAN" LIDDELL

For many years Liddell has been one of the most feared strikers in MMA. With a background in traditional karate and kickboxing, Liddell regularly throws looping punches that go around his opponent's guard. Sometimes accused of purposely throwing finger jabs, Liddell's inadvertent eye pokes reflect his years of training in Kempo karate. Unlike most striking specialists, Liddell has seen repeated success against many great grapplers. His success can be directly attributed to his years of collegiate wrestling experience at the California Polytechnic State University of San Luis Obispo. Liddell's actual wrestling record remains elusive, but it is known that he competed at the Division 1 level and has since adapted his wrestling to give him what is arguably the best sprawl in MMA.

2. JAKE ROSHOLT

A three-time National Collegiate Athletic Association Division I wrestling champion in two different weight classes, Rosholt is also a four-time All-American. With this pedigree there can be little doubt that Rosholt is easily one of the most accomplished wrestlers in the 185-pound weight class and brings to the ring ballistic takedowns and imposing strength. Unfortunately his submission game isn't yet up to snuff, and he has difficulty dealing with effective strikers, occasionally resulting in premature takedowns. Still a fairly young fighter, Rosholt's stand-up has improved in almost every bout, and after being cut from the Ultimate Fighting Championship in 2009, he has seen some success under lesser known promotions.

3. MIKE "MAYHEM" BROWN

An exceptionally strong fighter, Mike Brown is a gifted athlete who can dominate featherweight opponents with his strength alone. Most well-schooled fighters use Muay Thai as their primary striking art, but Brown instead combines boxing with traditional wrestling and Brazilian jiu-jitsu to give him an exceptionally effective skill set. Brown was a state wrestling champion during high school in Maine and went on to compete for Norwich University in Vermont.

4. SHANE ROLLER

Since beginning his mixed martial arts career with a loss to Jake Pruitt, Shane Roller has gone on to become a mainstay in the World Extreme Cagefighting promotion. A three-time All-American with a work ethic second to none, Roller spent his college career wrestling for Oklahoma State University. Using his tremendous grappling ability to limit the effectiveness of more experienced strikers, Roller lost a controversial decision against Ben Henderson when he grabbed his opponent's leg in order to avoid a downpour of accurate punches. To date his most important fight was against Melvin Guillard, who knocked him out in the first round of their match at UFC 132.

5. FRANK "THE ANSWER" EDGAR

Ranked as the top lightweight fighter in the world by several publications, Frank Edgar put his wrestling to the test when he took on and defeated UFC legend B. J. Penn, twice. Edgar first made a name for himself during high school when he went to the New Jersey State wrestling championships three different times. Then he competed for Clarion University of Pennsylvania, where he made it to the nationals all four years that he was in school. Often misidentified as a wrestler with just a few tricks up his sleeve, Edgar has fought and defeated many of the top names in MMA, including Tyson Griffin, Sean Sherk, and Hermes Franca.

6. BRADLEY GRAY "THE BULLY" MAYNARD

Far from the most distinguished wrestler to enter the octagon, Maynard is nonetheless a highly regarded wrestler who became a three-time All-American while wrestling for Michigan State. Another wrestler who emphasizes boxing as his primary stand-up art, Maynard has proven to be an efficient striker with the ability to punish opponents on their feet as well as on the mat. For such a powerful combatant, Maynard sports a disproportionate number of decision wins on his record, prompting some detractors to suggest that he lacks the killer instinct needed to put opponents away.

7. MATT "THE HAMMER" HAMILL

Matt Hamill is unique among mixed martial arts fighters in that he is deaf. That distinction has done nothing to limit his fighting ability, and from the beginning of his MMA career, Hamill has been fighting such worthy opponents as Seth Petruzelli and Michael Bisping. A much-loved contestant on *The Ultimate Fighter*, Hamill's solid fan base goes all the way back to when he was wrestling for the Rochester Institute of Technology. During his college career Hamill was a three-time NCAA Division III champion. After graduating from the institute, he went on to compete at the Deaflympics, where he won a gold in freestyle wrestling and a silver in Greco-Roman.

8. JON FITCH

A natural athlete who is willing to jump weight classes to fight all comers, Fitch is a welterweight who thinks nothing of packing on the pounds in order to fight better competition. He has amassed an impressive record with wins over the likes of Thiago Alves, Diego Sanchez, and Paulo Thiago. His wrestling coach at Purdue University was a former Pride fighter and introduced Fitch to mixed martial arts. Fitch then went on to cross train in various striking arts and has since gained notoriety as the second-best welterweight in the UFC, having lost only a single match to George St-Pierre and taken a draw against B.J. Penn.

9. JOSH "KOS" KOSCHECK

A standout wrestler during his college years, Koscheck is a former Division I NCAA champion and four-time All-American. Content either to stay on his feet or to go to the ground, Koscheck has knockout power in both hands but generally uses his outstanding wrestling skills to dominate opponents on the ground. He has proven himself as a durable fighter who brings a healthy dose of action to the cage. To date his best-known fights were against Diego Sanchez, who defeated him while a contestant on *The Ultimate Fighter*. They fought again two years later, and this time Koscheck was victorious.

10. MARK "THE SMASHING MACHINE" KERR

Mark Kerr had an incredible college wrestling career and went on to win a number of international championships before moving into MMA. A controversial figure from the start, Mark Kerr has been the subject of hundreds of news articles and even a highly acclaimed documentary. During his early MMA career, Kerr won three UFC tournaments, and it was widely believed that he would go on to become one of the greatest heavyweight fighters all time. Unfortunately Kerr encountered a series of setbacks, including chronic pain and drug issues. Still, Kerr will go down in history as a savage fighter whose athleticism upped the tempo of UFC fights and solidified ground and pound as a viable technique.

41

Gridiron Grapplers

They Loved the Football Field

Many mixed martial artists have excelled at other sports. The common sport of choice for mixed martial artists has been wrestling, given its demand for discipline, weight monitoring, grappling, and body control. Many mixed martial artists also have performed at a high level in other sports, including football. The following ten mixed martial artists pounded opponents on the football field before they ever stepped into a cage or a ring.

1. BROCK LESNAR

Brock Lesnar shocked the sporting world in 2004 when he announced that he was turning down a huge contract offer to become professional wrestling's "Next Big Thing" because he wanted to play in the National Football League. Lesnar had last played football in 1995 for Webster High School in South Dakota. He then wrestled at a junior college in North Dakota and the University of Minnesota. Glen Mason, then the University of Minnesota's football coach, tried to convince Lesnar in 2000 to play defensive end for the Golden Gophers, but Lesnar stuck with wrestling. Lesnar gave it a great effort with the NFL's Minnesota Vikings but was cut by the team before the regular season started. He had an opportunity to play in NFL Europe but passed on the offer. Fortunately for him, he has had even greater success when he moved from professional wrestling to mixed martial arts.

2. SHANE CARWIN

Before he detonated opponents in the octagon, Carwin laid them out in Division II football in college. Carwin earned All-American honors twice as a star linebacker for Western State College. In the 1997–1998 season, Carwin had more than a hundred tackles, seven sacks, and three interceptions. He played in the Senior Bowl after he graduated, hoping to attract interest from the professional level. Experts listed him as a possible NFL draft prospect; however, Carwin's draft disappointment did not derail him. He went on to obtain another degree and later found his athletic thrills in mixed martial arts, where he remains a top heavyweight contender.

3. RODNEY WALLACE

Rodney Wallace is a light heavyweight mixed martial artist who currently competes in the Ultimate Fighting Championship. Before beginning his professional MMA career, Wallace starred on the football field for Catawba College, a Division II school in Salisbury, North Carolina. Wallace earned first team All-South Atlantic Conference honors for the 2003 season. He finished his career as the school's all-time leading rusher with 3,769 career yards. During his career, he set two other school records—running twelve-hundred-yard games and making forty-one touchdowns.

4. HERBERT "WHISPER" GOODMAN

Herbert Goodman is a mixed martial artist who has competed in King of the Cage, Extreme Cagefighting, and Bellator

Before his career in MMA, Rodney Wallace was an all-conference running back at Catawba. *Courtesy of Catawba College Media Relations*

events. He has compiled a professional record of 18-10. Before turning to mixed martial arts in 2007, Goodman played two seasons with the NFL's Green Bay Packers in 2000–2001 and 2001–2002. Goodman surprised many by even making it to the NFL, as he had played college football at Graceland University, a tiny National Association of Intercollegiate Athletics (NAIA) school in Iowa. In 2002, he led NFL Europe in rushing while playing for the Scottish Claymores.

Goodman began his mixed martial arts career almost by accident. In 2007, he attended a local show to support his friend. He later told his friend that he wasn't impressed and that he could beat both his friend and his friend's opponent. A short time later Goodman made his professional debut with a knockout win in less than thirty seconds.

5. KEITH "THE DEAN OF MEAN" JARDINE

Keith Jardine is known for his unorthodox style, great nickname, fearsome appearance, and incredible toughness. He has defeated two former UFC light heavyweight champions—Chuck Liddell and Forrest Griffin—in his career. He also holds a win over the talented Brandon Vera and has battled the likes of Quinton "Rampage" Jackson, Ryan Bader, and Thiago Silva. Before he began his professional MMA career in 2001, Jardine played college football at New Mexico Highlands University, a Division II school in Las Vegas, New Mexico. There, he earned all-conference honors as a defensive end. After graduating, he served as an assistant coach at his alma mater and rose to the level of defensive coordinator.

6. MATT MITRIONE

Matt Mitrione is a UFC heavyweight fighter who achieved national exposure on season 10 of *The Ultimate Fighter*. While he did not win the show, he has earned his stripes in the UFC with victories in the octagon over both Marcus Jones and Kimbo Slice. Prior to his MMA debut, Mitrione was a standout defensive tackle for Purdue University. A three-year starter, he earned All–Big Ten honors during his junior and senior years in 1999 and 2000. He then played professionally with the NFL's New York Giants and Minnesota Vikings. He saw minimal action in his NFL career, suffering from a severe foot injury, but he did participate in nine games with the Giants in 2002 and made the Vikings' active roster in 2005.

7. HERSCHEL WALKER

Herschel Walker ranks among the greatest college football players in modern history. Walker led the University of Georgia in his freshman year to an undefeated season and the national championship. He won the Heisman Trophy in 1982 for his junior year. He left college and played football for the New Jersey Generals in the United States Football League (USFL). After leaving the defunct USFL, Walker played for several NFL teams, most notably the Dallas Cowboys and the Minnesota Vikings. He made the Pro Bowl in 1987 and 1988, rushing for more than fifteen hundred yards in 1988 and catching more than fifty passes. Meanwhile, Walker had long had an interest in the martial arts. In 2010, at the age of forty-seven, Walker made his professional mixed martial arts debut in Strikeforce by defeating Greg Nagy in the third round. In January 2011, he defeated Scott Carson via technical knockout. He looks to continue his MMA career even at his advanced age.

8. BRENDAN SCHAUB

Brendan Schaub played fullback for the University of Colorado, graduating in 2006. He then played professional football in the Arena Football League with the Utah Blaze and made the practice squad for the NFL's Buffalo Bills. In 2008, he made his professional debut in mixed martial arts. He finished second in the *The Ultimate Fighter*'s season 10 and now competes in the UFC.

9. MARCUS JONES

Marcus Jones stalked opposing quarterbacks as a star defensive lineman at the University of North Carolina and later for the NFL's Tampa Bay Buccaneers. He played seven seasons for the Buccaneers and was known as a dangerous pass rusher. In 2000, he ranked among the league's leaders in sacks with thirteen. In 2007, he made his professional debut in mixed martial arts with a win over Will Mora in the World Fighting Championships promotion. He appeared on season 10 of *The Ultimate Fighter* in 2009. During the show he defeated Mike Wessel and Darrill Schoonover to reach the semifinals, where he lost to Brendan Schaub. In his official octagon debut at the Ultimate Fighter: Heavyweights Finale in December 2009, he lost to Matt Mitrione in the second round. He announced his retirement after the bout.

10. JARED HAMMAN

Jared Hamman fights as a light heavyweight for the UFC. At the time of this writing, he has compiled an impressive professional MMA record of 13-3. Before he turned to mixed martial arts, Hamman played college football at the University of Redlands, a Division III school that competes in the Southern California Intercollegiate Athletic Conference. He earned all-conference honors in 2003 and won the team's most inspirational player award. He has also served as an assistant coach with his alma mater for several years.

42

Kickboxers in MMA

Heavyweight Kickers Turned to MMA

Leg strikes are an important aspect of mixed martial arts. Some of the greatest highlight reel knockouts in MMA history have occurred with brutal leg kicks. Consider Mirko Filipović's brutal leg kick knockout over Igor Vovchanchyn or Gabriel Gonzaga's nasty leg kick knockout over Cro Cop. The following ten heavyweights competed in professional kickboxing as well as mixed martial arts.

1. MAURICE SMITH

Maurice Smith was one of the greatest kickboxers of all time, winning more than sixty professional fights and several world titles. He won the World Kickboxing Association's heavyweight title in 1983 with a win over Travis Everett, and then proceeded on one of the most dominant streaks in all of sports by going a decade without losing a fight.

Smith shocked the mixed martial arts world in 1997 at the Ultimate Fighting Championship 14 when he used his precision striking and excellent takedown defense to defeat Mark Coleman for the UFC heavyweight championship. At the time Coleman, the godfather of ground and pound, was considered the dominant force in the sport. Smith showed that striking remained an important part of mixed martial arts.

2. MIRKO "CRO COP" FILIPOVIĆ

Cro Cop is one of the most feared strikers in MMA history. His famous saying, "Right leg, hospital; left leg, cemetery," epitomizes his power. Before making his transition to MMA in 2001, Cro Cop unleashed his devastating leg kicks in professional kickboxing. He made his pro debut in kickboxing in 1996 with a knockout victory over Jérôme Le Banner. He owns victories over Mark Hunt, Remy Bonjasky, and Peter Aerts in his kickboxing career. He could never, however, overcome Ernesto "Mr. Perfect" Hoost in kickboxing and lost three fights to the skilled Dutchman, whom many consider one of the greats of all time.

3. ALISTAIR OVEREEM

Alistair Overeem, the current Strikeforce heavyweight champion, is known for his aggressive style and devastating strikes. In 2007, he stopped Paul Buentello to win that Strikeforce belt. In 2010, he destroyed Brett "the Grim" Rogers to defend his title successfully. His striking ability also made him a great kickboxer. He has defeated the powerful Peter Aerts and the dangerous Badr Hari in K-1 competitions. Though Overeem competes in MMA now, he is still able to present a serious threat in kickboxing as well.

4. RICK "THE JET" ROUFUS

Rick Roufus has tried his hand at professional kickboxing, boxing, and mixed martial arts, but he enjoyed his greatest success in kickboxing. He won more than sixty professional matches and multiple titles in various organizations, including the International Kicking Federation and K-1. He holds a victory over Ernesto "Mr. Perfect" Hoost, one of the all-time greats in kickboxing history.

Roufus made his professional MMA debut in 2008 with a first-round loss to fellow kickboxing legend Maurice Smith in a Strikeforce event. Roufus has met with limited success in MMA but continued to fight into his early forties.

5. MARK HUNT

Mark Hunt is a heavyweight mixed martial artist who currently competes in the UFC, but this stout New Zealander of Samoan descent began his career in combat sports as a kickboxer in 1999. He competed regularly in international K-1 events, facing the likes of Jérôme Le Banner, Semmy Schilt, Ray Sefo, and Gary Goodridge in his career. In 2004, Hunt made his debut in mixed martial arts. He has defeated Mirko Cro Cop, Wanderlei Silva, and Dan Bobish in his career. He challenged (but lost to) the great Fedor Emelianenko for the Pride heavyweight championship in 2006. And after six straight losses, he defeated Chris Tuchscherer at UFC 127 in February 2011.

6. SEMMY "DUTCH DESTROYER" SCHILT

Semmy Schilt stands nearly seven feet tall and has delivered some of the greatest kick strikes in the history of combat sports. A former karate champion in Europe, Schilt has won the K-1 Grand Prix kickboxing tournament multiple times. He has defeated a virtual who's who of kicking greats, including Ernesto Hoost, Remy Bonjasky, Michael McDonald, Ray Sefo, and Jérôme Le Banner. Many consider Schilt one of the greatest kickboxers of all time.

Schilt also has competed in mixed martial arts, though he did not have as much success. In 2002, he lost consecutive fights to Fedor Emelianenko and Antônio Rodrigo Nogueira, the two greatest MMA heavyweights of the time.

Schilt has had his moments in MMA, including a stoppage of Pete Williams at UFC 31.

7. SIALA-MOU "MIGHTY MO" SILIGA

Mighty Mo is an American Samoan who has tried his hands and feet at boxing, kickboxing, and mixed martial arts. In mixed martial arts, he lost to Josh Barnett in 2010 by submission in the first round. He has had far greater success in kickboxing, where he has defeated the likes of Gary Goodridge, Remy Bonjasky, and Hong Man Choi. While taller fighters with longer limbs have outpointed him in several fights, his devastating right hand gives him a puncher's chance in any bout.

8. HONG MAN "THE TECHNO GOLIATH" CHOI

Hong Man Choi is one of the most unusual fighters in combat sports, and at seven foot two, the Korean is sometimes called the "Korean Colossus." He has performed better in kickboxing than he has in mixed martial arts. As a kickboxer, Choi has posted victories over many big-name opponents, including Semmy Schilt, Gary Goodridge, and Mighty Mo. In mixed martial arts, Choi has a losing record, though he has faced tough competition in Fedor Emelianenko and Mirko Cro Cop.

9. MICHAEL "THE BLACK SNIPER" McDONALD

Michael McDonald is a multiple K-1 World Grand Prix kickboxing champion who was born in England but reared in Jamaica and Canada. Nicknamed the Black Sniper, the muscular McDonald won the grand prix in 2002 and 2004. He has garnered more than fifty professional kickboxing wins in his career. McDonald has fought two professional MMA fights. In 2004, he fought the talented Brazilian Lyoto "the Dragon"

Machida, losing by submission. In 2008, he outpointed fellow kickboxer Rick "the Jet" Roufus.

10. GARY "BIG DADDY" GOODRIDGE

Gary Goodridge is best known for competing in mixed martial arts in the early days of the UFC and Pride. A former arm wrestling champion, Goodridge possessed powerful strikes but often fell victim to fighters with superior ground attacks. Goodridge also has fought more than thirty professional bouts as a kickboxer. Unfortunately, he has not fared well lately as a kickboxer, losing twelve of his last thirteen bouts.

43

Olympic Glory before MMA

They Won Gold Medals in the Olympics

Many professional mixed martial artists are gifted athletes; otherwise, they could not be fighting and competing in such a grueling sport. Some mixed martial artists were world-class athletes before they ever competed in mixed martial arts. A special few were good enough not only to qualify for but also to earn a gold medal in the prestigious Olympic Games before they turned to MMA. Kurt Angle, a professional wrestling star and former gold medalist, has announced his intention to fight professionally in mixed martial arts. The following ten athletes earned gold medals in wrestling, judo, or boxing and also fought professionally in mixed martial arts.

1. HIDEHIKO YOSHIDA

Hidehiko Yoshida is probably the most decorated judoka to compete in mixed martial arts. In judo, he won four world championships and competed at the 1992 and 1996 Olympics. At the 1992 Olympics in Barcelona, he won the gold medal in the 78-kilogram weight class. While he finished a disappointing fifth at the 1996 Olympic Games, he remained one of the best in the world. Yoshida also had his moments in mixed martial arts, including a sterling professional debut.

In his first fight at Pride 23, he submitted the great Don Frye. He also holds wins over Mark Hunt, David "Tank" Abbott, and Maurice Smith in his MMA career.

2. RULON GARDNER

Rulon Gardner is beloved in the annals of American sports history for his gold medal triumph at the 2000 Olympic Games in Sydney, Australia. In the gold medal match in the heavyweight division of Greco-Roman wrestling, Gardner faced the unbeatable Alexander "the Experiment" Karelin. The Russian Karelin had won gold medals at three previous Olympic Games, was undefeated in thirteen years of international competitions, and had not conceded in point in ten years. Gardner pulled the upset and won the gold medal.

In 2004, Gardner traveled to Japan for a mixed martial arts showdown with former Olympic judo gold medalist Hidehiko Yoshida. Gardner used his strength and wrestling prowess to ground out a unanimous decision victory. Gardner was not enamored with mixed martial arts, though, and never fought again.

3. RAY "MERCILESS" MERCER

Ray Mercer is best known for his distinguished professional boxing career, including his devastating knockout of Tommy Morrison to win the World Boxing Organization's world heavyweight championship. Some forget that Mercer had a distinguished amateur career in boxing, culminating in a gold medal at the 1988 Olympic Games in Seoul. In the gold medal match, he dispatched South Korean Baik Hyun-Man in the first round. Mercer turned pro in mixed martial arts with mixed results. He infamously lost to Kimbo Slice via guillotine choke, but he redeemed himself with a devastating nine-second knockout of former Ultimate Fighting Championship heavyweight champion Tim Sylvia.

4. KEVIN JACKSON

Kevin Jackson, the current wrestling coach at Iowa State University, captured the sport's highest honors at the 1992 Barcelona Olympics. He won the gold medal in freestyle wrestling in the 82-kilogram division. After his wrestling career ended, Jackson turned his attention to mixed martial arts. He won his first three bouts, including the UFC's middleweight tournament at UFC 14 in July 1997 after he stopped Todd Butler and Tony Fryklund. He suffered a setback, however, when he faced the great Frank Shamrock at another UFC event in December 1997. Shamrock submitted him in only sixteen seconds.

5. MARK SCHULTZ

Mark Schultz, along with his brother Dave, won a gold medal in freestyle wrestling at the 1984 Olympics in Los Angeles. Years later and on short notice, Schultz entered the octagon at UFC 9 to face the powerful Gary Goodridge, a dangerous striker. Dave Beneteau had been scheduled to square off against Goodridge but was sidelined with a broken hand. Schultz, who had received some training from the great Rickson Gracie, stepped in and, to the surprise of many, won the fight. He used his superior wrestling skills to score numerous takedowns and eventually won the bout. He went on to coach wrestling at Brigham Young University, until 2000. In 2003, he was submitted in a bout by Leopoldo Montenegro.

6. PAWEL NASTULA

Poland's Pawel Nastula, a decorated judo practitioner, was the world's best in his division in the mid- to late 1990s. He was the judo world champion in 1995 and 1997, but his highest glory was winning the gold medal in judo at the 1996 Olympic Games in Atlanta. He defeated South Korea's Min Soo Kim in the gold medal match. Unfortunately, Nastula's foray into mixed martial arts was not as successful when he turned professional in 2005. He compiled a professional mixed martial record of only 1-4, losing to Antônio Rodrigo Nogueira, Aleksander Emelianenko, Josh Barnett, and Dongi Yang.

7. KENNY MONDAY

Kenny Monday was one of the most decorated American wrestlers ever, accumulating both national and international awards. He competed in three different Olympic Games—1988, 1992, and 1996—as a freestyle wrestler. He garnered a gold medal at the 1988 Olympics in Seoul and a silver medal at the 1992 Olympics in Barcelona. After competing at the 1996 Olympic Games, Monday turned to mixed martial arts. In 1997, he challenged John Lewis in an Extreme Fighting promotion. He stopped Lewis in the second round.

8. SATOSHI ISHII

Satoshi Ishii, a gifted practitioner of judo from Japan, garnered a gold medal at the 2008 Olympics in Beijing, China. In December 2009, he made his professional MMA debut against fellow judoka and gold medalist Hidehiko Yoshida. Ishii lost a unanimous decision, falling to his more experienced countryman. However, he rebounded in 2010 with four victories and continues to improve. He recently sparred with Brazilian great Anderson Silva and had hoped to reach the highest pinnacles of MMA, just as he did in judo. In April of

2011, however, he announced he was leaving the sport to return to judo competition.

9. MAKOTO TAKIMOTO

Makoto Takimoto may not receive the press that his compatriots Hidehiko Yoshida and Satoshi Ishii enjoy, but he has similar credentials. Takimoto won a gold medal at the 2000 Sydney Olympics in the 81-kilogram division. He turned pro in mixed martial arts in 2004 with mixed results. He owns a victory over Murilo Bustamante and won his last two fights in Sengoku events before initially announcing his retirement in April 2009 at the age of thirty-five. He fought once more in September 2009. He posted a career record of 6-5.

10. ISTVAN MAJOROS

At the 2004 Olympic Games in Athens, Hungary's Istvan Majoros won a gold medal in Greco-Roman wrestling in the bantamweight division. He did not strike gold in mixed martial arts, however, when he squared off against dangerous Japanese striker Norifumi Yamamato at a K-1 MMA event in December 2006. Yamamoto stopped Majoros in the first round, and Majoros could not deal with Yamamoto's superior striking. It was his one and only professional MMA fight.

MMA Standouts

44

Greatest Grapplers
in MMA

Submission Specialists Who
Dominate on the Ground

It was the sport of mixed martial arts that brought submission grappling to the forefront of modern fighting systems. Without MMA, submission grappling would still be virtually unknown in the United States, and there can be no doubt that submission grappling has transformed the way in which combatants from all walks of life view fighting. Not only has submission grappling changed the nature of professional competition, it has even changed the way law enforcement and military personnel train for combat. Following is a list of some of the best submission grapplers to have ever fought in no-holds-barred competition, many of whom went on to become MMA champions.

1. RICKSON GRACIE
Rickson Gracie never fought in the Ultimate Fighting Championship, but members of the Gracie family credit him as being their best fighter. Helio's and Rolls's longtime student, Rickson became famous in Brazil when he defeated famed Brazilian fighter Casemiro "Rei Zulu" Nascimento Martins under vale tudo rules. During his younger years Rickson

spent nearly two decades as the no-weight world jiu-jitsu champion. During the mid-1990s he went on to showcase his abilities in Vale Tudo Japan, where he dominated all competition. Even though Rickson's record of 400-0 has been called into question, every grappler who has faced him, regardless of background, claims that he's the best Brazilian jiu-jitsu practitioner ever to walk the face of the earth.

2. WALLID "PARAÍBA" ISMAIL

Retired since 2002, Ismail was a student of Carlson Gracie's. He made a name for himself in mixed martial arts during the mid-1990s fighting in both Japan and Brazil and later in the UFC. Not exactly a household name in the United States, Ismail is well known in Brazil because he defeated four members of the Gracie family in competition: Royce, Ralph, Renzo, and Ryan. His most publicized match was against Royce, where he agreed to no time limits and loss only by submission. Ismail defeated Royce soundly and has agreed to a rematch only if he is paid an enormous sum of money.

3. CARLOS "THE RONIN" NEWTON

Although still fairly young, Newton has been a name in mixed martial arts since his first professional fight in 1996. Through the years he has competed against a number of famous combatants, including Matt Hughes, Renzo Gracie, and Pat Miletich, while winning the UFC welterweight belt along the way. With his athletic, fluid style, Newton has always been a crowd favorite, especially in Japan. His most intriguing fight was his first bout against Matt Hughes. Newton had Hughes in a triangle choke, but Hughes slammed Newton on the mat, knocking him out. It was later noticed that at the time of the slam Hughes was also unconscious and what had appeared to be a well-timed technique was in fact an uncontrolled fall.

4. RICCO "SUAVE" RODRIGUEZ

Ricco Rodriguez gained initial fame when he became one of the first Americans to win a title at the Brazilian jiu-jitsu world championship. With more than fifty fights under his belt, Rodriguez has had a long career and has fought all over the world. Most fans, however, will remember him from a slew of appearances in the UFC from 2001 to 2003. During that time he fought many of the great fighters of the era, even defeating Andrei Arlovski, Randy Couture, and Pete Williams. His career took a turn for the worse went he ran into Tim Sylvia, who knocked him out in the first round of their match. Since then his career has had its up and downs, but a string of recent victories suggests he may once again enter the UFC octagon.

5. JEFF "THE SNOWMAN" MONSON

To say that Jeff Monson is an accomplished grappler is an understatement. For almost ten years Monson has made it a point to enter every grappling event imaginable, an endeavor that resulted in a slew of national and international titles. Looking more like a cartoon character than a civilized human being, Monson sports tattoos advertising his anarchic worldview. A fan favorite by virtue of his unique look, Monson has also made the news because of his political ideology as well as his fighting ability. In 2009, for instance, Monson was arrested for vandalizing the Washington State Capitol with graffiti anti-establishment clichés. He was forced to pay $20,000 in compensation to the state and spent ninety days on work release. In April 2011, he won the Strength and Honor heavyweight championship, but lost a bout with Daniel Cormier, by decision, in June 2011 in a Strikeforce event.

6. FEDOR "THE LAST EMPEROR" EMELIANENKO

No list of great grapplers would be complete without paying

homage to Fedor Emelianenko. A combat sambo specialist who has won an untold number of competitions and tournaments, Emelianenko is also an experienced judoka and has even won the Russian National Judo Championship. Unlike many of the better-known MMA champions, Emelianenko has fought in just about every major promotion other than the UFC. Most experts consider him to be the best pound-for-pound MMA fighter ever. Emelianenko has the uncanny ability to do the right thing at the right time, regardless of how battered and hurt he is. His grappling ability defies explanation, in that he ignores many of the principles of Brazilian jiu-jitsu, including most guard work, and tends to fight from his back in a distinctly "Russian" manner. When combined with his unique striking, these grappling attributes make him one of the most feared fighters in mixed martial arts.

7. B. J. "THE PRODIGY" PENN

Few Americans have collected the submission grappling accolades that Penn has throughout his entire career. He earned his nickname the Prodigy and his black belt in Brazilian jiu-jitsu in an unheard-of three years as a result of his uncanny ability on the ground. His grappling skills are matched by his boxing ability, a combination that puts him in that rare category of martial artists who can meaningfully transition through fighting ranges. Penn's MMA accomplishments need not be recounted here; suffice it to say that he will go down in history as one of MMA's most accomplished and respected grapplers.

8. HIDEHIKO YOSHIDA

There are all kinds of grappling in the world, and before Brazilian jiu-jitsu became widespread in North America, judo dominated the combat grappling scene. Yoshida is arguably

Here David Martinez counters an armbar by slamming his opponent on his head. *United States Marine Corps*

the most accomplished judoka to ever step into the cage, with four world championships and an Olympic gold to his record. Not nearly as widely recognized as other fighters from his era are, Yoshida is nonetheless a highly respected figure in the MMA community. Early in his career Yoshida beat veterans Don Frye and Royce Gracie. Yoshida had a rematch with Gracie and fought him to a draw, but most who viewed the fight believed that Yoshida had soundly defeated Gracie.

9. FRANK "THE LEGEND" SHAMROCK

The name "Shamrock" will forever be enmeshed with the beginnings of MMA in North America. Frank Shamrock, the younger, adopted brother of the UFC veteran Ken Shamrock, came to MMA without any traditional martial arts training. Being the younger brother of a legend helps, however, and Frank soon began his MMA career. Frank goes down in history as a grappling legend because he has consistently shown up many grappling greats, including Renzo Gracie, to whom he lost by disqualification, and Cesar Gracie, whose submission attempts he repeatedly stuffed and whom he beat by a knockout. Shamrock's grappling skill stands in sharp contrast to most traditional fighters. He's strong, fast, and durable but has an ease of motion that few in MMA can emulate. When combined with good footwork and the dexterity of an acrobat, Shamrock makes some of his less dynamic opponents look downright comical.

10. MARIO "ZEN MACHINE" SPERRY

Another Brazilian who began grappling at an early age, Sperry has at least a dozen grappling championships under his belt, including eight at the world level. He is also a black belt under Carlson Gracie. His best amateur grappling win was over Royler Gracie, a victory that made him a household name in Brazil. He went on to have a substantial professional MMA career, defeating numerous BJJ stalwarts and gaining a submission victory over Vernon White. Sperry's impact on MMA continues even though his own fighting career has slowed down, as he, along with several BJJ personalities, went on to found the influential American Top Team.

45
Brains and Brawn
Highly Educated Mixed Martial Artists

For years the common assumption of a mixed martial artist was that of a barroom brawler who knew how to use his hands, feet, and perhaps other body parts but not his brain. Nothing could be further from the truth, as many mixed martial artists are highly educated individuals who have college, master's, and professional degrees. The following ten individuals are also known for their educational accomplishments.

1. NICK THOMPSON
Nick Thompson tries to lay down the law on his opponents, both in his vocation and in the sport of mixed martial arts. This veteran of more than fifty professional MMA fights is an intriguing person. A college wrestler at the University of Wisconsin, Thompson turned pro in 2003 and lost three of his first four fights. He gained more experience and began imposing his will on opponents. He fought twice in the Ultimate Fighting Championship, going 1-1 in the octagon. He has defeated the likes of Paul Daley and Josh Neer. Amazingly, he continued a professional MMA career while attending law school at the University of Minnesota. In 2008, a few days before taking the bar exam, Thompson fought Jake Shields

for the Elite XC welterweight championship. Though he lost the fight, he later found out that he had passed the Minnesota bar exam. He later joined a law firm in Wisconsin.

2. CHRISTIAN WELLISCH

This Hungarian-born heavyweight has as much brain as brawn, and that's saying a great deal since he tips the scales at more than 240 pounds. His family moved from Budapest to California when he was an eighth grader. He proceeded to graduate from Monterey High School, earned an undergraduate degree in philosophy from San Jose State, and matriculated to law school at McGeorge School of Law at Pacific University. He passed the bar exam in 2007 and has his own law office in Campbell, California.

3. RICH FRANKLIN

Rich Franklin, the former UFC middleweight champion, has both a college degree and a master's degree to his credit. He graduated from the University of Cincinnati with a degree in mathematics and earned a master's degree in education there as well. He later taught math at Oak Hills High School in Cincinnati. He also coauthored the book *The Complete Idiot's Guide to Ultimate Fighting*.

4. SHANE CARWIN

Shane Carwin has a dynamite right hand, knocking out in the first minute of the first round nearly every opponent he has faced in his young career. In July 2010, he nearly knocked out UFC heavyweight champion Brock Lesnar to capture the crown. While he harnesses undeniable power, Carwin also possesses a serious intellect. He earned an undergraduate degree in environmental technology from Western State College in Colorado. He then added a mechanical engineering degree from the Colorado School of Mines. He worked as an engineer for the North Weld County Water District, designing hydraulic models.

5. **KENNY FLORIAN**
Kenny Florian is a top UFC lightweight who challenged B. J. Penn for the crown in 2010. Though he lost that bout, Florian has defeated a bevy of contenders in his career. He is known for his dedication to his craft, sharp elbow strikes, and excellent submission skills. Florian also achieved well academically, earning a degree in communications from Boston College. He made the dean's list in college and earned Big East All-Star Academic status as a soccer player.

6. **EFRAIN ESCUDERO**
Efrain Escudero, who has competed in the UFC and won season 8 of *The Ultimate Fighter*, takes his education in and out of the cage seriously. In 2010, he earned his undergraduate degree in criminal justice from Grand Canyon University. He plans to pursue a master's degree in sociology. "School's actually helped me with my fighting," he told writer Mike Chiappetta in a piece for *Fanhouse*. "Overall, it kept me focused and out of trouble."

7. **TERRY MARTIN**
Terry Martin is an exciting striker who has competed at the highest levels of the sport, such as the UFC, Strikeforce, and Affliction. He has battled Chris Leben, Marvin Eastman, and Ivan Salaverry in the octagon. Martin also has a great life story, as he overcame gang activity and juvenile delinquency to become a real role model for inner-city youths and others. He was the first member of his family to graduate from high school. Martin later earned a master's degree in psychology

from Concordia University Chicago and is working toward a doctorate from the Adler School of Professional Psychology.

8. JEFF MONSON

Jeff Monson is a skilled grappler known for his excellent wrestling and submission skills. While he sometimes has garnered headlines for his leftist political views, Monson has accomplished much inside and outside the cage. In his MMA career, he once won sixteen fights in a row and challenged for the UFC heavyweight championship, dropping a decision to champion Tim Sylvia. He also has won the prestigious Abu Dhabi Submission Wrestling World Championship. Outside the cage, Monson earned an undergraduate degree from the University of Illinois at Urbana-Champaign and a master's degree both in psychology from the University of Minnesota.

9. DAVID GRIFFIN

David Griffin is a Charleston, South Carolina, firefighter during the day but a mixed martial artist by night. Years earlier Griffin graduated from the Citadel with his college degree. But, as a firefighter, he advanced his education by earning a master's degree. He plans to pursue a doctorate degree in education with a goal of becoming a full-time college professor. In his pro debut, Griffin went the distance with former UFC fighter Houston Alexander but lost the decision.

10. BRYAN VETELL

Bryan Vetell competed as a heavyweight in mixed martial arts, fighting bouts with both Roy Nelson and Ben Rothwell in the International Fight League. Vetell graduated from Hofstra University, where he majored in philosophy. He was working on his master's degree with visions of law school in his future when the lure of professional mixed martial arts pulled him into the fight scene.

46

Combat Craziness

Crazy Moments in MMA History

Mixed martial arts fighters tend to be dynamic, powerful, and a little crazy. While most fights tend to fall within the norm, there are always those fighters who bring a little bit of the unknown with them every time they enter the cage. Without these fighters MMA would be much less entertaining, and thousands of fans would probably go back to watching professional wrestling. The following lists memorable fighters and events—all of which definitely fall outside of the norm—that make MMA a more engrossing sport.

1. SCOTT "HANDS OF STEEL" SMITH VS. PETE "DRAGO" SELL

The television show *The Ultimate Fighter* has seen many unique fighters and a number of entertaining matches. Few bouts, however, can compare to the battle between Scott Smith and Pete Sell in season 4. The opponents were long-time friends who came out throwing bombs in what turned out to be a seesaw match. The action only slowed down when the fighters mutually decided that a few random high fives were in order even though they were trying to beat each other's heads in. The striking game almost came to an abrupt end when Sell landed a perfect left hook to Smith's floating ribs. Wincing in pain, Smith started retreating and looked as if he was about to go down. Sell rushed in for the kill only to eat a perfectly timed straight right that knocked him unconscious. Smith collapsed after throwing the telling shot, with his defeated opponent seemingly in far better condition than he was.

2. KEEGAN MARSHALL VS. MARCUS "LELO" AURELIO

Capoeira is an African martial art that slaves developed to resemble a dance so that their overseers wouldn't realize that they were training for combat. Acrobatic and expressive, Capoeira is rarely seen in the ring because it is a less direct approach to fighting than more traditional methods. The beautiful nature of the art, however, has attracted a few notable fighters so that on occasion prominent fighters use some elements of the system in their less-demanding matches. Marcus Aurelio's fight against Keegan Marshall saw the best example of Capoeira's use in the ring. As the match began, Auerlio's unorthodox style looked particularly ineffective and seemed to demand an inordinate amount of energy. Confused by the nature of the attack, Marshall slowly retreated toward his corner only to get caught with a double spinning back kick just as he hit the ropes. The second kick connected with an audible crack, and Marshall collapsed on the floor, the victim of what was perhaps the most elegant kick ever thrown in mixed martial arts history.

3. CHARLES "KRAZY HORSE" BENNETT

Charles Bennett didn't have to actually fight anyone to make this list. A showman by nature, Bennett does everything possible to get audience attention, from doing gymnastics off the top of the cage to throwing in an assortment of odd techniques, including using the ropes to pull off flying kicks. Although his bizarre persona and seemingly disrespectful attitude toward his opponent have earned the fans' ire, his unconventional antics have served him well in the ring against more orthodox opponents. Unfortunately, Bennett's behavior is just as strange outside the ring as it is inside it, and his antics have landed him in the loving arms of the law more than twenty times.

4. TOM "THE FILTHY MAULER" LAWLOR

Dancing and fighting seem to go together. Many fighters enter the ring while dancing to their favorite tunes, and some fighters even put on a pretty good floor show. Tom Lawlor is one weird fighter who combines dancing with his energetic personality and taste for the bizarre. Unlike other fighters who rely on pyrotechnics and professional entertainers to liven up their shows, Lawlor likes to surround himself with low-budget dancers and choreographs his own dance routines. To date Lawlor has had a number of awesome entrances. His best entrance was at Dream 9, where, festooned in a shiny jumpsuit and surrounded by Japanese schoolgirls, Lawlor hit the techno button and boogied his way to the ring as only a supremely confident human being could.

5. HEATH "THE TEXAS CRAZY HORSE" HERRING VS. YOSHIHIRO NAKAO

Mixed martial arts is one of the manliest sports ever devised. Locker room humor aside, any suggestion of overly aggressive male-on-male affection is strictly frowned upon because it can easily disrupt a gym. Granted, there are times when off-color humor is called for and widely accepted among friends, but sometimes things go a little bit too far, which is what happened at K-1's Dynamite show back in 2005. During the prefight stare down of what was supposed to be the evening's top bout, Yoshihiro Nakao leaned forward and gave Heath Herring a kiss on the lips. Herring retaliated with a punch that knocked Nakao unconscious. There was a brief skirmish between the corners, after which Herring was disqualified for throwing the foul punch. After K-1 officials determined that the kiss was also a foul tactic, they later changed the decision to a no contest, effectively disqualifying both opponents.

6. TIM "THE MAINE-IAC" SYLVIA VS. ASSUERIO SILVA

Professional fighters are a unique breed. Whether bleeding, injured, or sick, elite fighters will always answer the call of the bell, even if it means fighting at a disadvantage. Tim Sylvia is one of the most dominant heavyweight champions in Ultimate Fighting Championship history, yet he has been the subject of intense controversy. From accusations of poor conditioning to drug use and questionable grappling skills, Sylvia has nonetheless proven his durability against some of the best heavyweight fighters in MMA history.

When Sylvia took on Assuerio at the UFC Ultimate Fight Night 3, he was looking for a dominant victory in order to secure a rematch against Andrei Arlovski, who had taken his belt away a few months earlier. Sylvia came into the ring looking healthy and confident, but in reality he was suffering from an intestinal bug and had a high fever. As the fight progressed, Sylvia looked fine despite his illness, and he was never in any real trouble. Still, at some point during the match, fans noticed that Sylvia's shorts had taken on an unexpected color. It seems that not only did Sylvia have a fever, but he also had explosive diarrhea. Lesser men would have never stepped into the ring to begin with or would have thrown in the towel after soiling themselves, but not Sylvia. He fought most of match with a load in his pants and went on to win by unanimous decision.

7. QUINTON "RAMPAGE" JACKSON VS. RICARDO "BRAZILIAN TIGER" ARONA

With the release of the new *A-Team* movie, Quinton Jackson may soon be better known for his acting ability than his fighting prowess, but his legions of MMA fans will always remember him as a freakishly strong athlete who almost single-handedly upped the intensity level of the entire sport. For more than a decade, Jackson has battled the best fighters in half a dozen promotions and done so with a style that other fighters have sought to emulate. Even though Jackson has fought several legendary battles, one of his most unique victories came when he confronted the famed grappler Ricardo Arona on a Pride ticket in 2004. The standing game was nearly even, with Arona eating Jackson's punches and Jackson getting peppered with leg kicks. When the fight went to the ground, Arona was on the bottom and threw a series of upkicks, nearly knocking Jackson unconscious before pulling him back into the guard. Arona attempted submission after submission and eventually locked in a tight triangle choke. Jackson, however, had other ideas. Posturing up, the impressively athletic Jackson pulled Arona up *over* his head and smashed him back down in what is probably the best slam in all of MMA history. Arona was knocked out, and Jackson won the match.

8. ANDERSON "THE SPIDER" SILVA VS. RYO CHONAN

Nobody ever expects Anderson Silva to lose. As the best striker in all of mixed martial arts, Silva has a solid reputation for not just beating his opponents but making them look bad in the process. With the arms of a professional basketball player attached to a six-foot-two body, Silva is fast enough to keep opponents out of range and on the defensive for entire fights. And that is exactly what happened when he fought

Ryo Chonan. Not only did Silva pummel Chonan, but he did it in the same manner that three-year-olds beat up a piñata at a birthday party. For three rounds Chonan was beaten from one end of the ring to the other without him ever mounting an effective offense. Then, in the middle of the third round, Chonan stepped forward, pulled off a flying leg scissors, and transitioned into a heel hook, submitting Silva in less than three seconds. The entire MMA community was stunned. Chonan had shown once again that there is no such thing as an unbeatable champion.

9. YVES "THE TEXAS GUNSLINGER" EDWARDS VS. JOSH THOMPSON

There is one truism that everyone should understand about fighting: Never turn your back on your opponent. This cardinal rule makes just as much sense in the street as it does in the ring. UFC regulations ban striking to the back of the head, and on occasion fighters make the mistake of giving up their back in order to save their face.

When Edwards took on Thompson, everyone expected Thompson would win, but that isn't what happened. At the end of the first round, Thompson appeared lethargic and unconcerned, allowing his opponent to outwork him. After being tripped to the ground during an aborted slam, Thompson stood up with Edward's arms wrapped around his waist. Instead of immediately spinning around and locking up his opponent, Thompson decided to walk toward the opposite side of the ring. When Thompson belatedly tried to break the hold and turn around, Edwards threw an amazing leaping head kick that knocked him out cold. The fight was over, and MMA fans suddenly had another spectacular kick to turn into a screen saver.

10. TYLER BRYAN VS. SHAWN PARKER

This match is one of those fights that defies explanation. The bout occurred in 2008 at Legends of Fighting 25: Breaking Point. The fighters in question certainly weren't legends before their bout, but once the bout was over, both became instant Internet stars. The match began with the fighters appearing agitated and jumpy as they entered the cage. When the bell rang, they ran toward each other, exchanging two kicks. At eight seconds into the match, just as the action looked as though it was really going to get started, the fighters threw identical straight right hands that both connected, instantaneously knocking each other out. The fight was ruled a no contest, and the Legends of Fighting promotion suddenly received loads of free publicity as e-mail inboxes across the country became deluged with links to the video of this unusual bout.

47

Crazy Kickers

Hardest Kickers of the MMA

Most high-level professional boxers have avoided stepping into the cage because the paychecks in mixed martial arts can't compete with what they make in the world of boxing. The same cannot be said for professional kickboxers, who view the money to be made in MMA as a gold mine waiting to be tapped. So while the best punchers in the world tend to stick to the squared circle, the best kickers have no qualms about entering the cage, putting their striking skills to good use, and leveling the competition.

1. MIRKO "CRO COP" FILIPOVIĆ

Perhaps the best-known professional kicker in the world, Cro Cop has made a career out of kicking adversaries in the head the way that other people kick soccer balls. With wins over some of the most experienced fighters in MMA history, Cro Cop combines effective striking with a takedown defense that would make most Olympic wrestling coaches proud. Beginning his career in 1996 as a kickboxer fighting in the K-1 World Grand Prix, Cro Cop had a significant win over Jérôme Le Banner only to be derailed by the legendary Ernesto Hoost. Since then Cro Cop has gone on to have a hit-or-miss fighting career, battling many of the biggest names in mixed martial arts while jumping from one fight promotion to the next. In contrast with most professional fighters, who tend not to have serious jobs, Cro Cop is active in a variety of other venues including working as a counterterrorism officer and even serving in Croatia's Parliament.

2. CUNG LE

Born in South Vietnam but a longtime resident of the United States, Cung Le is an undefeated kickboxer and an established Sanshou competitor. Making his mixed martial arts debut in Strikeforce: Shamrock vs. Gracie, Le devastated his opponent by knocking him out in the first round. Kicking with the same dexterity that most fighters use to throw punches, Le attacks from all angles by packing a tremendous amount of power into the most innocuous strikes. A skilled grappler who is nearly as good with his hands as he is with his feet, Le always falls back on the same strategy when he feels threatened and kicks the hell out of whoever is in front of him. Perhaps the best example of this strategy was Le's fight against Frank Shamrock, when Shamrock used his superior grappling skills to ram Le into the cage at the end of the first round. Feeling himself at a disadvantage, Le quickly began playing a more multidimensional game by interspersing his hand strikes with powerful and disruptive kicks. At the end of the third round, a battered Shamrock successfully blocked one of Le's high kicks but ended up with a broken arm as a result. Le took the victory when Shamrock couldn't meet the bell.

3. THIAGO "PITBULL" ALVES

Considered by some to be the best kicker in his weight class, Alves is a Brazilian mixed martial artist who has a strong background in Muay Thai. A member of the ever-expanding

American Top Team, Alves has the uncanny ability to defend against takedowns while using his dominant striking skills to finish some of MMA's most feared grapplers. Perhaps not as highly skilled on the ground as some of his colleagues are, Alves combines an intense stand-up game with fast transitions to control the pace of the fight. During his 2008 fight against Matt Hughes, Alves pummeled the former champion while consistently stuffing his takedown attempts, eventually finishing the match with a beautifully executed flying knee to his opponent's face.

4. ANDERSON "THE SPIDER" SILVA

One of the most skilled and creative strikers in MMA, Silva has broken out of his traditional Muay Thai roots by adding advanced footwork and techniques from a variety of martial disciplines to meet competitive demands. Moving more like a skilled Savate practitioner than a Muay Thai fighter, Silva's dynamic striking abilities are complemented by his superb grappling skills, which he has used to stalemate such accomplished grapplers as Carlos Newton and Olympic wrestler Dan Henderson. Anderson Silva has fought just about everyone worth fighting in his weight class and is one of the few strikers in MMA who is considered technical enough to be a serious professional boxer.

5. PEDRO "THE ROCK" RIZZO

Known for his absurdly powerful low-line kicks, Rizzo sports a professional kickboxing record of more than thirty-one fights and *thirty knockouts*. He has wins over some of MMA's most stalwart warriors, including Mark Coleman and Dan Severn. It should be no surprise that Rizzo, with legs like tree trunks, is credited as being the hardest kicker in MMA, but it may surprise some to know that he rarely uses his incredible kicking ability in his bouts. Often relying more on his heavy hands than on his powerful legs, Rizzo tends to set up his opponents with leg strikes before following them up with punches to the head. Perhaps his two most notable kicking accomplishments are pounding Mark Coleman's legs until they were black and blue and launching a vicious head kick that left Andrei Arlovski open to a combination that put him on the canvas.

6. MAURICIO "SHOGUN" RUA

Another MMA fighter with a background in Muay Thai, Shogun has earned a well-deserved reputation as a deadly kicker. Generally forgoing anything but power shots, Shogun isn't afraid to throw anything that he thinks will knock an opponent out. More often than not, he uses a combination of low and high kicks, as exemplified by his performance against Quinton "Rampage" Jackson. During the fight Shogun continually peppered Jackson with a combination of kicks and knees, spending four minutes bouncing Jackson around the ring in the clinch before defeating him with a series of soccer kicks to the head.

7. BAS "EL GUAPO" RUTTEN

Easily the most recognizable figure in MMA, Bas Rutten is also known as one of the best kickers ever to enter the octagon. With a background in the traditional styles of Tae Kwon Do and Kyokushin karate, he is also an accomplished Muay Thai fighter. Just like Mike Tyson, Rutten's strikes were considered so powerful that many opponents were often intimidated before they got into the ring and became preoccupied with defense rather than offense. Not only is Rutten known for his powerful striking but he also has exceptional accuracy, particularly with his uncanny ability to target the liver specifically. It was, in fact, a liver shot that landed him the Ultimate Fighting Championship heavyweight championship when he knocked the steam out of former Olympic wrestler Kevin Randleman at UFC 20.

8. PETER "THE DUTCH LUMBERJACK" AERTS

Not exactly known for a stellar MMA career, Peter Aerts is certainly one of the most effective kickers to ever enter no-holds-barred competition. With a kickboxing record of 102 wins and 77 knockouts, Aerts is likely the most seasoned striker ever to enter MMA competition. He fought in the K-1 World Grand Prix more than fifteen times and battled such MMA stalwarts as Semmy Schilt, Bob Sapp, and Alistair Overeem. He has repeatedly displayed his ability to knock out extremely tough opponents with a deceptive-looking, rear roundhouse kick that doesn't look particularly threatening but packs a tremendous amount of power.

9. KEITH "THE DEAN OF MEAN" JARDINE

Another fighter known for his low-kick abilities, Jardine is also widely recognized as one of the strangest people in MMA. He is unusual in that he is more than willing to try just about every unorthodox technique imaginable, yet he still manages to put together some of the slickest punching and kicking combinations in the sport. The best example of his kicking ability was in UFC 76 when he was able to kick Chuck Liddell's left thigh and midsection at will. Blessed with a body that resembles a pile of wet rags stuffed into a sock, Jardine has nevertheless proven himself to be a dynamic competitor whose relaxed physique gives him a certain springiness that other fighters have a difficult time overcoming.

10. **PATRICK "HD" BARRY**

Not only is Barry a feared kickboxer, he is also an accomplished Sanshou competitor and was a silver medalist at the Kung Fu World Championships. Barry has also competed in the K-1 World Championships and even made an appearance in Chuck Norris's World Combat League. In 2008 he made his debut in the UFC, wrecking his first opponent with a nicely timed low kick to the knee. Barry is unusual for a heavyweight in that he can develop fluid cadence with his kicking, and with legs the size of small trees, he has shown time and again that he has the power to dominate his opponents.

Selected Bibliography

Arvantis, Jim. *The First Martial Art: Pankration from Myths to Modern Times*. Edited by Jon Thibault and Jeannine Santiago. Valencia, CA: Black Belt Books, 2009.

Buffong, Jonathan, and Brenda Downes. *Warriors of the Cage: The UK's Mixed Martial Arts Fight Club*. London: Pennant Books, 2009.

Couture, Randy. *Becoming the Natural: My Life In and Out of the Cage*. With Loretta Hunt. New York: Simon Spotlight Entertainment, 2009.

Crigger, Kelly. *Title Shot: Into the Shark Tank of Mixed Martial Arts*. Hong Kong, China: Victory Belt Publishing, 2008.

Franklin, Rich, and Jon F. Merz. *The Complete Idiot's Guide to Ultimate Fighting*. New York: Alpha Books, 2007.

Gentry, Clyde. *No Holds Barred: Ultimate Fighting and the Martial Arts Revolution*. London: Milo Books, 2002.

Gracie, Helio. *Gracie Jiu-Jitsu*. Valencia, CA: Black Belt Books, 2006.

Hudson, David L., Jr. *Combat Sports: An Encyclopedia of Wrestling, Fighting, and Mixed Martial Arts*. Santa Barbara, CA: Greenwood Press, 2009.

Hughes, Matt. *Made in America: The Most Dominant Champion in UFC History*. With Michael Malice. New York. Simon Spotlight Entertainment, 2008.

Jackson, Greg, and Kelly Crigger. *Jackson's Mixed Martial Arts: The Stand Up Game*. Hong Kong, China: Victory Belt Publishing, 2009.

Krakoff, Reed. *Fighter: The Fighters of the UFC*. New York: Viking Studio, 2008.

Krauss, Eric, Bret Aita, and Bob Shamrock. *Brawl: A Behind-the-Scenes Look at Mixed Martial Arts*. Toronto: ECW Press, 2002.

Lee, Bruce. *The Tao of Jeet Kune Do*. Burbank, CA: Ohara Publications, 1975.

Lerma, Chad. *Kajukenbo Kenpo-Karate: George W. Iversen Method*. Cannon Beach, OR: Blue Lotus Publishers, 2008.

Liddell, Chuck. *Iceman: My Fighting Life*. With Chad Millman. New York: Dutton, 2008.

Machida, Lyoto. *Machida Karate-Do Mixed Martial Arts Techniques*. With Glen Cordoza. Hong Kong, China: Victory Belt Publishing, 2010.

MacKinnon, Timothy J. *Never: Jens Pulver and the Wednesday Group That Will Change the World*. Bloomington, IN: iUniverse, 2007.

Mayeda, David T., and David E. Ching. *Fighting for Acceptance: Mixed Martial Artists and Violence in American Society*. Bloomington, IN: iUniverse, Inc., 2008.

Ortiz, Tito. *This Is Gonna Hurt: The Life of a Mixed Martial Arts Champion*. With Marc Shapiro. New York: Simon Spotlight Entertainment, 2008.

Penn, B. J. *Why I Fight: The Belt Is Just an Accessory*. With David Weintraub. New York: William Morrow, 2010.

———. *Mixed Martial Arts: The Book of Knowledge*. With Glen Cordoza and Erich Krauss. Hong Kong, China: Victory Belt Publishing, 2007.

Pulver, Jens. *Little Evil: One Ultimate Fighter's Rise to the Top*. With Erich Krauss. Toronto: ECW Press, 2003.

Shamrock, Frank. *Mixed Martial Arts for Dummies*. With Mary Van Note. Indianapolis: Wiley Publishing, 2009.

Shamrock, Ken. *Beyond the Lion's Den: The Life, the Fights, the Techniques.* With Erich Krauss. North Clarendon, VT: Tuttle Publishing, 2005.

Shamrock, Ken, and Richard Hanner. *Inside the Lion's Den: The Life and Submission Fighting System of Ken Shamrock.* Boston: Tuttle Publishing, 1998.

Sheridan, Sam. *A Fighter's Heart: One Man's Journey Through the World of Fighting.* New York: Atlantic Monthly Press, 2007.

Snowden, Jonathan. *Total MMA: Inside Ultimate Fighting.* Toronto: ECW Press, 2008.

Stann, Brian. *Heart for the Fight: A Marine Hero's Journey from Battlefields of Iraq to Mixed Martial Arts Champion.* With John R. Bruning. Minneapolis: MBI Publishing, 2010.

Wall, Jeremy. *UFC's Ultimate Warriors: The Top 10.* Toronto: ECW Press, 2005.

Wertheim, Jon L. *Blood in the Cage: Mixed Martial Arts, Pat Miletich, and the Furious Rise of the UFC.* Boston: Houghton Mifflin Harcourt, 2009.

Whiting, Jim. *Inside the Cage: The Greatest Fights of Mixed Martial Arts.* Mankato, MN: Capstone Press, 2010.

Index

Abbott, David ("Tank") 112, 130, 136, 178, 207, 222, **224–25**, 262
Abe, Hiroyuki, 69
Achhal, Iman, **114**
Adkins, Sam, 112, **193**, 222
Aerts, Peter, 257, **290**
Akiyama, Yoshihiro, **105–6**, 150, 191, 192, **219**
Aldo, José, **134–35**
Alexander, Houston, 278
Ali, Muhammad, 29
Allen, Kenneth, **234**
Al-Turk, Mustafa, 43
Alvarez, Eddie, 49
Alves, Thiago, 71, 213, **239–40**, 248
American Top Team, 19, 274, 288
Andrade, Alex, **43–44**
Angle, Kurt, 161, 261
Aoki, Shinya, **30**, **52–53**, **105**, 107
Arlovski, Andrei, 20, **25**, **32–33**, **74**, 97, **180–82**, 205, **240**, 271, 282, 289
Arona, Ricardo, 70, 81, **95**, 206, **283**
Arrichion of Phigalia, 4
Art of War Fighting Championship, **175–76**
Arum, Bob, 189
Arvanitis, Jim, **84–85**
Asahi, Noboru, 69
Attonito, Rich, 114
Aurelio, Marcus, 107, **280**
Azeredo, Luiz, 238

Backman, Atte, 40
Bader, Ryan, 195, 253
Baik Hyun-Man, 262
Bailey, Shamar, **113**
Bando, **8**
Barbosa, Ailton, 113
Barnett, Josh, 17, **34**, **49–50**, 73, 81, 101, **184**, 259, 264
Bartitsu, **5-6**
Baron, David, **113**
Baroni, Phil, **26–27**
Barrera, Dan, **113**
Barry, Patrick, **291**
Barton-Wright, Edward, 5
Baten, Chris, 117
Beebe, Chase, **231**
Belcher, Alan, 104–5
Belfort, Vitor, **32**, **55–56**, 68, **136**, 159, 196, **197**, 209, **226**
Beneteau, Dave, 130
Benítez, Wilfred, 199
Bennett, Charles, **150**, **280–81**
Bigelow, Scott, **159**
Bisping, Michael, 98, **230**
Bitetti, Amaury, 44
Blatnick, Jeff, 225
Blevins, Scott, **235**
Bloodsport, 166–67
Bobish, Dan, 149, 258
Bochenek, Joseph, **235–36**
Bonjasky, Remy, 99, 161, 257–58
Bonnar, Stephan, 116, 132, 239

Botha, Francois, **191**
Bowen, Melton, **191**
Boyes, Aaron, 133
Bravo, Eddie, **88**, 155
Brazilian jiu-jitsu, **11–12**
Brilz, Jason, 199, **231**
Broughton's Rules of 1743, 5
Brown, Mike, 19, 71, **246**
Brubaker, Larry, 131–32
Bryan, Tyler, **285**
Buentello, Paul, 100
Burns, Kevin, **47**
Bustamante, Murilo, 213, 265
Butler, Lionel, 193
Butler, Todd, 263

Cage, Nicholas, **152**
Cage Rage Championships (CRC),
    178
Camozzi, Chris, 112
Canseco, José, 140
Cantrell, Bo, 207, 222
Carano, Gina, **64–65**, 97, 150
Carpenter, Jason, 20
Carter, Rubin, 201
Carter, Shonie, **218**, **242**
Carwin, Shane, 158, **217–18**, **251**,
    276–77
Chappelle, Andrew, **125**
Chiappetta, Mike, 132
Choi, Hong Man, **139–40**, 161, **259**
Chonan, Ryo, **283–84**
Cikatić, Branko, **40–41**
Clark, LaVerne, 242
Clementi, Rich, 241
Clifton, Ross, **143**
Coleman, Mark,18, 54, 73, **75–76**,
    94, **132**, 164, **207–8**, **219–20**,
    256, **288–89**
Comacho, Art, 166
Combat Sambo, **14**
Combat Submission Wrestling, **14**
Combate Extremo, **175**
Confession of a Pit Fighter, 166
Copenhaver, Adam, 240
Cordova, Jason, 195
Correira, Wesley, 160, 192
Couture, Kim, 80

Couture, Randy, 11, 15, **29–30**,
    32, 70–71, 80, 102, **122–23**,
    130–31, 132, 134, 154, 158,
    162, **170**, 181, **184–85**, 189,
    197, 200, **208–9**, **230**, 271
Couture, Ryan, 80
Credeur, Tim, 201
Cruz, Dominick, 71
Cruz, Jamie, 82
Curran, Jeff, 71

Daley, Paul, 275
Danzig, Mac, 107
Datsik, Viacheslav, 240
Davis, David, **236–37**
De Jesus, Julio Cesar, 197
De La Hoya, Oscar, 20
DeLucia, Jason, **26**
DeMore, Joe, **118**
Denny, Marc, **85–86**
Diaz, Nate, 81-82
Diaz, Nick, 81-82, **135–36**, **196**
Diesel, Vin, **152**
Diniz, Edson, 113
Douglas, James, 205
Doyle, Sir Arthur Conan, 6
Duarte, Joe, **120**
Duffee, Todd, 101, 117, **217**
Durán, Roberto, 198, 199
Dux, Frank, 167

Eastman, Marvin, **55–56**, 177
Easton, Mike, **231**
Edgar, Frankie, **232**, **247**
Edwards, Yves, 241
Eilers, Justin, 240
Ejiofor, Chiwetel, 163
Eliminator, The, 165
Elite Fighting Championship (EFC),
    176–77
Ellis-Ward, Lisa, 62, 64
Emelianenko, Aleksander, 81, 97,
    141, **226**, 264,
Emelianenko, Fedor, 14, 62, **68**,
    72–77, **80–81**, 95, 97, 101,
    140–41, **147–48**, 178, **180–81**,
    205–6, **225–26**, 240, 258–59,
    271–72

Emelianenko, Ivan, 81
Emerson, Rob, **241**
Emperado, Adriano, **88**
Esch, Eric ("Butterbean"), 19, **192**
Escovedo, Cole, 71
Escudero, Efrain, 277
Evans, Rashad, **24**, 199, 229
Everett, Travis, 256

Faber, Urijah, **71**
Faircloth, Ron, **46–47**
Farrar, Chance, 71
Ferguson, Kevin ("Kimbo Slice"), 19, 117–18, **171–72**, **182**, 190, **207**, **222**, 253, 262
Ferreira, Valdomiro dos Santos, 131
Ferrozzo, Scott, 136
Fight Club, **167–68**
Filho, Paulo, **94**
Filipović, Mirko ("Cro Cop"), **34**, 43, **45–46**, **53–54**, 70, **73**, 80, **115**, **124**, 140, **209–10**, **226–27**, 256, **257**, 258–59, **286**
Finnfight, **179**
Fisher, Spencer, 82
Fitch, Jon, 71, **212–13**, **248**
Flannery, Sean Patrick, **153**
Florian, Kenny, **277**
Ford, Jeff, 17
Foreman, George, 129
Franca, Hermes, 241, 247
Francis, Julius, **192–93**
Franklin, Rich, 20, 68, **183–84**
Frazier, Joe, 29
Frazier, Zane, **51–52**
Free Fight Association (FFA), **176**
Frye, Don, 40, **111–12**, **172**, 193, **221–22**, 262, 273
Fryklund, Tony, 263
Fujii, Megumi, **61–62**
Fujita, Kazuyuki, 70
Funaki, Masakatsu, **34–35**, **104**

Gamlin, Stefan, **142**
Gannon, Sean, **117–18**
Garcia, Leonard, 147, **231**
Gardner, David, 120
Gardner, Rulon, **262**

Gassaway, Brian, **56**
Ghafarri, Matt, 76
Giron, Leo, **89**
Gomez, Lucas, 118
Gomez, Ulysses, 20
Gomi, Takanori, **104**, 113
Gono, Akihiro, **240–41**
Gonzaga, Gabriel, **53–54**, 97, **209–10**, 256
Goodman, Herbert **251–52**
Goodridge, Gary, 75–76, 112, 149, 258–59, **260**, 263
Gordeau, Gerard, **41**, 93, **101–2**
Gotch, Karl, 13
Gracie, Carlson,19, 78, 94, 270, 274
Gracie, Cesar, 81, 274
Gracie, Gastão, 78
Gracie, Helio, 78, **131**, 269
Gracie, Renzo, 83, 103, 159, 270, 274
Gracie, Rickson, 78–79, 93, 104, 131, 153, 263, **269–70**
Gracie, Rorion, 78, 131, 153
Gracie, Royce, 10, 13, **23–24**, 41, **67**, **78–79**, **93–94**, 101, 103, 129, 131, 133, 139, 151, 152, 159, 190, 270, 273
Gracie, Royler, 78, 88, 103, 105, 131, 159, 274
Gracie, Ryan, 103, 159
Gracie, Ryron, 20
Graham, Peter, 81
Greco-Roman Wrestling,**14–15**
Griffin, David, **278**
Griffin, Forrest, 68, **116**, 148, **171**, 195, **206**, 231, 238, **239**, 253
Griffin, Tyson, 104
Griggs, Chad, **112**, **210**
Guida, Clay, **240**

Hackleman, John, **18**
Hackney, Keith, **39–40**, **48**
Hagler, Marvin, 199
Hakes, Stacy, **233**
Hall, Skip, **132**
Hallman, Dennis, 107
Halme, Tony, **161–62**
Hamill, Matt, 136, **230**, **248**
Hamman, Jared, **255**

Hammortree, James, 112
Hansen, Joachim, **30**, **49**, 105, 107
Hardonk, Antoni, **102**
Hardy, Dan, 71, 113
Harris, Gerald, 200–201
Hartt, Dale, **56–57**
Hearns, Thomas, 199
Heath, Adam, 86
Heath, David, 44
Held, Marcin, **135**
Henderson, Dan, 15, 81
Hercules, 5
Herring, Heath, 72, 160, **173–74**,
    281–82
Hess, Jon, 136, **226**
Hill, Corey, **56–57**
Hinkle, Branden Lee, 118
Hioki, Hatsu, **229**
Hiraishi, Hisaki, **212**
Holyfield, Evander, 199, 200
Hoost, Ernesto, 99, 141, 258, 286
Hopkins Jr., Bernard, 129, 238
Horn, Jeremy, 70
Horton, Steve, **234**
Howe, Gordie, 129
Huang, Michael, 117
Hughes, Mark, **83**
Hughes, Matt, 18, **24**, **31**, **47–48**,
    56, **68–69**, 70–1, **83**, 94
Hume, Matt, **19–20**
Hunt, Mark, 70, 100, **258**, 262
Hurley, Joe, 136

Inosanto, Dan, 13, **86–87**
Inoue, Enson, 149
International Vale Tudo Champion-
    ships (IVC), **174–75**
Irvin, James, 68
Irwin, Steve, **151–52**
Ishida, Mitsuhiro, **107**
Ishii, Satoshi, **264–65**
Ismail, Wallid, **270**

Jackson, Eugene, 149
Jackson, Greg, **17**, 125
Jackson, Kevin, **263**
Jackson, Quinton ("Rampage"),
    24, **30–31**, 69–70, 103, 147,

149, 166, 177, 206, 214, 239,
    253, 289
James, Kevin, **153–54**, **263**
Jameson, Jenna, 71
Jardine, Keith, **148**, **195**, 222,
    253, **290**
Jeet Kune Do, **12**
Jennum, Steve, 191
Jimmerson, Art, **189–90**, 191
Johnson, Adam, **237**
Johnson, Anthony, **47**
Jolie, Angelina, 173
Jones, Jon, 81, 94, **136**
Jones, Marcus, **254–55**
Jones, Vinnie, 169
Jovovich, Milla, **154**
Judo, **12**
Jung, Chan Sung, **147**, **231**

Kali, **9**
Kampfringen, **6**
Kang, Denis, 100, 105
karate, **15**
Karelin, Alexander, 262
Kato Pankration, **3–4**
Kawajiri, Tatsuya, **49**
Kelly, John, **112–13**
Kennedy, Tim, **122**
Kerr, Mark, 40, 140, **164**, **249**
Kikuchi, Akiro, 105
Kim, Min Soo, **182–83**
Kondo, Yuki, 71
Kongo, Cheick, **43**, **45–46**
Koscheck, Josh, 71, 116, 239,
    248–49
Kotani, Naoyuki, **50**
Kyle, Mike, **42**

Laimon, Marc, **20**
LaMotta, Jake, 200
Landi-Jons, José, **56**
LaRosa, Tara, **62–63**
Lashley, Bobby, 112, **123**, **210**
Lauzon, Dan, **82–83**, **135**
Lauzon, Joe, **82–83**
Lawlor, Tom, **281**
Le Banner, Jérôme, 257, 258, 286
Le, Cung, 216, **287**

Leben, Chris, 20, 106, **150**, **219**, 277
Lee, Bruce,12, 14, 165
Leites, Thales, **96**
Leko, Stefan, 76
Leonard, ("Sugar") Ray, 198, 199
Leopoldo, Kimo, 67, 159, 239
Lerma, Michael, **192**
Lesnar, Brock, 17, **26**, **157–58**, **182–83**, **185**, **217–18**, **250–51**, 276
Lester, Frank, **124–25**
Lewis, Lennox, 191
Liborio, Ricardo, **19**
Liddell, Chuck, 15, 18, **29–30**, **70**, 122, 147–48, **183–84**, 195, **209**, **245–46**, 253, 290
Lighty, Scott, **200**
Lindland, Matt, 197, 235
Lytle, Chris, **111**, 113, **195**, 206

M-1 Global, **178–79**
MacDonald, Robert, **117**
MacDonald, Rory, **137**
Machida, Lyoto, 15, 94, **95**
Maeda, Mitsuyo, 68
Majoros, Istvan, **265**
Manhoef, Melvin, **100**, 101, 105
Marcello, Christiano, 107
Marshall, Keegan, **280**
Martin, Terry, 150, **277–78**
Matsumoto, Miku, **63–64**
Matua, John, **224–25**
Matyushenko, Vladimir, 71
Maynard, Gray, **247**
Mayweather, Jr. Floyd, 189
McCarthy, John ("Big"), 46, **116**, 220–21, 225, 228
McDonald, Brad, 136
McDonald, Michael, **259–60**
McIntyre, Nat, 17
McKee, Antonio, **132–33**, **211**
Melanson, Neil, **87**
Melendez, Gilbert, 107
Mercer, Ray, **190–91**, 207, **262–63**
Mezger, Guy, 99, 104
Miletich, Pat, **18**, 19, 56, 270
Miller, Dan, 82
Miller, Jason, 142

Miller, Jim, 82
Mir, Frank, **26**, 43, **52**, 158
Misaki, Kazuo, **219**
Mitrione, Matt, **253**
Miyata, Kazuyuki, 105
Modafferi, Roxanne, 62–63, **66**
Monday, Kenny, **264**
Monson, Jeff, 208, **271**, **278**
Moore, Archie, 129
Moorer, Michael, 129
Morais, Ricardo, **140–41**
Morecraft, Christian, **220**
Moreira, Joe, 193
Morrison, Tommy, 193
Mousasi, Gegard, **100**, 241
Muay Thai Kickboxing, **11**
Muñoz, Mark, 104

Nagata, Yuji, **226–27**
Nakai, Yuki, 41
Nakamura, Kazuhiro, **213**
Nakao, Yoshihiro, **281–82**
Nastula, Pawel, **263–64**
Navratilova, Martina, 129
Nelson, Greg, **17**
Nelson, Roy, **181–82**, 278
Never Back Down, **164–65**
Newton, Carlos, 56, 68, **270**
Nogueira, Alexandre, **69**, **72–73**
Nogueira, Antônio Rodrigo, 68, **79–80**, **96**, 101, 141–42, 148, **181**, **184–85**, 195, **215**, 225, 258, 264
Nogueira, Antônio Rogerio, **79–80**, **195**
Nolan, Shawn, **236**
Noons, K. J., 150, **196**
Norris, Chuck, 291

Odoms, Richard, **118**
Ogawa, Naoya, **76–77**
Okami, Yushin, **104–5**
Olsen, Jeff, 42
Omigawa, Michihiro, **229**
O'Neill, Ed, **153**
Ong-Bak, **167**
Ortiz, Tito, **28**, **33–34**, 70, **71**

Overeem, Alistair, **46**, 81, 97, **100–10**, 102
Overeem, Valentijn, 100, **102**

Pacquiao, Manny, 20
Page, Greg, 201
Palahniuk, Chuck, 168
Palling, Stephen, 69
Pankey, Josh, **235**
Parisyan, Karo, **53**
Parker, Shawn, **285**
Paulson, Erik, 14, **16–17**, 19
Pearson, Joe, 71
Pearson, Ross, **199**
Penn, B. J., 19–20, **24–25**, **27**, 69, 71, 107, **134**, **149**, 186, 194, **208–9**, 213, 224, **232**, 241, 247–48, 277
Perry, William, 141
Petruzelli, Seth, **182**, **207**, **222–24**, 248
Pit Fighter, **166**
Pittman, Craig, **161**
Polchlopek, Michal, **160–61**
Pulver, Jens, 18, **24–25**, 71, 104, 107, **194**, 241

Queensbury Rules, 5

Radach, Benji, **201**
Ramirez, Steve, **225**
Ramirez, Thomas, 112, **221–22**
Randleman, Kevin, 73, **74–75**, 81, 99, 213, **228–29**, 239, 290
Redbelt, **163–64**
Renken, John, **120–21**
Reynolds, Burt, 172
Ring, Nick, **196**
Rizzo, Pedro, 196, **230**, **288–89**
Roach, Freddie, **20**, 74
Rodriguez, Ricco, **271**
Rogan, Joe, 57, 154, **155**, 217
Rogers, Brett, 101
Roller, Shane, 20, **246–47**
Rosholt, Jake, 20, **246**
Rosier, Kevin, 101
Rothwell, Ben, 278
Roufus, Rick, **257**

Rowan, Chad ("Akebono"), **138–39**
Rua, Mauricio ("Shogun"), **54**, 81, **94**, 95, 136, **206–7**
Rua, Murilo, 81, **229**
Ruddock, Donovan, **201**
Russow, Mike, **116–17**, **217**
Rutten, Bas, **26**, **34**, **99**, 104, 154, 156, 165, **169–70**, **228–29**, **289–90**

Sakara, Alessio, **46–47**, 96
Sakuraba, Kazushi, **31–32**, **103**, 104, **158–59**, 190
Sakurai, Hayato, 69, 104, **106–7**, 113, 196, 241
Sambo, **14**
Sanchez, Diego, **53**
Sandler, Adam, 172
Santana, Givanildo, **148**
Santiago, Jorge, 150
Santos, Cristiane ("Cyborg"), **64**, 65–66, **97–98**, **150**, 195, **239**
Santos, Junior dos, 80, 97, 137, 205
Sapp, Bob, 20, 80, 123, **141**, 142, **158**, 160, **172**, 178, 215, 290
Sato, Rumina, 107
Saunders, Ben, 19, 113, 213
Schafer, Eric, 117
Schaub, Brendan, **254**
Schilt, Semmy, 68, **76**, **101**, **141–42**, 214, **258–59**, 290
Schrijber, Bob, **41–42**, **101**
Schultz, Mark, **263**
Sde-Or, Imrich ("Imi"), **87**
Sefo, Ray, 258
Sell, Pete, **279–80**
Serra, Matt, 20, **24**, 70–71, 111
Severn, Dan, 67, **129–30**, 208, 239, 288
Sexton, Rosi, **55**, **65**
Shamrock, Bob, 79
Shamrock, Frank, **26–27**, **34**, 79, 99, 104, 208, 263, **274**, 287
Shamrock, Ken, 12, 19, **23–24**, **28**, **33–34**, 71, 94, 104, 133, 143, **170**, 182, 207, 222, **274**
Shamrock, Ryan, 79
Shamrock, Sean, 79

Sherk, Sean, 17, 69
Shields, Jake, 71, 275
Shinashi, Satoko, **65**
Shoot Wrestling, **12–13**
Shooto, **175**
Shuai Jiao, **7–8**
Silat, **8–9**
Siliga, Siala-Mou ("Mighty Mo"), **49–50**
Silva, Anderson, 11, 20, **68**, 80, 96, 104, 107, 197, **216–17**, 220, **238**, **283–84**, **288**
Silva, Assuerio, **282**
Silva, Paulo ("Giant"), 139, **142**, **160**
Silva, Thiago, 19
Silva, Wanderlei, **30–32**, **48–49**, **69–70**, 71, **98**, **148–49**
Sims, Wes, **42–43**
Sinosic, Elvis, 71
Skliaudys, Darius, **50**
Smashing Machine, The: The Life and Times of Extreme Fighter Mark Kerr, **164**
Smith, Maurice, 99, **207–8**, **256**, 258, 262
Smith, Patrick, **133**
Smith, Scott, 196, **216**, **279–80**
Snipes, Wesley, **154–55**
Sobral, Renato, **44**, 70, 100, 209
Son, Joe, 40, **48**
Sonnen, Chael, 68, 94
Sonnon, Scott, **89**
Soszynski, Krzysztof, 43, 120
Southworth, Bobby, **133**
Spartacus, 4
Sperry, Mario, 81, **274**
Stann, Brian, **119–20**, 223
Statham, Jason, **155–56**, 169
Steffens, Lyle, **114**
Stelly, James, **123–24**
Stiebling, Alex, 83
Stout, Sam, **198**
St-Pierre, Georges, 15, 17, 19–20, **27**, **31**, 69, **70–71**, 82, **173**, 176, **185–86**, **206**, 212–13, 248
Struve, Stefan, 101, **137**, **220**
Sudo, Genki, 105, 192
Sugie, Daisuke, 107

Sunaba, Tomomi, **55**, **62**, 64
Suttles, Mike, **234**
Swick, Mike, 104
Sylvia, Tim, 18, **25**, **32–33**, **52**, **73–74**, 80, **181**, 191, 196, **208**, 216, 240, 263, 271, 278, **282**

Takada, Hiroya, **77**
Takada, Nobuhiku, 149
Takimoto, Makoto, **265**
Taktarov, Oleg, 130
Tamada, Yasuko, **211–12**
Tanner, Evan, 71, 104
Tavares, Brad, 112
Telligman, Tra, 136, **196**
Terkay, Sylvester, **161**
Thiago, Paulo, **115–16**, 213, 248
Thomas, Din, 107, 149
Thompson, James, **226**
Thompson, Nick, 17, 122, **275–76**
Tillman, Pat, 1, 20
Toida, Katsuya, 69
Tokyo Zombie, **165–66**
Toney, James, 11, 189, 200
Toughill, Erin, **66**
Trigg, Frank, **47–48**, 69
Tsuji, Yuka, **62**
Tuli, Teila, 101
Tyson, Mike, 191

Universal Reality Combat Championship (URCC), 177–78
Uno, Caol, 105–6, **107**, 149, **224**, **241**
Usui, Hayate, **212**

Valentino, Rudy, **18–19**
Vajramushti, **6–7**
Van Clief, Ron, **131**
Van Damme, Jean-Claude, 167
Varelans, Paul, **140**
Vaulin, Yuri, **193**
Velasquez, Cain, 158
Vera, Brandon, 195, 253
Vetell, Bryan, **278**
Villaseñor, Joey, **201**
Vincent, Steve, 194
Volkmann, Jacob, 133

Vovchanchyn, Igor, **49**, 196, 213, 256
Vunak, Paul, **85**, 86, 305

Walker, Herschel, **254**
Wallace, Rodney, **251–52**
Watson, Tom, 81
Wattree, Darvin, **225**
Wellisch, Christian, **276**
Werdum, Fabricio, 81, **96–97**, 101, 148, **205–6**
White, Dana, 28, 71, 113, 173, 183
White, Ralph, 41
White, Vernon, **34–35**
Williams, John, **131–32**

Williams, Pete, 75
Williams, Rubin, 190
Williams, Shawn, 153
Wisniewski, Keith, **52–53**
Wnek, Eric, xiii, 305
Worsham, Cal, **51–52**

Yamamiya, Keiichiro, **213**
Yamamoto, Norifumi ("Kid"), **105**, 265
Yarborough, Emmanuel, 39–40, **139**
Yoshida, Hidehiko, **261–62**, **272–73**
Yvel, Gilbert, **40**, 42, **48–49**, 102, 149, **184**, **200–201**

About the Authors

Adam T. Heath is a publishing professional and lifelong martial arts practitioner. He is a certified instructor in Jeet Kune Do, the Filipino Martial Arts, and Progressive Fighting Systems under Paul Vunak and Eric Wnek. He is also a personal student of Dennis Hill in Combat Sambo and Ken Zaborowski in tai chi chuan. He lives in Charleston, South Carolina.

David L. Hudson Jr. is a licensed boxing judge who covers mixed martial arts and boxing for Fightnews.com. He has also written articles for *FIGHT!* magazine. He is the coauthor of *Boxing's Most Wanted™: The Top 10 Book of Champs, Chumps, and Punch-Drunk Palookas* (Potomac Books, 2004) and two other books in the Most Wanted™ series. He has written or cowritten thirty-two books and resides in the Middle Tennessee area with his wife, Carla.